CUSTOM WOODWORKING

Shop-Built
Jigs & Fixtures

TIME®
LIFE
BOOKS

OTHER PUBLICATIONS

COOKING
Weight Watchers® Smart Choice Recipe Collection
Great Taste-Low Fat
Williams-Sonoma Kitchen Library

DO IT YOURSELF
Golf Digest Total Golf
How to Fix It
The Time-Life Complete Gardener
Home Repair and Improvement
The Art of Woodworking

HISTORY
Our American Century
What Life Was Like
The American Story
Voices of the Civil War
The American Indians
Lost Civilizations
Mysteries of the Unknown
Time Frame
The Civil War
Cultural Atlas

TIME - LIFE KIDS
Student Library
Library of First Questions and Answers
A Child's First Library of Learning
I Love Math
Nature Company Discoveries
Understanding Science & Nature

For information on and a full description of any of
the Time-Life Books series listed above,
please call 1-800-621-7026 or write:

Reader Information
Time-Life Customer Service
P.O. Box C-32068
Richmond, Virginia 23261-2068

CUSTOM WOODWORKING

Shop-Built
Jigs & Fixtures

By the editors of Time-Life Books
and *Woodsmith* magazine

Time-Life Books, Alexandria, Virginia

CONTENTS

CUSTOM WOODWORKING

Shop-Built Jigs & Fixtures

Jointer Push Block

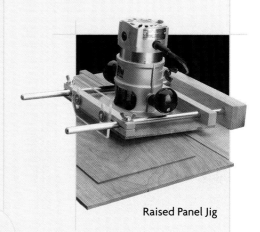

Raised Panel Jig

MACHINE TOOL JIGS   76

Taper Jig

SAFETY ACCESSORIES

Good woodworkers know how to protect themselves in the workshop and routinely practice safe tool-handling. The best of them use their woodworking talents to custom-build accessories that combine safety, precision, and practicality.

On the table saw, for example, nearly every workshop has a push block, but few can boast the easily replaceable body that our design offers. Our version of the shop-built featherboard locks itself right into the miter gauge slot for real convenience, and the small-piece clamp adds safety and accuracy to detail cutting.

Our versatile hold-down clamps provide accuracy and security for many woodworking applications. And the heavy jointer push block helps you joint stock with confidence.

Push Block

A push block doesn't have to be a simple scrap piece that you throw away after one use. This version is designed with a comfortable, practical handle and a replaceable body.

Using a push block on a table saw is just good sense: it keeps the workpiece under control and it provides a protective barrier between your hand and the saw blade.

Unlike a push stick that stays behind the workpiece and offers little control over longer boards, this push block keeps the workpiece under control through the entire cut.

The size and angle of the handle make it comfortable and practical to use, but that's not the only reason for the distinctive shape. It's designed to exert forward pressure to push the workpiece through the blade, as well as downward pressure to prevent chattering. The 2x4 body rides on edge to put extra inches of solid wood between your fingers and the blade.

REPLACEABLE BODY. Ordinary push blocks get chewed up after being run over the saw blade. This one is designed so the body and the heel can be replaced as often as needed.

This push block is particularly useful for ripping thin strips, because the heel pushes both the workpiece *and* the waste completely past the blade without the danger of kickback (see "Using a Push Block" on page 11). If you need to cut lots of narrow stock, you may prefer a block specifically designed for the purpose. You'll find it in the Shop Tip box on page 11.

MATERIALS. The body is nothing more than 2x4 scrap, and the heel is cut from hardboard. I cut the handle out of 2x4 scrap as well. However, since the handle is the part that will last a long time, you could also make it out of hardwood, if there's a suitable piece in your scrap bin.

While you're making this push block, it's worth taking time to cut several extra bodies and heels. This way you will always have replacements on hand whenever you need them.

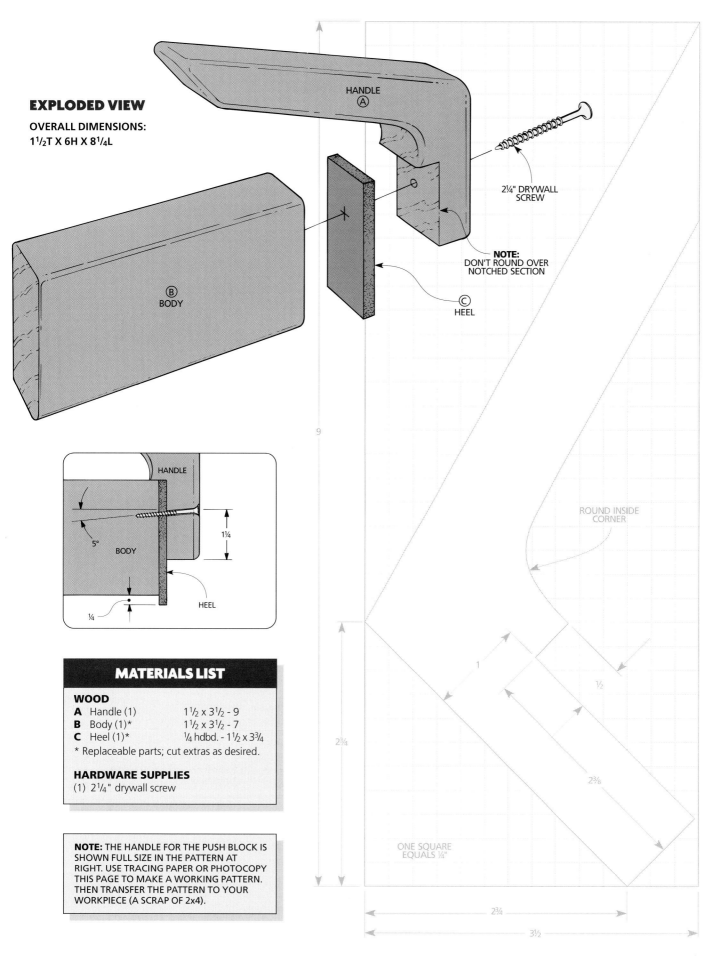

EXPLODED VIEW

OVERALL DIMENSIONS:
$1^1/_2$T X 6H X $8^1/_4$L

HANDLE
Ⓐ

$2^1/_4$" DRYWALL
SCREW

NOTE:
DON'T ROUND OVER
NOTCHED SECTION

Ⓑ
BODY

Ⓒ
HEEL

HANDLE

5°

BODY

$1^1/_4$

$^1/_4$

HEEL

ROUND INSIDE
CORNER

1

$^1/_2$

$2^3/_4$

$2^3/_8$

ONE SQUARE
EQUALS $^1/_4$"

$2^3/_4$

$3^1/_2$

9

MATERIALS LIST

WOOD

A	Handle (1)	$1^1/_2$ x $3^1/_2$ - 9
B	Body (1)*	$1^1/_2$ x $3^1/_2$ - 7
C	Heel (1)*	$^1/_4$ hdbd. - $1^1/_2$ x $3^3/_4$

* Replaceable parts; cut extras as desired.

HARDWARE SUPPLIES

(1) $2^1/_4$" drywall screw

NOTE: THE HANDLE FOR THE PUSH BLOCK IS
SHOWN FULL SIZE IN THE PATTERN AT
RIGHT. USE TRACING PAPER OR PHOTOCOPY
THIS PAGE TO MAKE A WORKING PATTERN.
THEN TRANSFER THE PATTERN TO YOUR
WORKPIECE (A SCRAP OF 2x4).

This push block has only three parts: a replaceable body (made from a scrap of 2x4), a $1/4$" hardboard heel that hooks over the end of the workpiece (the heel is also replaceable), and a handle.

HANDLE. The handle (A) is the key to the whole design of this push block system, so it's worth making a good one. I cut the handle out of a scrap piece of 2x4, but any $1^1/2$"-thick stock will do.

Start by cutting the handle blank $3^1/2$" wide by 9" long (see the full-size pattern on page 9).

Now, lay out the pattern shown in the diagram on the blank. Then cut the handle to shape using a band saw or a sabre saw.

After cutting out the shape, round over the sharp edges of the handle by filing and sanding them smooth.

DRYWALL SCREW. Attach the handle to the 2x4 body through the heel with a $2^1/4$" drywall screw (see the detail in the Exploded View on page 9).

Drill a shank hole for this screw at a slight angle (about $5°$). This way, when the screw is tightened down it will pull the body and heel tight into the notch in the handle.

BODY AND HEEL. When the handle is complete, the next step is to cut out the body.

For the body (B), cut a scrap piece of 2x4 to a length of 7". You could also use any other type of $1^1/2$"-thick stock, but

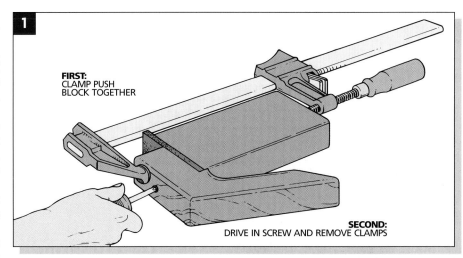

FIRST:
CLAMP PUSH
BLOCK TOGETHER

SECOND:
DRIVE IN SCREW AND REMOVE CLAMPS

since the body will be replaced several times, you will probably want to use inexpensive material.

The heel (C) is cut from a piece of $1/4$"-thick tempered hardboard. It's the same width as the body, or slightly less. It needs to be narrow enough not to catch on the rip fence, but also wide enough to catch the workpiece steadily on either side of the blade when ripping thin strips (refer to *Fig. 2*). It should extend $1/4$" below the bottom edge of the body.

Note: Since the body and the heel are eventually going to get chewed up, it's a good idea to cut several of each of these pieces and keep them on hand for replacements.

ASSEMBLY. To assemble the push block, set the parts on a flat surface and

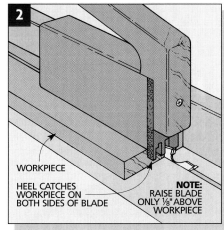

WORKPIECE

HEEL CATCHES
WORKPIECE ON
BOTH SIDES OF BLADE

NOTE:
RAISE BLADE
ONLY $1/8$" ABOVE
WORKPIECE

clamp them together *(Fig. 1)*. Then drive a drywall screw through the shank hole in the handle and into the body. Then remove the clamp. ∎

SHOP TIP . . . . *Reusing the Body*

When I was assembling the push block (see above), I decided to use a drywall screw rather than a standard woodscrew. The reason is that a drywall screw doesn't require a pilot hole.

This is especially handy when it comes time to replace the heel and body of the push block after they've become too chewed up to use. Drilling a new pilot hole for the screw every time would defeat half the purpose of having a conveniently replaceable body.

When the body and heel first get chewed up, you don't even have to replace them with new pieces. Instead, just flip both parts over and let the other edge get chewed (see drawing).

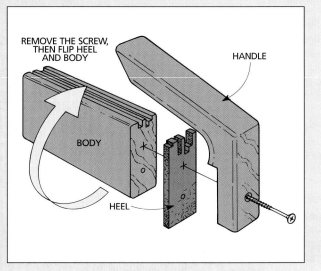

REMOVE THE SCREW,
THEN FLIP HEEL
AND BODY

HANDLE

BODY

HEEL

TECHNIQUE..... Using the Push Block

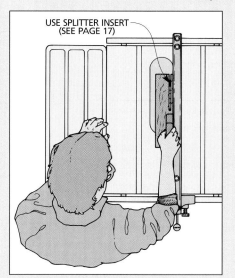

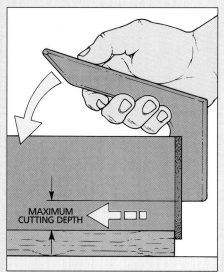

USE SPLITTER INSERT (SEE PAGE 17)

NOTE: GUARD REMOVED FOR CLARITY

MAXIMUM CUTTING DEPTH

Ripping Thin Strips. *This push block can be very helpful when ripping thin strips on the table saw. The body keeps the thin strip steady, while the heel pushes the thin strip smoothly through the blade without kickback.*

Preventing Pull. *To prevent a workpiece from pulling away from the rip fence during a cut, center the push block between the blade and fence. Then apply gentle pressure toward the fence throughout the cut.*

Two-Way Force. *The angled handle not only provides a comfortable grip for your hand, but also force in two directions. It allows you to push straight ahead and also press the workpiece down (to prevent chattering).*

SHOP TIP .... Thin Strip Push Block

Sometimes when ripping very narrow stock, I don't feel altogether comfortable using a push block that's designed mainly for wider stock. And it's nice having more than one option in the workshop. So I also built a push block that straddles my rip fence (refer to *Fig. 2*).

This version is made from two face pieces of $\frac{1}{4}$" hardboard and a spacer. And for different thicknesses of stock, I cut stair-step notches on the front end of the hardboard face nearest the blade.

To make this push block, start by cutting a $\frac{3}{4}$"-thick spacer to width to match the thickness of your rip fence. The width is critical because the push block should fit snugly over the rip fence, but not so tight that it binds.

Cut the two hardboard face pieces 7" long and high enough to clear any adjustment bolts on the top of the rip fence, plus $\frac{3}{4}$" for the thickness of the spacer (*Fig. 1*).

To cut the stepped cuts on the piece that faces the saw blade, lay out and cut a stair-stepped design. Each step is $\frac{1}{4}$" high and $\frac{1}{2}$" wide. (I cut mine using the band saw.)

Next, glue the face pieces to the spacer so their bottom edges ride on top of the saw table and the spacer clears the top of the rip fence.

Then, to get a secure grip on the push block, I drilled a $\frac{3}{4}$"-dia. hole and glued a $\frac{3}{4}$" dowel near the back of the spacer.

To use this push block to rip narrow stock, first set it over the fence with the notch on the push block over the workpiece.

To help hold the stock tight against the fence, you can use a featherboard (see page 12) or just hold a piece of scrap against the piece while cutting (*Fig. 2*).

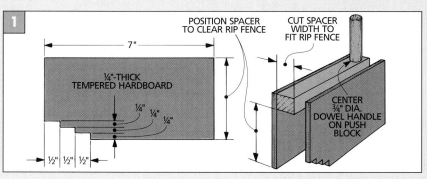

1

7"

POSITION SPACER TO CLEAR RIP FENCE

CUT SPACER WIDTH TO FIT RIP FENCE

$\frac{1}{4}$"-THICK TEMPERED HARDBOARD

$\frac{1}{4}$" $\frac{1}{4}$" $\frac{1}{4}$"

$\frac{1}{2}$" $\frac{1}{2}$" $\frac{1}{2}$"

CENTER $\frac{3}{4}$" DIA. DOWEL HANDLE ON PUSH BLOCK

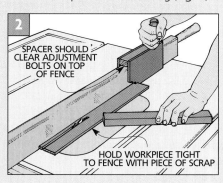

2

SPACER SHOULD CLEAR ADJUSTMENT BOLTS ON TOP OF FENCE

HOLD WORKPIECE TIGHT TO FENCE WITH PIECE OF SCRAP

No-Clamp Featherboard

Clamping a featherboard to your table saw can be difficult. This sturdy featherboard solves that problem with an expandable runner that fits tight in your saw's miter gauge slot.

To get safe and accurate results when I'm using a fence on the table saw, I like to use a featherboard like the shop-made one shown in the photo above.

A featherboard is designed to apply constant pressure to the side of the workpiece as it passes through the saw blade. This helps to prevent drift as well as kickback (see the article "Avoiding Kickback" on pages 16-17).

This pressure is created by cutting several long kerfs in one end of the featherboard. The lengths of narrow stock that remain (the finger-like barbs) act like springs, putting pressure on the side of the workpiece and holding it securely against the rip fence.

EXPANDABLE RUNNER. For me, the biggest problem with using a featherboard has always been finding a way to hold it in place, especially on a table saw where clamping can be difficult. Many clamps don't have enough reach, especially for a small featherboard, and the underside of a table saw is usually not an ideal surface for a clamp.

To solve this problem, I made a featherboard with a runner that expands to fit tight in the miter gauge slot of my table saw. However, this system only keeps the runner in place, not the featherboard itself.

To keep the featherboard from turning, I glued a stop block to the top of the runner. By mitering the end of

the stop 30° each way, the featherboard can be used in two directions. For information on using the featherboard, see the box on page 15.

MATERIALS. All the parts for the featherboard shown in the photo above were made from scrap hardwood stock. But you have more than one option in choosing the type of material you use to make a featherboard.

For hardware, you can purchase a metal wing nut, but the one shown in the photo above is wooden, made right in the shop. I find the wooden wing nut more comfortable to use. For plans on making a wooden wing nut, as well as other shop-made knobs, see the Woodworker's Notebook on pages 116-117.

EXPLODED VIEW

OVERALL DIMENSIONS:
$1^7/_8$T X $4^1/_2$W X 10L

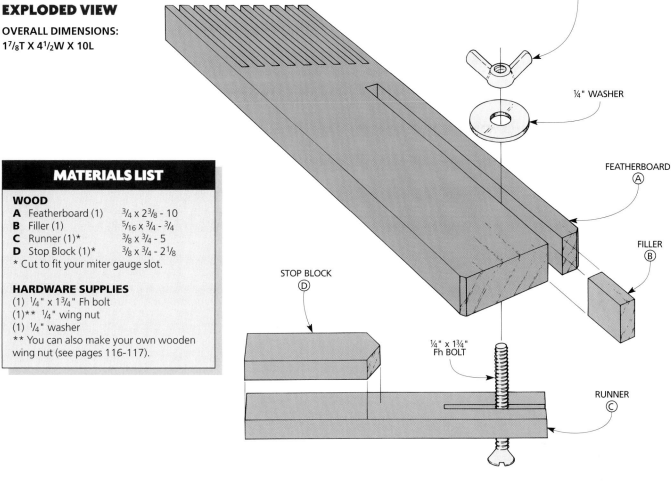

¼" WING NUT

¼" WASHER

FEATHERBOARD
Ⓐ

FILLER
Ⓑ

STOP BLOCK
Ⓓ

¼" x 1¾"
Fh BOLT

RUNNER
Ⓒ

MATERIALS LIST

WOOD
A Featherboard (1) $3/_4$ x $2^3/_8$ - 10
B Filler (1) $5/_{16}$ x $3/_4$ - $3/_4$
C Runner (1)* $3/_8$ x $3/_4$ - 5
D Stop Block (1)* $3/_8$ x $3/_4$ - $2^1/_8$
* Cut to fit your miter gauge slot.

HARDWARE SUPPLIES
(1) ¼" x 1¾" Fh bolt
(1)** ¼" wing nut
(1) ¼" washer
** You can also make your own wooden
wing nut (see pages 116-117).

WOODWORKER'S NOTEBOOK

MATERIALS FOR FEATHERBOARDS

A featherboard should be strong and durable, but also have enough give or "spring" in its barbs to run against a workpiece properly. Not every material will work.

Softwood is not strong enough, and hardboard and plywood would break since they don't have the grain to support the kerfs.

PLASTIC. Many featherboards are made of plastic (see top photo at right). But while cutting the kerfs, the sharp edges of some stiff plastic can be hard on a blade. Plastic can also give off an unpleasant odor while being cut, and can even melt if the blade isn't clean.

If you do use plastic, choose a polycarbonate, as acrylic tends to chip rather easily.

HARDWOOD. The material I like to use most is hardwood (see bottom photo). Its density, tight grain and springiness make it an ideal material for a featherboard.

Most hardwoods will work fine, but the best may be maple. It has all the necessary qualities, and is usually readily available and inexpensive.

Note: Choose wood that is free of knots, cracks and splits.

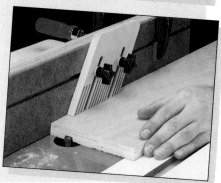

To make the featherboard (A), I started with a ³/₄"-thick hardwood blank, about 14" long. First, rip this blank to a finished width of 2³/₈" and cut a 30° miter on one end *(Fig. 1)*. Leave the blank at rough length. It will be trimmed to a finished length of 10" later.

BARBS. After cutting the blank, the next step is to cut the barbs at one end. To keep all of the barbs the same uniform length, I marked a stop line parallel to and 2³/₄" from the angled end *(Fig. 1)*. Each of the barbs is ¹/₈" wide and can be cut with a hand saw, a band saw, or a table saw.

Note: If you use a table saw, remember to raise the blade to its full height. That way the ends of the notches will be as straight and vertical as possible. This is necessary to leave room for an adjustment slot that will be added later.

Safety Note: When using the table saw to cut the notches, turn off the saw when you reach the end of each notch,

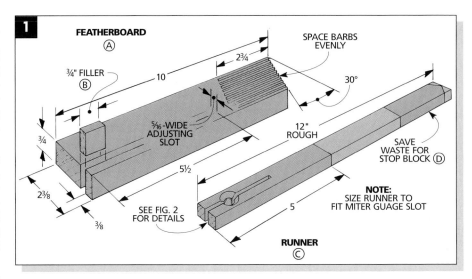

and wait for the blade to stop before pulling the stock out. This will prevent the possibility of kickback.

Finally, cut the featherboard to its finished length of 10" *(Fig. 1)*.

ADJUSTMENT SLOT. To allow the featherboard to be used with varying widths of stock, cut an adjustment slot near the short edge.

To make the slot, start about ³/₈" in from the edge, and cut a ⁵/₁₆"-wide groove that extends 5¹/₂" from the square end of the featherboard *(Fig. 1)*. Then for added strength, cut a small filler block (B) and glue it in place.

RUNNER. When the featherboard itself is complete, the next step is to cut a 12"-long runner (C) to fit in the miter

---

SHOP JIG .... *Featherboard Jig*

When you plan to make several featherboards, this jig allows you to make them quickly and easily.

The jig rides in the miter gauge slot of your table saw, holding the featherboard blank at an angle. This allows you to cut a series of consistent kerfs.

THE JIG. To build the jig, start by cutting a base, runner, index key, and fence to finished size (see drawing).

KERFS. There are two kerfs in the base of the jig; one for the index key and one for the saw blade. The spacing between these kerfs (¹/₈") determines the width of the finger-like barbs.

Set your rip fence 8" away from the

blade and cut a 2"-long kerf for the index key. After gluing the index key into the kerf, move the fence another ¹/₄" away from the blade and cut the second kerf.

Without moving the rip fence, glue the runner to the bottom of the base with the base tight against the fence. This will ensure that the kerf in the jig will always line up with the blade.

Once the glue has set up, secure the runner with screws. Then attach the

fence at a 30° angle to complete the jig (see detail).

USING THE JIG. To make a featherboard using this jig, bevel both ends of your blank at 30°. Then clamp a stop block to your rip fence to control the length of the barbs (see photo).

With one side of the blank against the index key, cut a kerf. Continue cutting kerfs along the edge of the blank, placing each newly-cut kerf over the index key before cutting the next.

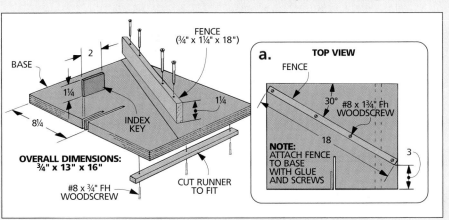

gauge slot of your table saw *(Fig. 1)*. (Be sure to measure your own miter gauge slot before cutting the runner. On my table saw the miter gauge slot measures $3/4$" x $3/8$".)

Once the runner is cut, the next step is to drill the hole for the bolt and cut the expansion slot in one end. Do this by following the steps shown in *Fig. 2*. Then cut the runner to a finished length of 5" *(Fig. 1)*.

STOP BLOCK. Next, to make the stop block (D), I used the remainder of the board left over from cutting the runner to length *(Fig. 3)*. Cut two 30° angles on one end of the block (so they meet in the middle at a point).

Then trim the stop to length, and glue it to the top of the runner. It should be flush and square with the non-slotted end of the runner *(Fig. 3)*.

Finally, assemble the featherboard and the runner with a $1/4$" x $1^3/4$" flat-head bolt *(Fig. 4)*.

As the wing nut is tightened, the runner actually expands in the miter gauge slot (see detail 'a' in *Fig. 4*). This way, the featherboard doesn't shift during use. ■

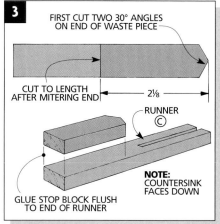

2
½" DIA.
¾
FIRST: DRILL ½" DIA. COUNTERSINK

¼" HOLE
SECOND: DRILL A ¼" HOLE THROUGH CENTER OF COUNTERSINK HOLE

2¼
THIRD: CUT A ⅛" KERF 2¼" LONG CENTERED ON HOLE

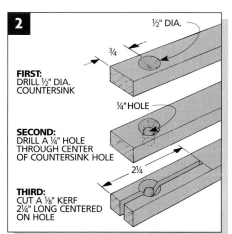

3
FIRST CUT TWO 30° ANGLES ON END OF WASTE PIECE
CUT TO LENGTH AFTER MITERING END
2⅛
RUNNER Ⓒ
GLUE STOP BLOCK FLUSH TO END OF RUNNER
NOTE: COUNTERSINK FACES DOWN

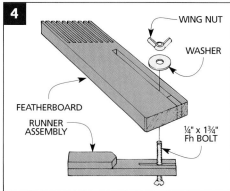

4
WING NUT
WASHER
FEATHERBOARD
RUNNER ASSEMBLY
¼" x 1¾" Fh BOLT

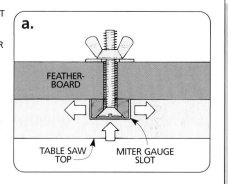

a.
FEATHER-BOARD
TABLE SAW TOP
MITER GAUGE SLOT

TECHNIQUE .. *Using the Featherboard*

Once you make the featherboard shown on page 12, you'll want to use it whenever you're ripping a board that may drift away from the fence. To use the featherboard effectively, first place the runner (C) in the miter gauge slot of your table saw. Then adjust and lock the table saw fence for the cut you want to make and position your workpiece against the fence.

Now you can slide the featherboard against the edge of your workpiece, but not so tight that the barbs are bent back (see the photo on page 12). The idea is to exert just enough pressure to keep the workpiece snug against the fence as it passes through the saw blade, but not so much that it slows the cut.

To prevent the saw blade from binding during a cut, be sure to position the featherboard an inch or so in *front* of the cutting edge of the blade (see the drawing at right). If you were to place the featherboard *alongside* the blade, the waste piece could pinch the kerf

and bind up the blade, creating a potentially dangerous situation (see "Avoiding Kickback" on pages 16-17).

Once you're satisfied that the featherboard is in the proper position, tighten the wing nut that locks it to the runner and locks the runner in the miter gauge slot. Be certain the featherboard doesn't shift while tightening, or you will have to loosen the wing nut and reposition it.

Safety Note: Besides using a featherboard, always remember to use a push block when ripping on the table saw. (For information on building a push block with a replaceable body, see the article beginning on page 8.)

Also, although a featherboard helps prevent kickback, it's always good to avoid standing directly behind the workpiece whenever you're ripping lumber.

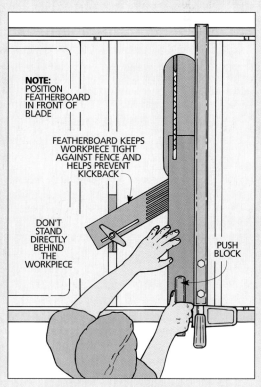

NOTE: POSITION FEATHERBOARD IN FRONT OF BLADE

FEATHERBOARD KEEPS WORKPIECE TIGHT AGAINST FENCE AND HELPS PREVENT KICKBACK

DON'T STAND DIRECTLY BEHIND THE WORKPIECE

PUSH BLOCK

I have a friend who has a piece of wood embedded in the wall behind his table saw. It's a reminder to others entering his shop not to stand directly behind the saw when it's in use. And it's a reminder to himself as to how dangerous kickback can be.

Kickback shouldn't be taken lightly. It's as serious as an unguarded saw blade or an exposed router bit. The secret to preventing kickback (and a serious injury) is to understand where and when it's most likely to occur and what causes it.

TWO TOOLS. There are two tools in the shop where the potential for kickback is high: the table saw and the router or shaper.

With the table saw, kickback is often the result of a workpiece getting pinched between the blade and fence. Or sometimes the saw kerf closes up around the blade. In either case, the blade grabs the workpiece and propels it backwards — quicker than you can blink an eye.

FENCE POSITION. On the table saw, the first step in ensuring that you will make a straight, bind-free cut is to be sure the rip fence is set absolutely parallel to the saw blade. Having the fence set parallel to the blade allows the workpiece to slide smoothly past the blade without binding.

To make sure the fence is parallel to the blade, you can simply measure between the fence and one of the miter gauge slots — at both ends of the fence (see drawing below right).

Note: This assumes that your saw blade is parallel to the miter gauge slot. You can check this by measuring between the blade and slot at the front and back of the blade. But if you do, rotate the blade to be sure your measuring tool touches the same tooth at the front and back.

Along with a properly set fence, there are a number of inexpensive things you can do to reduce your chances of kickback.

PAWLS. One thing you should always do is use your blade guard with its anti-kickback pawls (see photo above). As long as these pawls are sharp and well-maintained, they should dig in and "catch" the workpiece in the event that it's kicked back.

SPECIAL INSERT. When I can't use the blade guard, I often use a special insert with a built-in splitter (see "Splitter Insert" on the opposite page). This splitter prevents the saw kerf from closing up around the saw blade.

Two additional ways you can help prevent kickback on the table saw are to use a pair of anti-kickback rollers or a featherboard.

FEATHERBOARD. A featherboard works much like the anti-kickback rollers. It also keeps the workpiece tight against the fence or table top to help you get a straight cut. And the fingers help prevent a workpiece from kicking back at you should the blade begin to grab it.

Plans for making and using a no-clamp hardwood featherboard are shown on pages 12-15. To purchase ready-made featherboards, see page 126 for sources.

SAFETY TIPS. Whenever possible, it's also a good idea to use a push block (see "Using the Featherboard" on page 15). It won't prevent kickback, but it just might save a finger or two if something does go wrong.

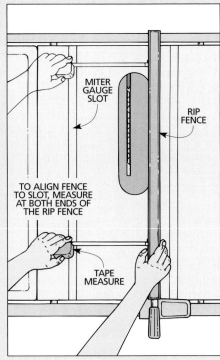

MITER GAUGE SLOT

RIP FENCE

TO ALIGN FENCE TO SLOT, MEASURE AT BOTH ENDS OF THE RIP FENCE

TAPE MEASURE

And finally, never remove the waste piece from the top of the table saw until the power is off and the blade has come to a stop.

SPLITTER INSERT

It's always a good policy to use the blade guard and kerf splitter on your table saw when cutting. But there are some times when I have to remove my blade guard for a certain cut. When this occurs, I like to protect myself by replacing the metal insert in my table saw with a special shop-built insert that has a built-in splitter (see drawing).

This splitter helps protect me from any kickback that might be caused by a workpiece closing up around the saw blade — even when the blade guard has been removed.

CONSTRUCTION. The splitter insert I made is just a scrap piece of hardwood that is cut and sanded to match the shape and thickness of the original metal insert.

Make sure the piece ends up flat and square so it will remain flush with the top of your table saw. This will help ensure that your workpiece will ride smoothly over the top of the splitter

insert, just as it would have with the original metal one.

SPLITTER. A long kerf cut in from one end of the insert accepts a hardwood splitter. This splitter will physically prevent the workpiece from pinching the blade by holding the kerf open while the cut is made. The splitter is just a piece of $1/8$" hardboard cut to a length of 3" and a height of $1^1/8$" (see drawing at right).

File a point on the front of the splitter (the end facing the table saw blade). This will keep the workpiece from catching on the splitter as it's pushed through the blade.

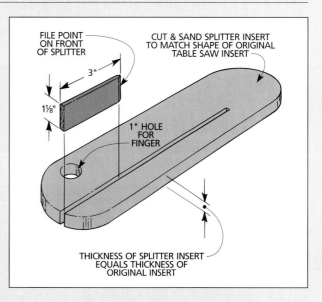

FINGER HOLE. For convenience, I added a 1"-dia. finger hole to make it easier to remove the insert once I'm finished (see drawing).

ROUTER TABLE KICKBACK

Working with a router table can be deceptive. It might have a smaller motor and use a smaller cutter than a table saw, but a serious accident can occur here, too.

CAUSES. A workpiece can kick back if it's fed into a router bit too quickly. Or if you try to remove too much wood in one pass. And even if the bit hits a knot in the workpiece. So it's a good idea to inspect the workpiece carefully first, before turning on the router.

Also keep in mind the other rules for a router table. Rout in a right-to-left direction — whether you're using a fence or a bit with a bearing (see drawing). You should *never* backrout — this is very dangerous.

With backrouting, there's always a chance the router bit will grab the workpiece and pull it, along with your fingers, into the sharp cutters.

Never rout with the workpiece *between* the bit and the fence. And always keep your fingers safely out of the way. For small pieces, use a featherboard and a push block.

ANTI-KICKBACK BITS. You can also reduce your chances of getting kickback by using special anti-kickback bits (see photo above right). Unlike standard router bits, these bits have less

cutter surface exposed (see detail 'a' in drawing below).

As the workpiece passes through the cutter, less wood can be removed per revolution of the bit. The less wood you remove at a time, the less chance there is of kickback.

MULTIPLE PASSES. And one of the simplest ways to prevent kickback is to nibble away at the wood with a series of shallow passes (see detail 'b' below). As an added benefit, this produces a clean cut with less burning or chipout.

Anti-kickback Bits. *A bit with less cutter surface exposed lessens the likelihood of kickback.*

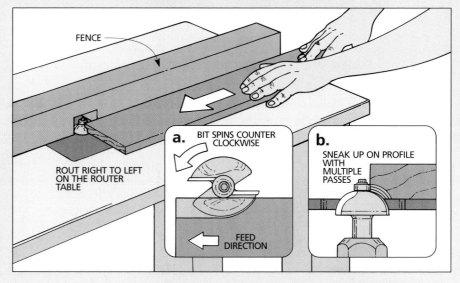

Small-Piece Clamp

Cutting small pieces on a table saw can be difficult if you don't have a way of protecting your hands. This versatile clamp attaches to your miter gauge for safe and accurate cutting.

Recently I was in my shop building a project that required cutting several small pieces on the table saw. Of course, cutting any number of small pieces can be nerve-racking if you don't have an appropriate way of protecting your fingers. So rather than take any chances, I made a special small-piece clamp jig that attaches to my miter gauge.

There is nothing very complicated about this project. The basic idea of the jig is that two "arms" hold the workpiece securely (like a vise) and keep your fingers a safe distance away from the blade (see photo above).

ANGLE. The jig also keeps the workpiece steady at exactly 90° to the blade, since small pieces can be more likely to drift or jump during a cut.

You can also make a slight modification to the small-piece clamp to make 45° miter cuts (see "Using the Clamp" on page 20).

ADJUSTABLE. The clamp consists of just three pieces: a back jaw, a front jaw, and an adjustable spreader. A slot cut in the spreader allows you to adjust the distance between the jaws so you can cut different size pieces.

A carriage bolt and wing nut at the other end provide the clamping pres-sure. When the nut is tightened down on the bolt, it pinches the two jaws together like a vise to hold the work-piece in place as you make a cut.

MATERIALS. All three parts of the small-piece clamp are made from 3/4"-thick hardwood.

You can probably find enough scrap wood to make this jig, but remember to end up with pieces that are flat, square and true (for accurate cuts).

MINI-CLAMP. For a smaller, hand-held version of the clamp that you can use to grind down or sand small wooden parts or hardware, see the Woodworker's Notebook on page 21.

EXPLODED VIEW

OVERALL DIMENSIONS:
15³/₄W X 3¹/₂D X 2H

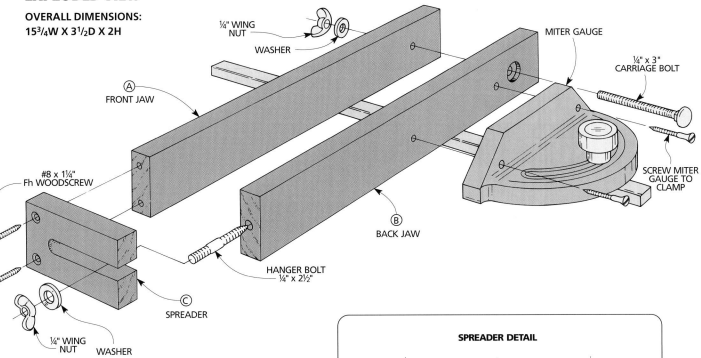

¹/₄" WING NUT

WASHER

Ⓐ
FRONT JAW

MITER GAUGE

¹/₄" x 3"
CARRIAGE BOLT

SCREW MITER
GAUGE TO
CLAMP

#8 x 1¹/₄"
Fh WOODSCREW

Ⓑ
BACK JAW

HANGER BOLT
¹/₄" x 2¹/₂"

Ⓒ
SPREADER

¹/₄" WING
NUT

WASHER

TIP: THE SMALL-PIECE CLAMP SHOWN HERE IS VERY EFFECTIVE FOR HOLDING SMALL PIECES STEADILY AND SECURELY THROUGHOUT THE CUT. HOWEVER, FOR ADDED PROTECTION AGAINST SLIPPING ON THE TABLE SAW, YOU MAY CHOOSE TO LINE THE INSIDE FACE OF EACH JAW WITH ADHESIVE-BACKED SANDPAPER.

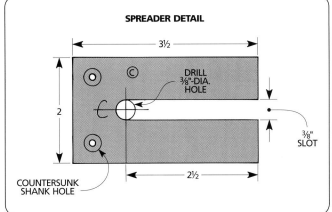

SPREADER DETAIL

3¹/₂

Ⓒ

DRILL
³/₈"-DIA.
HOLE

2

³/₈"
SLOT

COUNTERSUNK
SHANK HOLE

2¹/₂

MATERIALS LIST

WOOD
A	Front Jaw (1)	³/₄ x 2 - 15
B	Back Jaw (1)	³/₄ x 2 - 15
C	Spreader (1)	³/₄ x 2 - 3¹/₂

HARDWARE SUPPLIES
(2) No. 8 x 1¹/₄" Fh woodscrews
(1) ¹/₄" x 3" carriage bolt
(2) ¹/₄" wing nuts
(2) ¹/₄" flat washers
(1) ¹/₄" x 2¹/₂" hanger bolt

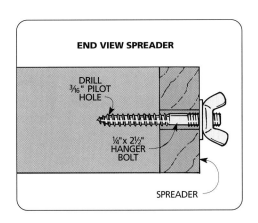

END VIEW SPREADER

DRILL
³/₁₆" PILOT
HOLE

¹/₄" x 2¹/₂"
HANGER
BOLT

SPREADER

I began work on the small-piece clamp by cutting the two jaws and the spreader. All three parts are made from $^3/_4$"-thick hardwood (refer to the Exploded View on page 19).

I cut both the front jaw (A) and the back jaw (B) to a final width of 2" and a final length of 15". The spreader (C) is 2" wide and $3^1/_2$" long.

SPREADER. The spreader has a slot cut in from one end to make the clamp adjustable. To cut this slot, first drill a $^3/_8$" hole $2^1/_2$" from the end. This hole should be centered top-to-bottom (see the Spreader Detail in the Exploded View on page 19).

Then make two parallel cuts up to the hole with a band saw or sabre saw. You can sand down any rough spots to allow the hanger bolt to move smoothly.

After the slot is cut, drill two counter-sunk shank holes at one end of the spreader. Then screw the spreader to the end of the front jaw with No. 8 x $1^1/_4$" flathead woodscrews *(Fig. 1)*.

HANGER BOLT. The slotted end of the spreader fits over a hanger bolt. The spreader is then tightened down over the hanger bolt with a wing nut *(Fig. 1)*.

Screw the hanger bolt into the end of the back jaw (see the End View Spreader in the Exploded View). For more information on attaching the hanger bolt to the back jaw, see the Shop Tip on the opposite page.

After the bolt is installed, thread on a washer and wing nut. When you tighten

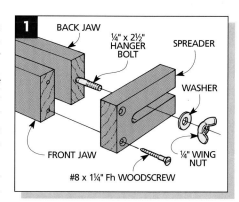

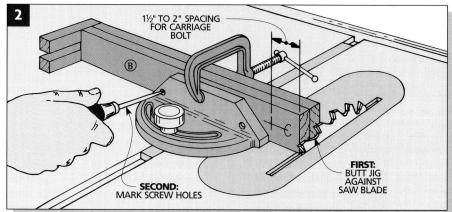

TECHNIQUE .... *Using the Clamp*

The first thing to do when using the clamp is to loosen the wing nut on the spreader (at the left end of the clamp) and adjust the jaws to the width of your workpiece. Then tighten the nut.

Next, insert the workpiece between the jaws at the right end of the clamp, and tighten the wing nut on the carriage bolt *(Fig. 1)*.

Note: When clamping pieces wider than 1", the top edges of the jaws may tip in. To prevent this, cut a spacer the same width as the workpiece and insert it between the top edges of the jaws.

MITER CUTS. When you tilt the miter gauge to 45°, the end of the clamp is too far away from the blade to safely hold and support a small workpiece. So you need to reposition the clamp on the miter gauge for 45° miter cuts *(Fig. 2)*.

To do this, unscrew the clamp and tilt the miter gauge to 45°. Then slide the clamp along the miter gauge until the front corner of the back jaw just touches the edge of the blade.

Mark new locations for the screws, and drill pilot holes. Then screw the clamp to the miter gauge.

Now turn on the saw, and trim off the back corner of the back jaw.

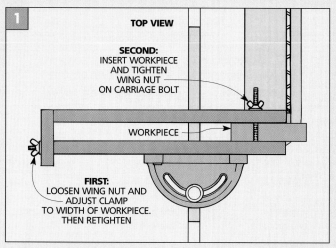

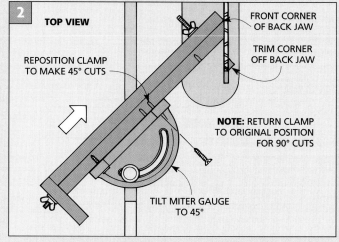

down the wing nut, it pinches the spreader, locking one end of the front jaw in place.

Note: Be sure to use a washer so the wood in the spreader won't get damaged when you tighten the wing nut.

ATTACHING THE CLAMP. To attach the small piece clamp to your miter gauge, first you need to find the correct locations for the screws.

To do this, first set the miter gauge at 90°. Then place the back jaw against the miter gauge *(Fig. 2)*.

Next, slide the clamp over so the end just touches the saw blade. Now use the miter gauge to mark the position of the two screw holes in the back jaw (I used a scratch awl). Finally, drill pilot holes for the two woodscrews.

CARRIAGE BOLT. A 3"-long carriage bolt is used to close the jaws around the workpiece at the right end of the clamp (refer to *Fig. 3*).

Mark the position of the bolt on the back jaw *(Fig. 2)*. Then counterbore a hole to accept the head of the bolt *(Fig. 3a)*. Finally, drill a ¼" hole through both jaws for the carriage bolt.

Screw the clamp to the miter gauge, insert the carriage bolt and washer, and tighten the wing nut *(Fig. 3)*. ∎

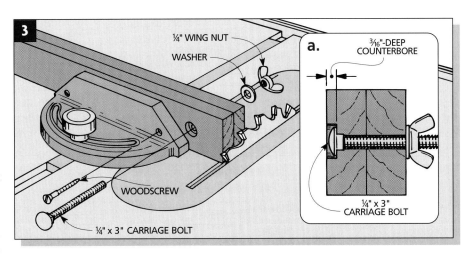

¼" WING NUT

WASHER

a. ³⁄₁₆"-DEEP COUNTERBORE

WOODSCREW

¼" x 3" CARRIAGE BOLT

¼" x 3" CARRIAGE BOLT

SHOP TIP *Installing Hanger Bolts*

A hanger bolt is a bolt that is threaded at both ends. Since there is no flat surface, trying to screw one into a workpiece (like the back jaw of the clamp) can be as challenging as climbing a greased pole.

To get around this problem, thread two nuts onto the shaft and then tighten them together. This gives your wrench something to grab onto when screwing the bolt into the workpiece (see drawing).

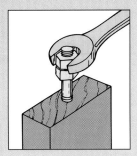

WOODWORKER'S NOTEBOOK

MINI-CLAMP

Sometimes I need to grind or sand small parts. I could use a pair of locking pliers to hold them, but they can mar the surface of the part.

So instead, I made a mini-clamp out of wood. The soft jaws hold objects tightly without marring them, and they don't transfer heat like metal jaws.

The clamp has two loosely connected jaws. A wedge driven in at one end causes the jaws to close at the other (see detail 'a').

To make this mini-clamp, you need a short dowel, a bolt, a wing nut, and a few washers.

CONSTRUCTION. Drill a slightly oversize bolt hole through the center of the dowel. Then round off one end with a sander for the jaws.

After cutting the dowel lengthwise on a band saw, place the washers between the jaws to act as spacers. A bolt and wing nut hold everything together (see drawing).

A small wedge fits into the back of the clamp, allowing the jaws to "bite" down on the object being held. The further the wedge is pushed in, the tighter the grip.

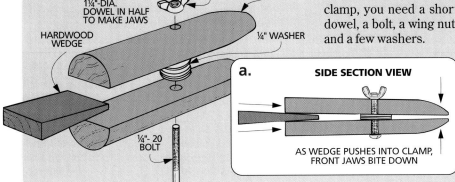

NOTE: CUT 1¼"-DIA. DOWEL IN HALF TO MAKE JAWS

WING NUT

JAW

HARDWOOD WEDGE

¼" WASHER

¼"- 20 BOLT

a. SIDE SECTION VIEW

AS WEDGE PUSHES INTO CLAMP, FRONT JAWS BITE DOWN

Hold-Down Clamp

Take the time to make one or more of these versatile shop-made hold-down clamps.
Then use them over and over for different thicknesses of stock and on different tools and projects.

This hold-down clamp is simple to make but has a variety of applications around the shop. It is designed to be mounted easily to a workbench to hold stock. For example, it's ideal for holding a workpiece down on a flat surface for freehand routing, carving, and planing.

VERSATILITY. The hold-down can also be mounted to a drill press table to hold stock securely, or used as part of a ripping jig for the table saw. Chip carving on a large piece of stock also becomes easier when this hold-down clamp is used to steady the piece.

For photographs and information about these other uses for the hold-down clamp, see the Woodworker's Notebook on page 25.

SIMPLE TO BUILD. Besides being versatile, the hold-down clamp is fairly satile. One or more of them can be mounted through the dog holes in a traditional cabinetmaker's bench, or attached in various ways to power tool jigs.

simple to construct, whether you decide to make one or several.

There are only two wooden parts for this clamp: an arm and a semi-circular pivot block. They are both cut from the same piece of stock, using a band saw or sabre saw.

MULTIPLES. Once you have one clamp, you can use it as a template to make more. Many jigs and fixtures require more than one clamp, so it makes sense to build extras while you have the shape, materials and tools available.

DIFFERENT SIZE PIECES. The hold-down clamp is not only versatile enough for working with different types of tools and projects. It's also useful for clamping down different sizes and thicknesses of stock.

The clamp is designed with one side of the arm shorter than the other (refer to the Arm Pattern on the opposite page). It is held in place with the pivot block. This allows more freedom than some other clamps, as it gives you a range of options in the thickness of stock you can clamp (up to 3").

MATERIALS AND HARDWARE. The arm and pivot block are both made from $1^1/_2$"-thick stock.

The clamp assembly is secured with a threaded rod or bolt and a wing nut, which makes it easy to tighten down the assembly (for information on building your own shop-made wooden wing nut, see the Woodworker's Notebook on pages 116-117).

This type of clamp is extremely ver-

EXPLODED VIEW

OVERALL DIMENSIONS:
$1^1/_2$T X $7^3/_4$L X 6H

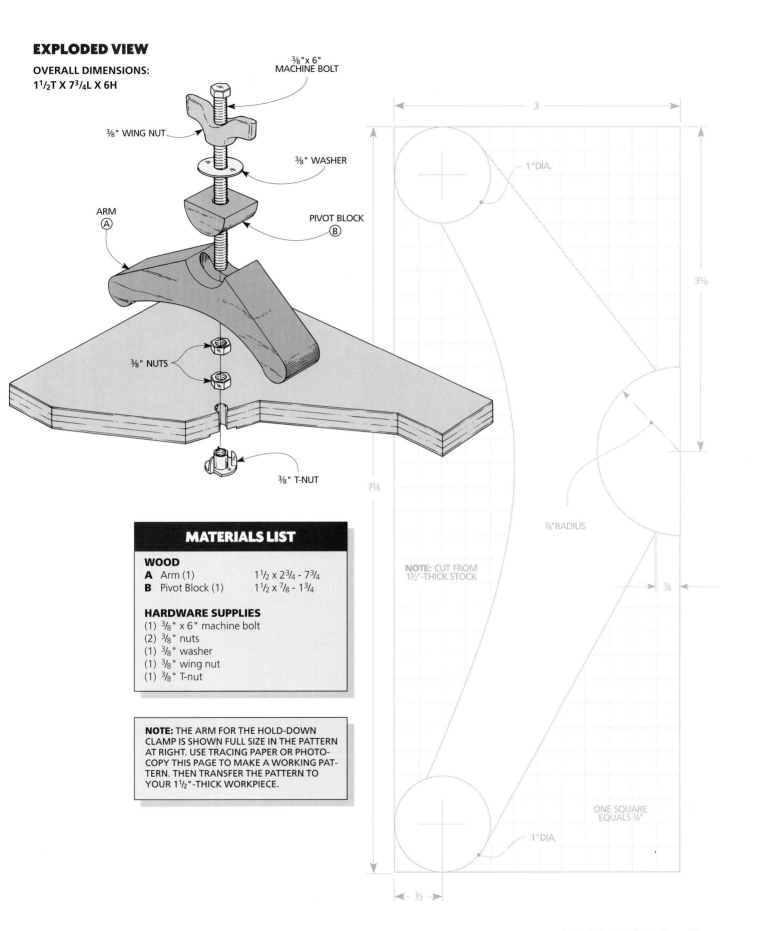

$3/_8$"x 6" MACHINE BOLT

$3/_8$" WING NUT

$3/_8$" WASHER

ARM
Ⓐ

PIVOT BLOCK
Ⓑ

$3/_8$" NUTS

$3/_8$" T-NUT

1"DIA.

3

$3^3/_8$

$7/_8$"RADIUS

NOTE: CUT FROM $1^1/_2$"-THICK STOCK

$1/_4$

$7^3/_4$

1"DIA.

ONE SQUARE EQUALS $1/_4$"

$1/_2$

MATERIALS LIST

WOOD
A	Arm (1)	$1^1/_2$ x $2^3/_4$ - $7^3/_4$
B	Pivot Block (1)	$1^1/_2$ x $7/_8$ - $1^3/_4$

HARDWARE SUPPLIES
(1) $3/_8$" x 6" machine bolt
(2) $3/_8$" nuts
(1) $3/_8$" washer
(1) $3/_8$" wing nut
(1) $3/_8$" T-nut

NOTE: THE ARM FOR THE HOLD-DOWN CLAMP IS SHOWN FULL SIZE IN THE PATTERN AT RIGHT. USE TRACING PAPER OR PHOTO-COPY THIS PAGE TO MAKE A WORKING PATTERN. THEN TRANSFER THE PATTERN TO YOUR $1^1/_2$"-THICK WORKPIECE.

To build the hold-down clamp, I started with the arm.

ARM. To make the arm (A), the first step is to lay out the pattern (refer to the Arm Pattern on page 23) on a blank of $1^{1}/_{2}$"-thick hardwood.

Before cutting out the shape of the arm, bore a $^{7}/_{16}$"-dia. hole through the top of the block for the machine bolt to pass through *(Fig. 2)*.

PIVOT BLOCK. Next, cut out the semi-circular pivot block (B) from the same $1^{1}/_{2}$"-thick blank of wood, and save this piece *(Fig. 3)*.

To allow the arm to pivot around a machine bolt (as shown in *Fig. 1*) or a threaded rod, you need to bore out a clearance slot. To do this, bore a series of overlapping holes through the bottom of the block with a drill, all the way through to the pivot area *(Fig. 4)*.

Note: Do not drill into the pivot block.

Now you can cut the arm to shape on a band saw (or with a sabre saw). Then clean out the slot with a chisel and file, and soften the edges of the arm and pivot block with sandpaper.

ASSEMBLY. To assemble the hold-down clamp, insert a 6"-long machine bolt through the arm and screw it into a T-nut mounted in a jig or bench *(Fig. 1)*. To keep the bolt from going too far, lock two hex nuts together to form a stop.

To use the clamp on a thick benchtop with dog holes, you will need to use a longer machine bolt or a threaded rod (refer to photo on page 22). Instead of a T-nut, you will need a large fender washer and a lock nut.

To tighten down the arm, you can make your own wing nut out of wood (see pages 116-117). To find sources for the wing nut shown in the photographs and other hardware for this hold-down clamp, see page 126.

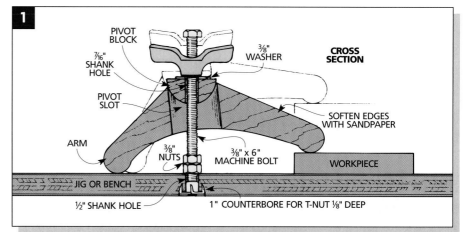

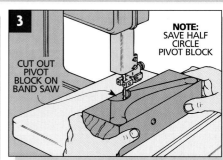

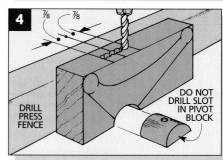

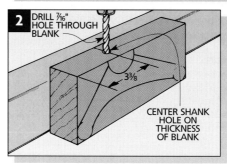

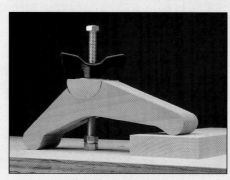

SHOP TIP . . . . *Different Thicknesses*

The hold-down clamp is made with versatility in mind. This includes using it for different applications (see the Woodworker's Notebook on the opposite page), and for different thicknesses of wood — up to a maximum of 3".

The arm of the clamp has a clearance slot for flexibility, and one side is longer than the other. This design allows more options when clamping down workpieces.

To clamp a workpiece flat with its *face* against the surface of the bench or tabletop, position the clamp so the longer side of the arm is holding down the piece (see left photo below).

To clamp workpieces that are standing *on edge*, or to clamp several pieces of wood stacked together, position the clamp with the shorter side holding down the wood (see right photo).

This clamp design also gives flexibility in *where* the arm contacts the piece to hold it down.

WOODWORKER'S NOTEBOOK

CLAMP APPLICATIONS

You will find many applications for the hold-down clamps, from basic shop tasks to help with detailed carving. Below are three examples of uses for this versatile project.

■ Once you have finished making two or more of the wooden hold-down clamps shown on page 22, you will find that they will come in handy for a large variety of applications and projects around the shop.

You have already seen the hold-down clamps as they would be used for freehand routing and planing, but three additional examples of uses for the clamps are shown below. They help to illustrate the wide variety of tasks that can be made easier by adding the clamps to a bench or tabletop, or even a power tool jig.

But this is only a small portion of the applications you may find once you start using them. Ordinary shop duties such as filing and sanding, as well as additional jigs become more efficient with these clamps.

And you don't even have to build the clamps exactly as shown. You can experiment, making the same basic style in different sizes and shapes to fit other tools and jigs (for an example of an alternate style, refer to the Taper Jig on pages 102-107).

RIPPING JIG

■ At times if the edge of a board is especially crooked (or if you don't have a jointer), you may have to turn to the table saw to rip a straight edge.

And if there is no straight edge to run against the rip fence of your table saw, this requires a simple jig (see photo above right). The hold-down clamps on this jig provide a good way of securing the workpiece.

The jig is just a piece of plywood that acts as a "sled," carrying the board through the saw blade.

To position the board, use the edge of the plywood sled as a reference to show where the blade will cut through.

To do this, start by ripping the plywood so it's wider than the workpiece you want to rip (see photo above).

Without moving the rip fence, position the board so the edge you want to remove hangs over the plywood.

To attach the workpiece to the sled, you could use woodscrews. But by using hold-down clamps fastened to the sled, you avoid putting unnecessary screw holes in the workpiece.

DRILL PRESS HOLD-DOWN

■ A drill press may seem safe in comparison to other tools, but especially with large bits, the drill can "grab" a workpiece and swing it around, making for a dangerous situation.

The hold-down clamps help solve this problem. Not only will they hold the workpiece down securely, but they can also improve accuracy.

To use the hold-downs on a drill press table, you can make an auxiliary table (see photo) and thread T-nuts into it (refer to *Fig. 1* on page 24). The auxiliary table can then be clamped or bolted to your drill press table.

Note: You could also add a series of T-nuts to a drill press table, like the one shown on page 82.

CARVING HOLD-DOWN

■ It isn't just machine tool tasks like ripping and drilling that the hold-down clamps can make safer and more efficient. They can also allow for a worry-free session of detailed carving (see photo at left).

The clamps are easy to reposition, and small enough to stay out of the way.

Also, since they are wooden, if you do hit one with a carving tool, the tool won't get damaged as easily as it would if it hit a metal dog or clamp.

Most importantly, the clamps hold your carving securely. The last thing you want is for the piece to slip, causing you to ruin your project.

Jointer Push Block

This push block lets you apply forward and downward pressure on a board as you run it through a jointer. It also keeps your hands safely away from the cutterhead.

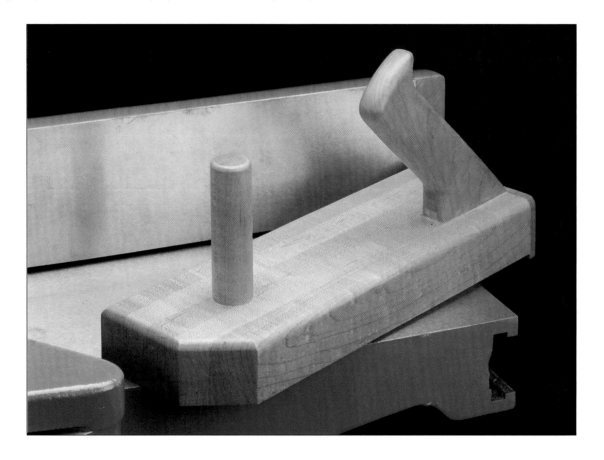

A power jointer can be a very useful tool to have in your workshop. Its main job is squaring up the edges of a workpiece, making it the tool of choice when readying boards for edge gluing. The jointer is also the perfect tool to use for smoothing the faces of unsurfaced boards, and even for flattening boards that have become cupped or bowed.

SAFETY. In principle, a jointer seems significantly safer than other machine tools, such as a table saw or router, but there is still risk involved, especially when working with rough or twisted boards. Keeping your hands behind the cutterhead as you start to push a board through the machine is a good practice.

The real safety concern, however, is when the end of the board passes over the cutterhead: how do you apply even pressure all the way along the workpiece — right out to the end — without putting your hands in jeopardy?

To make using the jointer safer and more efficient, I made a jointer push block. It isn't very complicated, and it's made from materials most woodworkers already have around the shop: $3/4$"-thick stock, a hardwood dowel, and a piece of $1/4$"-thick tempered hardboard. If you use your jointer for flattening boards, you'll find yourself reaching for it every time.

DUAL PRESSURE. This push block allows you to apply pressure in two directions: forward to move the workpiece over the cutterhead, and downward to keep the board flat against the jointer table. That constant, even pressure is especially useful in creating a consistent cut over the entire length of the workpiece.

The shape and placement of the two handles make it a very natural push block to use, even for long boards. (For more on using the push block, see the Technique section on page 29.)

Most important, whether you're handling long boards or short, the push block's thick body offers ample protection and the two-handed grip keeps your hands exactly where they belong all the way through the pass.

EXPLODED VIEW

OVERALL DIMENSIONS:
12¼L X 3¾W X 7H

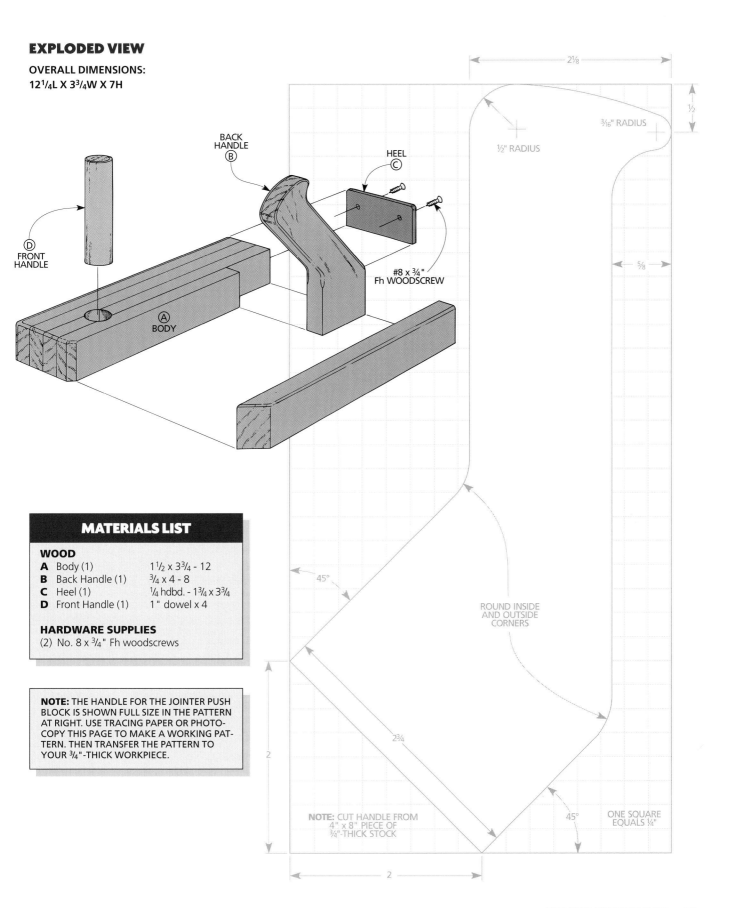

FRONT
HANDLE
Ⓓ

BACK
HANDLE
Ⓑ

HEEL
Ⓒ

Ⓐ
BODY

#8 x ¾"
Fh WOODSCREW

2⅛

½

3⁄16" RADIUS

½" RADIUS

5⁄8

45°

ROUND INSIDE
AND OUTSIDE
CORNERS

2¾

2

45°

ONE SQUARE
EQUALS ¼"

NOTE: CUT HANDLE FROM
4" x 8" PIECE OF
¾"-THICK STOCK

2

MATERIALS LIST

WOOD
A	Body (1)	1½ x 3¾ - 12
B	Back Handle (1)	¾ x 4 - 8
C	Heel (1)	¼ hdbd. - 1¾ x 3¾
D	Front Handle (1)	1 " dowel x 4

HARDWARE SUPPLIES
(2) No. 8 x ¾" Fh woodscrews

NOTE: THE HANDLE FOR THE JOINTER PUSH
BLOCK IS SHOWN FULL SIZE IN THE PATTERN
AT RIGHT. USE TRACING PAPER OR PHOTO-
COPY THIS PAGE TO MAKE A WORKING PAT-
TERN. THEN TRANSFER THE PATTERN TO
YOUR ¾"-THICK WORKPIECE.

To make the jointer push block, I began by building the body.

BODY. To distribute the pressure from your hands evenly over a board during a cut, the body (A) of the push block is 12" long and $1^1/2$" thick. But it's not made from a single piece of stock. It's glued up from five $3/4$"-thick strips *(Fig. 1)*. I did this for two reasons.

First, by building up the body in strips, it's less likely to warp or twist. This is important since the whole purpose of jointing is to end up with a board that has a flat face.

Second, by cutting one of the strips shorter than the rest, it's easy to create a "pocket" for the back handle that's added later *(Fig. 1)*. Trying to cut a notch out of a solid piece of stock would be less efficient.

POCKET. To provide some "knuckle room" between the handle and the jointer fence, the pocket is not centered on the body. Rather, it is located off-center by $3/4$". To do this, start by gluing up three 12"-long strips and one $9^1/4$"-long strip *(Fig. 1)*.

BACK HANDLE. After gluing up the four strips, set them aside for a moment. The next step is to make the back handle *(Fig. 1)*.

The shape of this handle is patterned after the handle on a bench plane. This allows it to fit your hand comfortably and also apply pressure in the proper directions (see "Using a Push Block" on the opposite page).

LAY OUT SHAPE. To make the back handle (B), start by laying out the shape on a piece of $3/4$"-thick stock that is 4" wide and 8" long (refer to the Handle Pattern on page 27).

Next, cut out the shape (using a band saw or sabre saw) and round over the edges that will be exposed *(Fig. 1)*.

Note: To ensure that the handle fits tightly in the pocket, don't round over the bottom edges.

ATTACH HANDLE. When the back handle is complete, the rest of the body can be assembled.

This is just a matter of gluing the handle into the pocket, then gluing the outside (12") strip in place *(Fig. 1)*.

BEVEL CORNER. At this point, the body of the push block is nearly complete. There are only two more steps.

First, to prevent the push block from catching the cutter guard when jointing narrow pieces, I cut a 45° bevel on the

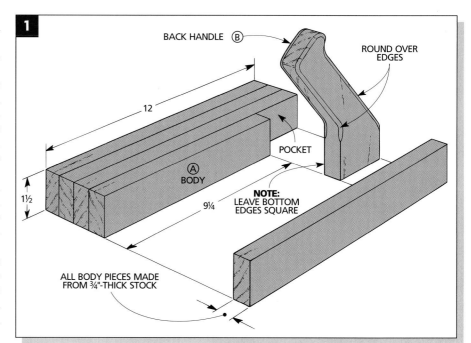

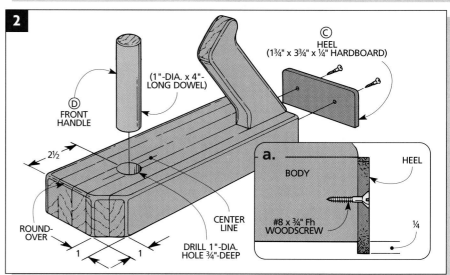

front outside corner of the body *(Fig. 2)*. This bevel should be cut in 1" from both the front and side of the body.

Second, round over the front and side edges of the body the same way you did with the back handle *(Fig. 2)*. This will ensure a smooth ride through the jointer each time, as well as making the block more comfortable to handle.

HEEL. After beveling the corner and rounding over the sharp edges of the body, the next step is to make the heel (C) *(Fig. 2)*.

The heel is made to "hook" over the end of a workpiece, which allows you to push it over the cutterhead. This heel is made from a piece of $1/4$" tempered hardboard that is cut to a length of $3^3/4$" (to match the width of the body).

The heel's width is $1^3/4$" (wider than

the thickness of the body), because it needs to extend $1/4$" below the bottom of the body to catch the workpiece.

Once you've cut the heel to size, drill two $3/16$"-dia. shank holes through it. Then position the heel against the body and drill pilot holes. Finally, glue and screw it in place with two No. 8 x $3/4$" flathead woodscrews *(Fig. 2a)*.

FRONT HANDLE. All that's left is to add the front handle (D) *(Fig. 2)*. This handle provides a safe place for your left hand as you apply downward pressure on the workpiece.

The front handle is just a 1"-dia. hardwood dowel that's cut to a length of 4" *(Fig. 2)*. To accept this dowel, drill a $3/4$"-deep hole in the body of the push block, centered $2^1/2$" from the front. Then simply glue the dowel in place. ■

TECHNIQUE ...... Using a Push Block

The jointer push block shown on page 26 is designed with a couple of simple but important things in mind.

First, it allows you to hold a workpiece down flat on the jointer table throughout a cut, even if it is a long or irregular board.

And second, it keeps your hands a safe distance away from the jointer's cutterhead, without sacrificing stability or accuracy.

Using the push block is fairly straightforward, but there are several things to keep in mind.

POSITION BOARD. Before you ever start using the push block to joint the face of a board, first be sure to orient your workpiece correctly. If the board is cupped, be sure you lay the board on the jointer table so the cupped side faces down. This way, the board can ride on the two edges, rather than "rocking" on a curved face.

Also try to position the board so the grain is running *down* toward the back of the board. In other words, just look at the edge of the board and make sure the grain is angled downward from front to back. This will help reduce the amount of tearout, due to the rotation of the cutterhead (toward the back of the board). Some boards have wild grain, so it may be difficult to choose which position will cause the least tearout, but do the best you can.

POSITION BLOCK. Once you have the board situated in the most favorable position, it's time to bring in the jointer push block.

The hardboard heel of the block is "hooked" over the back end of the workpiece, and the body of the block should rest flat against the upper face of the board *(Fig. 1)*.

Note: If the board is cupped or bowed slightly, make sure the $1/4''$ extension of the heel is catching enough of the workpiece to hold it securely throughout the cut. You don't want the push block to slip off the board, causing you to lurch forward toward the cutterhead.

BEGIN THE CUT. Now you are ready to begin pushing the workpiece forward over the cutterhead with the back handle *(Fig. 1)*.

On a long board, the downward pressure is provided initially by placing your left hand on top of the workpiece in back of the cutterhead.

Note: Be sure to keep your left hand a safe distance behind the cutterhead. Do not trust the board alone to protect your hand.

The idea here is to maintain consistent pressure as you feed the workpiece underneath your hand. You don't want to stop and start again on a jointer; rather you want to keep a smooth motion the whole time.

FINISH CUT. When the push block is almost touching your left hand, keep holding the block steady with your right hand and transfer the downward pressure (with your left hand) from the board to the front handle.

Then you can complete the cut, without stopping or shifting *(Fig. 2)*.

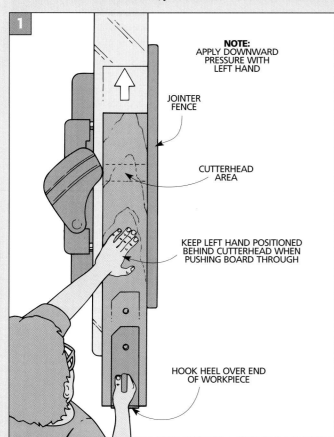

Beginning of cut. To begin, push with the back handle while your left hand presses down on the board (behind the cutter).

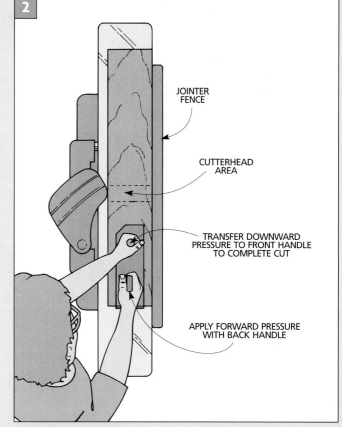

End of cut. To complete the cut, transfer the downward pressure (with your left hand) to the front handle.

PORTABLE TOOL JIGS

These jigs help you get smoother surfaces, more accurate layout, truer cuts, and add custom touches to any project. They'll teach your old tools new tricks.

Flush Trim Jig

While many jigs are built to do only one job, this one for your router can perform double duty. Made to trim two surfaces flush with each other, it's also easily modified to cut perfect rabbets.

Getting a piece of hardwood edging perfectly flush with the surface of a workpiece seems like a simple thing to do.

But it often requires a lot of scraping and sanding. I always worry that I might stray off the edging and scratch the workpiece. And if this surface is covered with thin veneer or a piece of plastic laminate, I don't like to risk it.

ROUTER. So to make it easy to trim edging flush, I made a simple jig for my router. The router is mounted to a platform that sits on the worksurface, so that a straight bit just barely touches it. As you slide the jig across the work-piece, the router bit "planes" the edging strip flush with the adjoining surface.

ADJUSTABLE STOP. To allow you to rout right up to (but not past) where the edging meets the surface, there's an adjustable stop under the end of the platform. This stop is simply a bearing that rides against the edging (see inset photo).

EDGE GUIDE. Another nice thing about this jig is that with a quick modification, it can be used for more than flush trimming. Just replace the stop with a shop-made edge guide as shown

in the Woodworker's Notebook on page 37. Now you can use a straight bit to rout a rabbet without having to clamp a fence to your workpiece.

MATERIALS. The main platform is made of 3/4" medium density fiberboard (MDF) with a base of 1/4" hardboard. The handle and the arm to hold the guide bearing can be made from scraps of hardwood.

EXPLODED VIEW

OVERALL DIMENSIONS:
6W X 20L X 3½ H

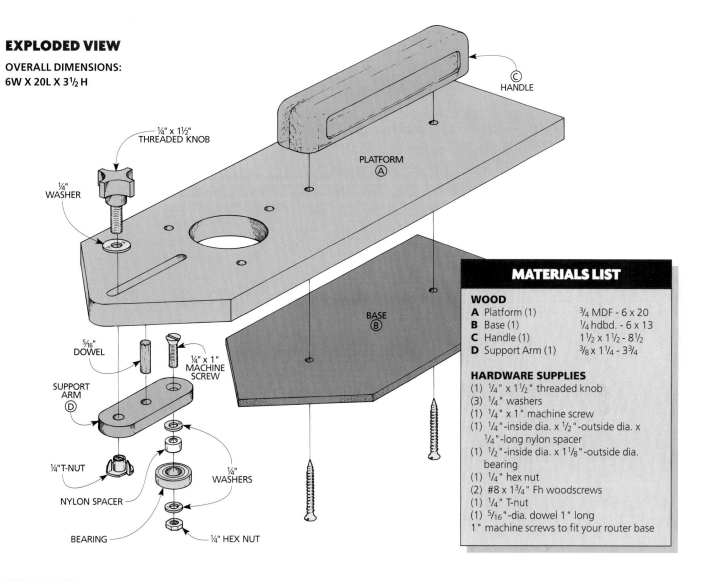

¼" x 1½"
THREADED KNOB

¼"
WASHER

PLATFORM
Ⓐ

HANDLE
Ⓒ

⁵⁄₁₆"
DOWEL

SUPPORT
ARM
Ⓓ

¼" x 1"
MACHINE
SCREW

BASE
Ⓑ

¼" T-NUT

NYLON SPACER

BEARING

¼"
WASHERS

¼" HEX NUT

MATERIALS LIST

WOOD
A	Platform (1)	¾ MDF - 6 x 20
B	Base (1)	¼ hdbd. - 6 x 13
C	Handle (1)	1½ x 1½ - 8½
D	Support Arm (1)	⅜ x 1¼ - 3¾

HARDWARE SUPPLIES
(1) ¼" x 1½" threaded knob
(3) ¼" washers
(1) ¼" x 1" machine screw
(1) ¼"-inside dia. x ½"-outside dia. x
    ¼"-long nylon spacer
(1) ½"-inside dia. x 1⅛"-outside dia.
    bearing
(1) ¼" hex nut
(2) #8 x 1¾" Fh woodscrews
(1) ¼" T-nut
(1) ⁵⁄₁₆"-dia. dowel 1" long
1" machine screws to fit your router base

SHOP JIG .... *Finger Recess Jig*

A hand-held router with a core box bit makes quick work of cutting the finger recess in the handle of the flush trim jig. All you need to guide the bit is a guide bushing and a template made from ¼" hardboard (see drawing).

First, cut an opening in the template shaped like the recess. The opening has to be slightly *larger* than the desired size of the recess. The reason for this is simple. When the bushing is attached to the base of your router, it rides against the edge of the opening. This means the bit won't cut right up next to the edge (see detail).

To determine the size of the opening, first measure the distance from the outside edge of the core box bit to the outside edge of the bushing.

Then to account for both sides of the opening, add *twice* that amount to the desired size of the finger recess.

After cutting the opening in the template, center the opening on the side of the handle blank.

Then, to keep the template from shifting, screw two wood pinch blocks to the bottom so they fit snug against the handle (see detail). Tightening these blocks in a vise holds the handle in place while you rout the recess.

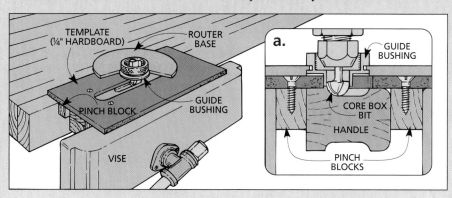

TEMPLATE
(¼" HARDBOARD)

ROUTER
BASE

PINCH BLOCK

GUIDE
BUSHING

VISE

a.

GUIDE
BUSHING

CORE BOX
BIT

HANDLE

PINCH
BLOCKS

The flush trim jig starts out as a simple platform (A) that supports the router (*Fig. 1*).

The platform is a piece of ¾"-thick MDF with the corners at one end cut at a 90° angle. The point left at the tip is then rounded with a file to a 1" radius (Detail in *Fig. 1*).

To accept the stop (added later), an adjustment slot is cut near the angled end. And a hole provides an opening for the router bit to stick through. (I made the hole large enough so I could see the workpiece as I'm routing.)

MOUNTING HOLES. With the platform complete, the next step is to mark holes for mounting the router. The best way to do this is to use the base plate from your router as a template (*Fig. 1*).

What you want to do here is position the base plate so you'll have an unobstructed view through the opening in the side of the router and the hole in the platform. In my case, this meant laying out the holes so the handles of the router would be about 45° to the platform (refer to photo on page 32).

Now it's just a matter of drilling the holes. To prevent the screws that hold the router in place from scratching the surface of a workpiece, don't forget to countersink the holes on the bottom of the platform.

BASE. The next step is to add a ¼" hardboard base (B) (*Fig. 2*). The base raises the platform above the surface of the workpiece so it extends over the edging as you rout. By lowering the router bit below the platform, the edging can be trimmed flush with the workpiece surface.

To provide support right up to (but not touching) the bit, the end of the base is also cut at a 90° angle (*Fig. 2a*). Then the base is glued in place, smooth side down.

HANDLE. While you're routing, it's important that the end of the jig that's opposite the router is held down firmly against the workpiece. Otherwise the jig could tip and cause the bit to cut too deeply or even gouge the edging.

I started with an oversize blank (C) (*Fig. 3*) so I could safely rout a ⅛"-deep finger recess using a core box bit. When the recess is routed, the handle is cut to shape and all but the bottom edges are rounded over. Then it's glued and screwed to the platform (*Fig. 3*).

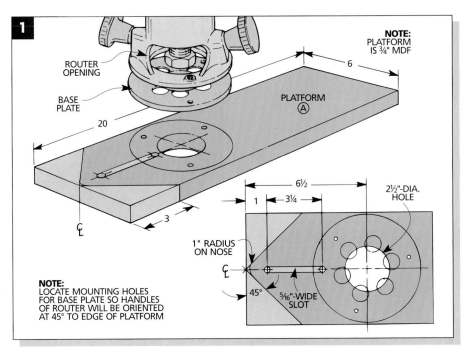

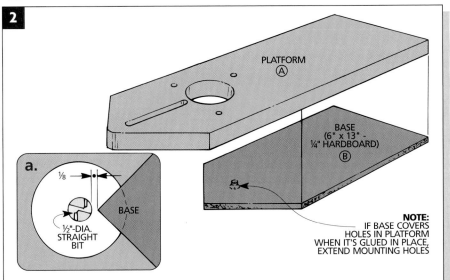

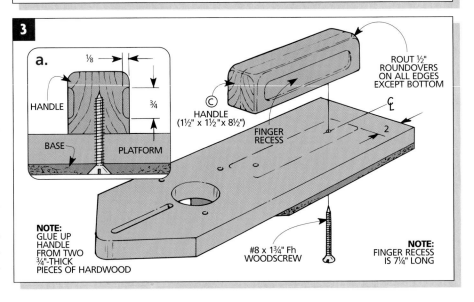

STOP. Now all that's left is to add the adjustable stop. It's just a bearing that's attached to a hardwood support arm (D) *(Figs. 4 and 4a)*.

The bearing is held to the bottom of the support arm with a machine screw and hex nut. But to ensure that it spins freely, a nylon spacer fits in the hole in the bearing. And a pair of washers "sandwich" the bearing *(Fig. 4)*.

To make the stop adjustable, a $^5/_{16}$"-diameter dowel that's glued into the support arm slides back and forth in the slot in the platform.

And to lock the stop into position, a threaded knob runs through the platform of the jig and into a T-nut in the support arm. By tightening the threaded knob, you pull the stop tight to the bottom of the platform, locking it in place *(Fig. 4b)*.

SETUP

Once you've completed the flush trim jig, set up takes only a few minutes.

MOUNTING ROUTER. The first step is to mount the router to the platform. First, remove the plastic base from your router. Since the platform is made of $^3/_4$"-thick material, you may have to buy longer mounting screws. And since some routers use metric screws, it's a good idea to take your router with you when you go buy them. That way you can check that the screws fit properly.

STOP. After mounting the router, the next step is to set the adjustable stop. The goal here is simple. You want to position the bearing on the stop so the bit will cut right up next to (but not past) the point where the edging meets the plastic laminate (or veneer) *(Fig. 5a)*.

When setting the stop, place a square against the edging and the base of the jig. This keeps the platform perpendicular to the edging. So even if you angle the jig while you're routing, the bearing will prevent the bit from cutting too far in from the edge.

DEPTH OF CUT. The last thing to do is adjust the depth of cut. The idea is to adjust the bit so it's perfectly flush with the base *(Fig. 6)*. This way, the bit will trim the edging flush with the surface that the base is riding on.

To do this, set a metal ruler on the hardboard base of the jig. The ruler should extend over the bit opening. Then adjust the height of the bit until it *barely* grazes the ruler. Lock the bit in place and your jig is ready to use. ∎

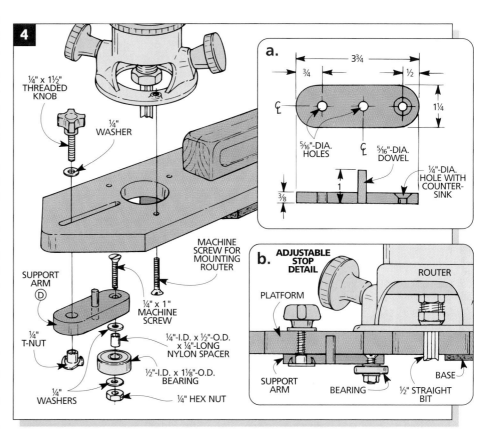

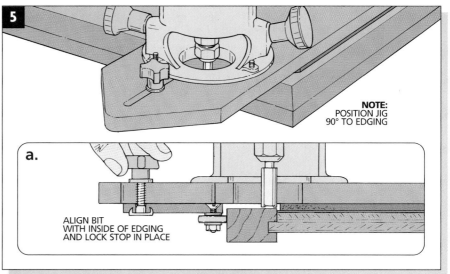

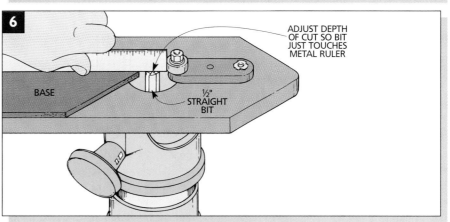

TECHNIQUE.. *Using the Flush Trim Jig*

Proper setup is only the first part of getting the most from the Flush Trim Jig. Before you fire up the router, there are a couple of techniques you should know that will help you get the best results possible.

FIRST PASS. Once the jig is set up, you can't just set the bit on top of the edging strip and turn on the router. That's because the bit is set to cut *deeper* than the part of the edging that sticks up above the plastic laminate on the surface.

So to avoid accidentally gouging the edging, you'll need to lower the spinning bit onto the workpiece. To do this, raise the nose of the jig slightly so the bit clears the edging. Slowly move the jig back until the guide bearing contacts the edging. Then lower the bit onto the workpiece.

Make the first pass (and all other passes) by routing from right to left along the inside edge *(Fig. 1)*. Use a steady feed rate to get the best results.

If the edging on the project wraps around more than one side (for example on a countertop or table top), make a pass on all the edging strips with this setup.

Where two pieces of edging meet at a corner, the bit won't cut clear to the end of either piece. That's because the base of the jig will hit the lip formed by the adjacent piece of edging *(Fig. 2)*. You'll need to lift the router when it bumps into this lip, then reposition it over the next piece of edging and resume routing. The corners will be cleaned up later.

SECOND PASS. After you finish the first pass, there's no need to reset the stop. Just reposition the jig at the right end of the edging and make another pass freehand. Don't worry about straying off a perfectly straight line. The stop will prevent you from routing past the edging.

Then make more passes as needed to remove the remaining waste.

CORNERS. As you work your way toward the outside edge, the jig's base will contact the waste at the corner left by the previous pass. This forms a scalloped border at the corners *(Fig. 2a)*.

To clean this up, you'll need to "nibble" away at the waste from both sides *(Fig. 3)*. To do this, simply start at the inside of the corner of one side and gradually work toward the outside edge.

Save this corner cleanup until last, after you have the bulk of the waste trimmed from the edging.

When the edging is flush, a light sanding will remove any remaining swirl marks left by the router bit. To keep from scratching the surface of the workpiece as you sand close to the joint line, put some masking tape next to the edging.

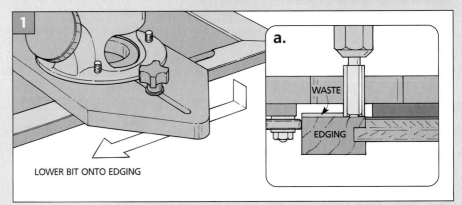

1
LOWER BIT ONTO EDGING

a.
WASTE
EDGING

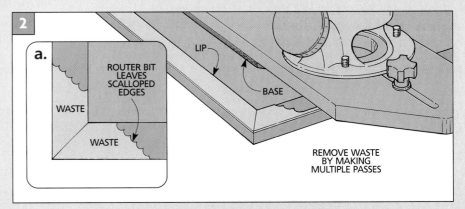

2
a.
ROUTER BIT LEAVES SCALLOPED EDGES
WASTE
WASTE

LIP
BASE
REMOVE WASTE BY MAKING MULTIPLE PASSES

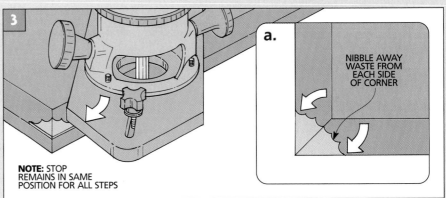

3
a.
NIBBLE AWAY WASTE FROM EACH SIDE OF CORNER

NOTE: STOP REMAINS IN SAME POSITION FOR ALL STEPS

WOODWORKER'S NOTEBOOK

With this simple modification, you can turn the flush trim jig into a jig for cutting precise rabbets. Plus you can rout the rabbets with a regular straight bit instead of a special rabbet bit.

EDGE GUIDE

As an option, you can replace the adjustable stop with an edge guide that helps you rout rabbets quickly and accurately. The edge guide also lets you cut rabbets wider than regular rabbet bits will cut.

The edge guide consists of a triangular-shaped support plate (E) with a fence (F) glued to the edge *(Fig. 1)*.

To make the edge guide adjustable, the support plate slides in and out. Use the same idea as with the support arm on the flush trim jig — a dowel glued into a hole drilled near the center of the support plate (Detail in *Fig. 1*).

To keep the edge guide aligned as it slides in and out, a threaded knob tightens into a T-nut to lock it in place *(Fig. 1a)*.

Clearance for the router bit is provided by cutting a semi-circular opening in the edge with the fence (Detail in *Fig. 1*).

To set the rabbet width, measure from the face of the fence to the opposite side of the router bit.

MATERIALS LIST

NEW PARTS
E Support Plate (1) $1/2$ x 6 - 10
F Fence (1) $1/2$ x 1 - 10

HARDWARE SUPPLIES
(1) $1/4$" T-nut

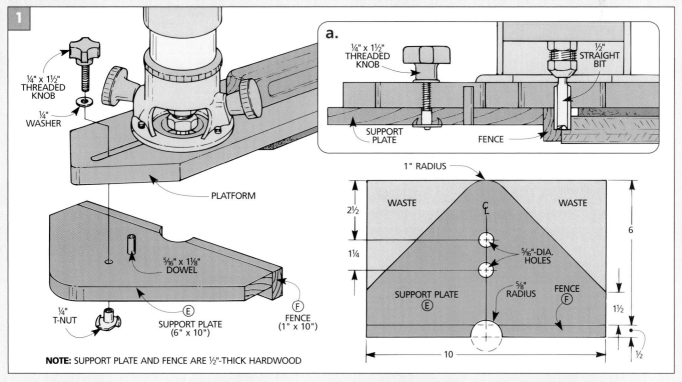

1

$1/4$" x $1\frac{1}{2}$" THREADED KNOB

$1/4$" WASHER

a.

$1/4$" x $1\frac{1}{2}$" THREADED KNOB

$1/2$" STRAIGHT BIT

SUPPORT PLATE

FENCE

PLATFORM

$5/16$" x $1\frac{1}{8}$" DOWEL

$1/4$" T-NUT

SUPPORT PLATE (6" x 10")

FENCE (1" x 10")

1" RADIUS

$2\frac{1}{2}$

WASTE

WASTE

$1\frac{1}{4}$

$5/16$"-DIA. HOLES

6

SUPPORT PLATE (E)

$5/8$" RADIUS

FENCE (F)

$1\frac{1}{2}$

10

$1/2$

NOTE: SUPPORT PLATE AND FENCE ARE $1/2$"-THICK HARDWOOD

Shelf Pin Drilling Guide

*Drill holes for your shelf pins in the right place every time with this adjustable guide.
Or you can make a simple-to-build fixed version of this useful jig.*

The idea for this jig came to me after I had built a cabinet with adjustable shelves like the one in the inset photo. When I set the first shelf in place, it rocked back and forth on only three of the four shelf pins.

The reason was simple. One pin wasn't aligned with the other three.

INDEX. I built this drilling guide to prevent that mistake from happening again. It automatically indexes the holes for the shelf pins in *two* directions. First, it sets the distance in from the edge of the workpiece. And second, it accurately and consistently indexes the spacing between each hole.

LOCKING SYSTEM. This accuracy starts with a unique locking system. Once you set the guide for the desired distance from the edge of the workpiece, tightening a couple of nuts locks in the adjustment.

INDEX PIN AND GUIDE HOLES. To keep the spacing between each hole identical, an index pin fits into the last hole drilled. A slot in the drilling guide fits over the pin and automatically determines the spacing for the next hole.

I designed my jig to drill $1/4$"-dia. holes either 2" or 3" apart. If you want different spacing, just drill these holes where you need them when building

the jig. To prevent the bit from enlarging the guide holes after repeated use, the holes are lined with bronze bushings.

VARIATION. There's also a different way to build the jig without as much hardware. In this simpler version, you can't adjust the distance from the holes to the edge of the workpiece. But since it's quick to make, it's ideal for use on a specific project. See the Woodworker's Notebook on page 43 for details.

EXPLODED VIEW

OVERALL DIMENSIONS:
$6^3/8$"W X 7L X $2^3/8$H

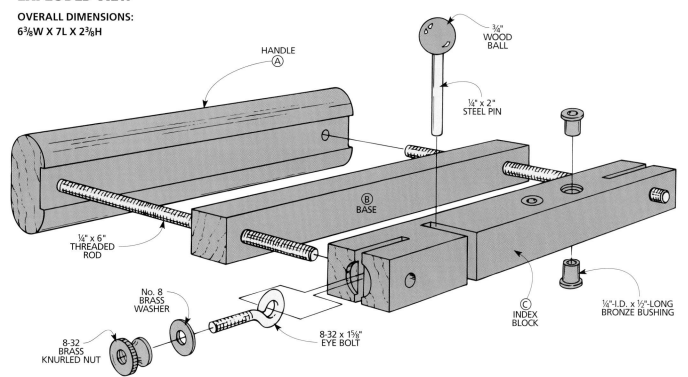

HANDLE
Ⓐ

¾"
WOOD
BALL

¼" x 2"
STEEL PIN

Ⓑ
BASE

¼" x 6"
THREADED
ROD

No. 8
BRASS
WASHER

8-32
BRASS
KNURLED NUT

8-32 x 1⅝"
EYE BOLT

Ⓒ
INDEX
BLOCK

¼"-I.D. x ½"-LONG
BRONZE BUSHING

MATERIALS LIST

WOOD
A Handle (1)   ¾ x 2 - 7
B Base (1)   ¾ x 1 - 7
C Index Block (1)   1 x 1½ - 7

HARDWARE SUPPLIES
(2) ¼" x 6" threaded rods
(2) 8-32 x 1⅝" eye bolts
(2) 8-32 knurled nuts

(2) No. 8 washers
(4) ¼"-in. dia. x ½" bronze bushings
(1) ¼" x 3" bolt
(1) ¾"-dia. wood ball

HARDWARE

KNURLED NUT AND EYE BOLT. *Tightening a knurled nut pulls an eye bolt against a threaded rod to lock in the adjustment.*

CUTOFF BOLT AND BALL. *An index pin made from a cutoff bolt and a wood ball positions the guide for the next hole.*

BRONZE BUSHINGS. *To reduce wear from repeated drilling, each guide hole is lined with a pair of bronze bushings.*

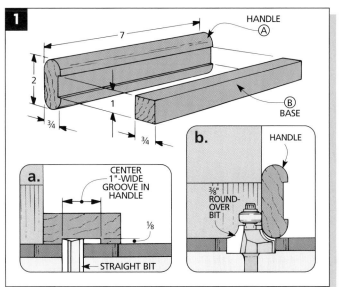

1

HANDLE Ⓐ

7

2

¾

¾

1

Ⓑ BASE

a.
CENTER 1"-WIDE GROOVE IN HANDLE

⅛

STRAIGHT BIT

b.
HANDLE

⅜" ROUND-OVER BIT

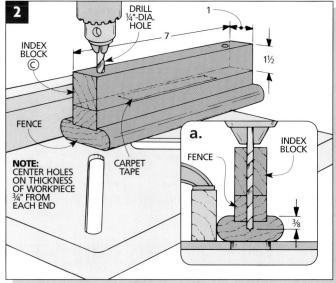

2

DRILL ¼"-DIA. HOLE

INDEX BLOCK Ⓒ

1

7

1½

FENCE

NOTE: CENTER HOLES ON THICKNESS OF WORKPIECE ¾" FROM EACH END

CARPET TAPE

a.
FENCE

INDEX BLOCK

⅜

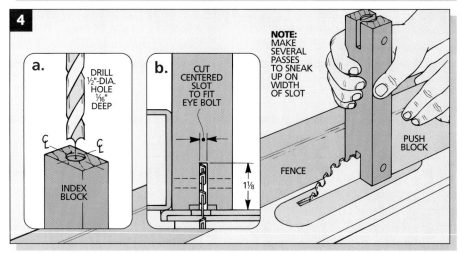

3

Ⓐ HANDLE

INDEX BLOCK Ⓒ

BASE Ⓑ

EPOXY THREADED ROD IN FENCE

INDEX BLOCK SLIDES BACK AND FORTH ON THREADED RODS

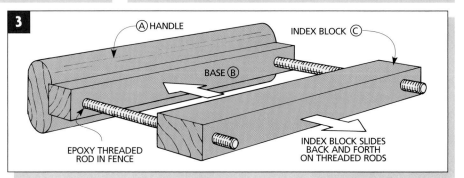

4

a.
DRILL ½"-DIA. HOLE 1/16" DEEP

INDEX BLOCK

b.
CUT CENTERED SLOT TO FIT EYE BOLT

1⅛

NOTE: MAKE SEVERAL PASSES TO SNEAK UP ON WIDTH OF SLOT

PUSH BLOCK

FENCE

5

AUXILIARY FENCE

a.
CUT WIDTH OF SLOT TO FIT PIN

1⅞

1

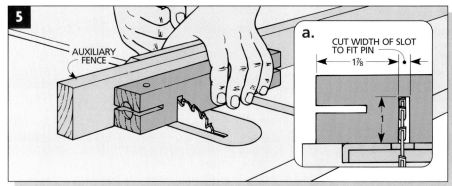

CONSTRUCTION

The drilling guide consists of two parts. The handle (A) and base (B) form a fence that positions the guide on the workpiece *(Fig. 3)*. And an index block (C) slides on a pair of threaded rods to set the location of the holes.

FENCE. The handle (A) and base (B) are ¾"-thick hardwood *(Fig. 1)*. To accept the base, there's a wide, shallow groove routed in the handle *(Fig. 1a)*. Before gluing these pieces together, I rounded the edges of the handle to provide a comfortable grip *(Fig. 1b)*.

THREADED RODS. Now you can start to add the threaded rods. They pass through holes drilled in the index block and into the handle *(Fig. 2)*. So it's important to keep the holes aligned.

To do this, first cut a blank for the index block (C) and temporarily fasten it to the base (B) using carpet tape. Then drill the holes and epoxy the rods in the fence *(Figs. 2 and 3)*.

LOCKING MECHANISM. What's unique about this drilling guide is the index system. It sets the distance in from the edge of the workpiece. And it ensures identical spacing between each hole. To make this work, there's a simple mechanism that locks the index block on the threaded rods.

The key to this mechanism is a pair of eye bolts. Each eye bolt fits in a slot in the end of the block (refer to *Fig. 9*). The "eyes" of these bolts provide openings for the threaded rods to pass through (refer to *Fig. 9a*). This way, when you tighten a knurled nut (and washer) on the end of the bolt, it pulls tight against the rod and locks the index block in place.

Before cutting the slots for the eye bolts, it's easiest to drill a shallow counterbore for the washer centered on each end *(Fig. 4a)*. Then just cut the centered slots so the eye bolts fit snug *(Figs. 4 and 4b)*.

There's one more slot to cut. But this time it's on the edge of the index block *(Fig. 5)*. The purpose of this slot is simple. It slips over an index pin (added later) that's placed in the last hole you've drilled in the workpiece. This automatically indexes the drilling guide for the next hole.

To prevent any "play," it's important to cut the slot so the index pin fits snug. I used a $\frac{1}{4}$"-dia. bolt for the pin and took several passes over the table saw to sneak up on the final width of the slot *(Fig. 5a)*.

GUIDE HOLES. Once the slot for the index pin is cut, the next step is to lay out two holes that will be used to guide the bit when drilling the holes for the shelf pins.

To provide two options for the spacing between the pins, one hole is located 2" from the center of the slot, and the other is 3" *(Fig. 6)*.

HAIRLINES. To make it easy to align the drilling guide later, I used a knife to scribe "hairlines" through the centerpoint of each hole and extended them around the block *(Fig. 6)*. Finally, a simple drilling sequence ensures that the bronze bushings (added later) will align (Details in *Fig. 6*).

HARDWARE INSTALLATION

To prevent enlarging the guide holes through repeated drilling, I "lined" each of the holes with two bronze bushings *(Fig. 7)*. Use a vise to press the bushings snugly into the holes *(Fig. 7a)*.

INDEX PIN. After assembling the drilling guide, all that's left is to add the index pin *(Fig. 8)*. This is simply the unthreaded shank of a $\frac{1}{4}$" bolt, cut off and glued with epoxy into a hole drilled in a wood ball.

To make it easy to center the hole in the ball, first use your drill press to drill a $\frac{1}{2}$"-dia. hole in a piece of scrap. Then without moving the scrap, chuck a $\frac{1}{4}$" bit into the drill press. Now cradle the ball in the hole (a screw clamp works well for this) and drill the hole into the ball *(Fig. 8a)*. ∎

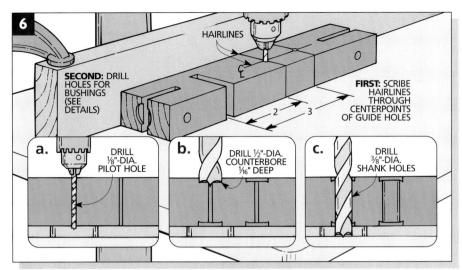

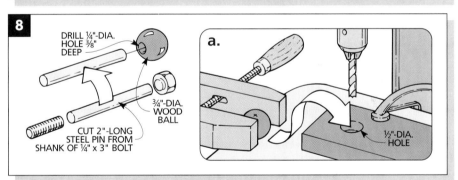

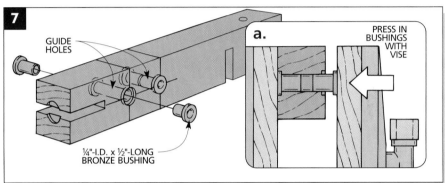

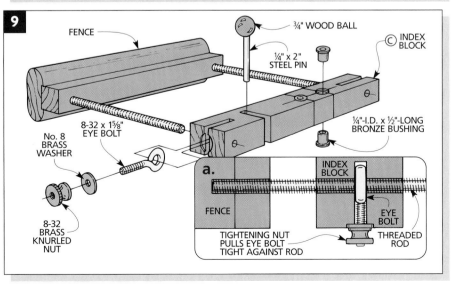

Building this Shelf Pin Drilling Guide is pretty straightforward. Using it is also a simple process. But getting the results you hope for all begins with an accurate layout at the start.

Before you start drilling holes, take some time to decide where you want the first set of shelf pins to be.

You can start from the top of the cabinet and work down or from the bottom and work up. Just remember that you won't need holes too close to either the top or bottom edges. After all, you need space for things to sit on the shelves.

Once you've decided on the position of the first shelf, use a framing square to mark a line across the piece at this height *(Step 1)*. While you're measuring, it's a good idea to mark this height on both cabinet sides.

Next, you need to determine how far in from the edges you want the shelf pins to be. It's easiest if you make this the same measurement for both the front and back pins. If these distances are different, you'll need to drill all the holes along one edge of each workpiece, then reset the guide to drill the holes on the other edges.

When you determine how far in you want the holes, set the jig's index block using a ruler. Make sure you measure

from the *handle* of the fence, not the base piece *(Step 2)*.

All that remains in setting up to use the jig is to drill the first hole. After that, the jig takes care of positioning the remaining holes.

To locate the first hole, use the hairlines on the jig to position one of the guide holes on the layout line. Fasten a stop collar on your drill bit to set the hole's depth and drill the hole *(Step 3)*.

Then use the index pin to position the jig for the remaining holes *(Step 4)*.

When it's time to drill the holes on

the other edge of the cabinet, flip the jig over and repeat the process *(Step 6)*.

Note: To prevent drilling in the wrong guide hole, put a piece of tape over it (see photo below).

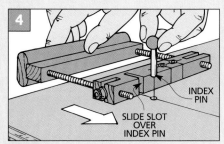

Lay Out Line. *Once you decide how far from the top (or bottom) to start the holes, square a line across the piece.*

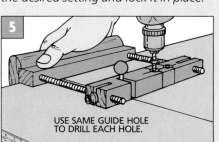

Set the Guide. *To locate the holes in from the edge, slide the index block to the desired setting and lock it in place.*

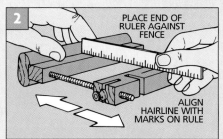

Position Guide. *Position the hairline on the layout line. Hold the fence tight against the edge and drill the first hole.*

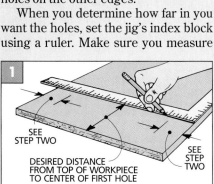

Set Pin. *Now fit the pin in the hole and slide the slot over it to automatically index the guide for the next hole.*

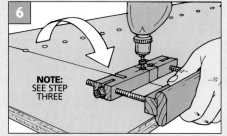

Drill Holes. *Use the appropriate guide hole to drill the next hole. Then continue indexing and drilling the holes.*

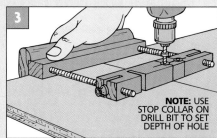

Flip Guide. *To drill the opposite row of holes, flip the guide over and line it up again on the original layout line.*

WOODWORKER'S NOTEBOOK

If you don't need adjustability, and time is a factor, this Shelf Pin Drilling Guide can be put together quickly from scrap. And you can easily customize it to the job at hand.

SIMPLE DRILLING GUIDE

■ This drilling guide consists of just two parts, the handle (A) and the index block (C). The index block is just a piece of 3/4"-thick solid wood. Plywood or MDF would also work.

■ The handle (A) is the same as on the adjustable guide, with two small changes. First, the groove cut in the handle is only 3/4" wide to accept the index block (C). Also, cut this groove 1/4" deep instead of 1/8" deep to provide extra support.

■ Next, cut an index block from 3/4"-thick stock to a width of 6" and a length of 7" *(Fig. 2)*.

■ Now lay out the locations for the holes for the indexing pin and guide holes *(Fig. 2)*. Carry the lines for the guide holes onto the outside edge of the index block *(Fig. 1)*.

Note: Change the position of these holes (if necessary) to suit the layout of your project.

■ Drill 1/4"-dia. holes for the index pin. Drill 5/16"-dia. holes for the guide holes. These oversize holes allow for the bronze bushings added next.

■ Using a vise, press a 3/4"-long bronze bushing into each of the guide holes.

■ Glue and clamp the index block into the handle. Make sure it sits snugly against the bottom of the groove.

■ A simple indexing pin can be made from a 1/4" x 3" bolt. Cut the threads off the bolt to leave a 2"-long pin.

■ To use the jig, mark a line across the workpiece to mark the height of the first row of holes. Then use the mark on the edge of the guide to align one of the guide holes with the layout line on the workpiece.

A piece of masking tape can be wrapped around the bit instead of using a stop collar to indicate the drilling depth (see photo).

MATERIALS LIST

CHANGED PARTS
C Index Block (1)   3/4 x 6 - 7

HARDWARE SUPPLIES
(4) 1/4"-I.D. x 5/16"-O.D. bronze bushings
Note: Do not need part B, threaded rods, knurled nuts, eye bolts, washers, flanged bushings or wood ball.

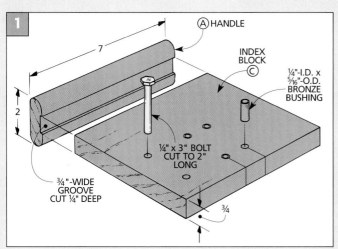

1
7
(A) HANDLE
INDEX BLOCK (C)
1/4"-I.D. x 5/16"-O.D. BRONZE BUSHING
2
1/4" x 3" BOLT CUT TO 2" LONG
3/4"-WIDE GROOVE CUT 1/4" DEEP
3/4

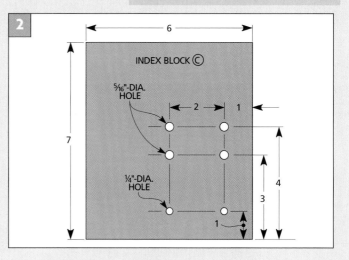

2
6
INDEX BLOCK (C)
5/16"-DIA. HOLE
2   1
7
1/4"-DIA. HOLE
4
3
1

Straight-Edge Guide

There's no chance of your circular saw wandering off course in the middle of a cut with this guide. And with the optional router attachment, you can also cut perfectly straight dadoes and rabbets.

Sometimes a power tool seems to have a mind of its own. Take a circular saw, for instance. Even when you clamp a straightedge to the workpiece, the saw can still wander off course in the middle of a cut.

Before I ruined another sheet of expensive plywood, I built a cutting guide for my circular saw to produce a cut with dead-on accuracy.

CARRIAGE. The unique thing about this cutting guide is the carriage that holds the circular saw snugly and that hooks onto the cutting guide. Because the carriage is "captured" by the cutting guide, it's impossible for the saw to

stray off the line as you slide the tool along to make a cut.

TWO SECTIONS. Since I wanted to be able to cut the full length of a sheet of plywood, the cutting guide is over eight feet long. In fact, to support the carriage at the start and finish of a cut, it's a full nine feet long.

But storing something that long can be a hassle. So I built it in two sections – one is five feet long and the other is four feet long. With just the long section clamped in place, you can cut across the width of a full sheet of plywood. Or simply connect the two parts to cut along the full length of a sheet.

LAYOUT TOOL. Because of the way you build the jig, the edge of the guide shows you exactly where the saw will cut. So it's easy to quickly and accurately align the guide with layout marks on your workpiece.

ROUTER. After using this guide for a while, it dawned on me it could be easily adapted to keep my router on track as well. So I built a simple carriage for my router that hooks onto the guide just like the saw carriage. I've used this set-up to cut dadoes, rabbets, and even to clean up some edges. Details for making this carriage are found in the Woodworker's Notebook on page 49.

EXPLODED VIEW

OVERALL DIMENSIONS:
$7^3/_8$W X $2^1/_2$H X 108L

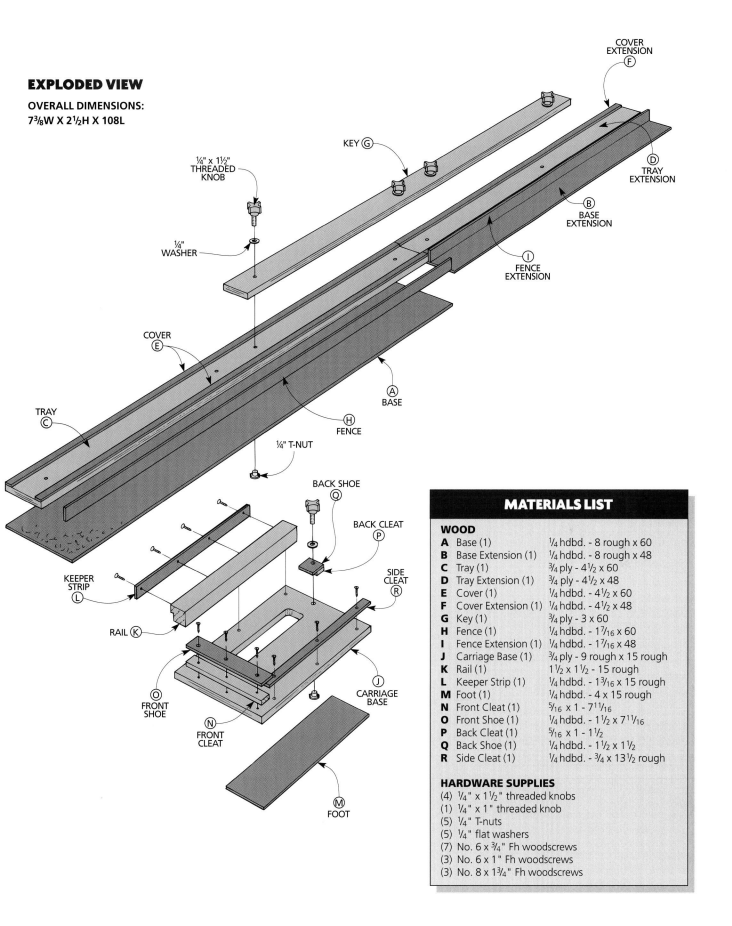

COVER
EXTENSION
(F)

KEY (G)

TRAY
EXTENSION
(D)

BASE
EXTENSION
(B)

FENCE
EXTENSION
(I)

$1/_4$" x $1^1/_2$"
THREADED
KNOB

$1/_4$"
WASHER

COVER
(E)

BASE
(A)

TRAY
(C)

FENCE
(H)

$1/_4$" T-NUT

BACK SHOE
(Q)

BACK CLEAT
(P)

SIDE
CLEAT
(R)

KEEPER
STRIP
(L)

RAIL (K)

FRONT
SHOE
(O)

FRONT
CLEAT
(N)

CARRIAGE
BASE
(J)

FOOT
(M)

MATERIALS LIST

WOOD

A	Base (1)	$1/_4$ hdbd. - 8 rough x 60
B	Base Extension (1)	$1/_4$ hdbd. - 8 rough x 48
C	Tray (1)	$3/_4$ ply - $4^1/_2$ x 60
D	Tray Extension (1)	$3/_4$ ply - $4^1/_2$ x 48
E	Cover (1)	$1/_4$ hdbd. - $4^1/_2$ x 60
F	Cover Extension (1)	$1/_4$ hdbd. - $4^1/_2$ x 48
G	Key (1)	$3/_4$ ply - 3 x 60
H	Fence (1)	$1/_4$ hdbd. - $1^7/_{16}$ x 60
I	Fence Extension (1)	$1/_4$ hdbd. - $1^7/_{16}$ x 48
J	Carriage Base (1)	$3/_4$ ply - 9 rough x 15 rough
K	Rail (1)	$1^1/_2$ x $1^1/_2$ - 15 rough
L	Keeper Strip (1)	$1/_4$ hdbd. - $1^3/_{16}$ x 15 rough
M	Foot (1)	$1/_4$ hdbd. - 4 x 15 rough
N	Front Cleat (1)	$5/_{16}$ x 1 - $7^{11}/_{16}$
O	Front Shoe (1)	$1/_4$ hdbd. - $1^1/_2$ x $7^{11}/_{16}$
P	Back Cleat (1)	$5/_{16}$ x 1 - $1^1/_2$
Q	Back Shoe (1)	$1/_4$ hdbd. - $1^1/_2$ x $1^1/_2$
R	Side Cleat (1)	$1/_4$ hdbd. - $3/_4$ x $13^1/_2$ rough

HARDWARE SUPPLIES

(4) $1/_4$" x $1^1/_2$" threaded knobs
(1) $1/_4$" x 1" threaded knob
(5) $1/_4$" T-nuts
(5) $1/_4$" flat washers
(7) No. 6 x $3/_4$" Fh woodscrews
(3) No. 6 x 1" Fh woodscrews
(3) No. 8 x $1^3/_4$" Fh woodscrews

BASE

The base of the cutting guide consists of two sections. Although the sections are different in length, they're built exactly alike. Each section consists of four parts: a base, tray, cover, and fence *(Fig. 1)*. And there's a single "key" that joins the two sections together.

BASE. To provide a platform for the carriage to ride on, I began by making the base (A) and base extension (B) *(Fig. 1)*. These are strips of ¼"-thick hardboard that are cut to finished lengths and a rough width of 8" *(Figs. 2 and 3)*. (The Woodworker's Notebook on page 55 has tips on working with hardboard.) Later, when you make your first cut with a circular saw, the base pieces will be trimmed to final width.

TRAY. The next step is to add a plywood tray (C) and tray extension (D) to help stiffen the bases *(Fig. 3)*. I used contact cement to join these pieces. Contact cement bonds the two pieces instantly, so they don't slide out of position as they might do if glue were used.

Next, you need to cut a wide, shallow groove that runs the length of the tray pieces. This groove accepts the key (G) (added later).

Forming this groove is a simple two-step process. First, use contact cement to glue on a hardboard cover (E) and cover extension (F) that are the same size as the tray pieces *(Fig. 3)*. Second,

cut a 3"-wide groove centered on the width of the cover pieces. The width doesn't have to be precise, just consistent. The key is cut to fit next.

KEY. After attaching the tray pieces to the base (here again, I used contact cement), the next step is to cut a plywood key (G) to fit the groove *(Fig. 3)*. The key spans the two sections of the cutting guide and locks it together when you want a nine-foot-long guide.

To make this work, the key is held in place with threaded knobs that tighten into T-nuts installed in the bottom of the cutting guide *(Fig. 1a)*. The holes are located so you can also bolt the key to the long section for storage.

FENCE. Now all that's left is to add the fence pieces (H and I) *(Fig. 4)*. To form a lip that tracks the carriage, these pieces are cut taller (wider) than the thickness of the tray, then glued and clamped in place. (I used yellow glue.)

Note: To keep the carriage from binding, be sure to wipe off the excess glue before it dries.

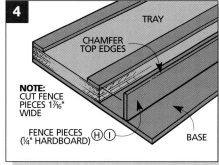

CROSS SECTION   **a.**

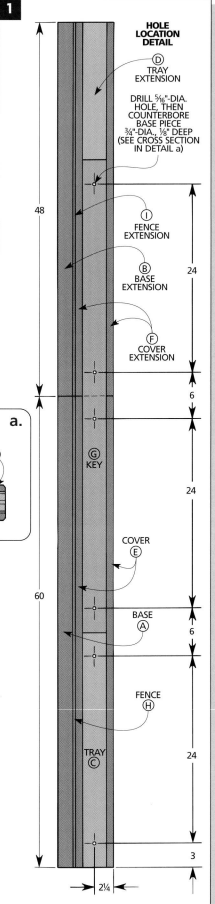

2
FIVE-FOOT SECTION — G KEY (¾" PLY)
60
8
A BASE
H FENCE
E COVER
C TRAY (¾" PLY)
NOTE: BASE, FENCE, AND COVER ARE ¼" HARDBOARD

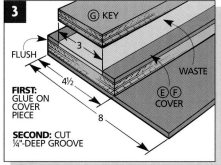

3
G KEY
FLUSH
3
WASTE
4½
8
E F COVER
FIRST: GLUE ON COVER PIECE
SECOND: CUT ¼"-DEEP GROOVE

4
TRAY
CHAMFER TOP EDGES
NOTE: CUT FENCE PIECES 1⁷⁄₁₆" WIDE
FENCE PIECES H I (¼" HARDBOARD)
BASE

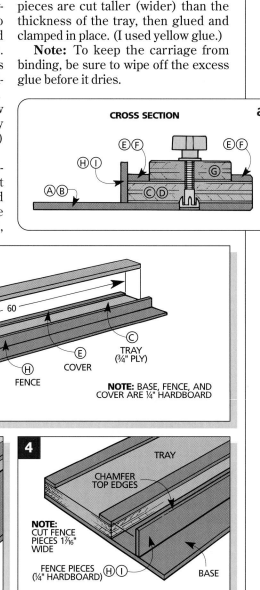

1
HOLE LOCATION DETAIL
D TRAY EXTENSION
DRILL ⁵⁄₁₆"-DIA. HOLE, THEN COUNTERBORE BASE PIECE ¾"-DIA., ⅛" DEEP (SEE CROSS SECTION IN DETAIL a)
48
I FENCE EXTENSION
B BASE EXTENSION
F COVER EXTENSION
24
6
G KEY
24
60
COVER E
BASE A
6
FENCE H
TRAY C
24
3
2¼

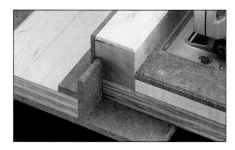

SAW CARRIAGE

Once the cutting guide was finished, I started building a carriage for my circular saw. It features a special hanger that hooks over the fence on the cutting guide to track the tool in a straight line.

BASE. The saw carriage starts out as a ³/₄" plywood base (J) for the saw to rest on *(Fig. 5)*. To allow for a system of brackets that hold the saw in place, cut the base 2" longer and wider than the metal base of your saw.

OPENING. After the base is cut to size, the next step is to make an opening in it for the saw blade and guard. To locate this opening, it's easiest if you first raise the blade of the circular saw above the shoe so the shoe will sit flat on the base (J).

Now position the saw so the shoe is ³/₄" in from one long edge of the base *(Fig. 6)*. This distance allows for a side cleat (added later). Then mark the opening and cut out the waste with a sabre saw.

After the opening is cut, reposition the saw on the base with the blade and guard sticking through the hole. Check that the saw's blade guard still moves freely through the opening.

HANGER. Now you're ready to add the hanger. The hanger has a groove that slips over the fence *(Fig. 6a)*. This groove "locks" the carriage to the guide so the saw won't wander off course.

This groove is built up from two parts: a hardwood rail (K) and a hardboard keeper strip (L). First, a ¹/₄" rabbet is cut in the rail *(Fig. 6a)*. Then the keeper strip is glued and screwed in place to form the groove.

After the hanger is assembled, it's glued and screwed to the base with the bottom of the rabbet flush with the edge of the base (J) *(Fig. 6a)*. Make sure the screws are countersunk into the base so the carriage will slide smoothly across the cutting guide.

FOOT. Once the hanger is fastened to the base, the next step is to add a hard-

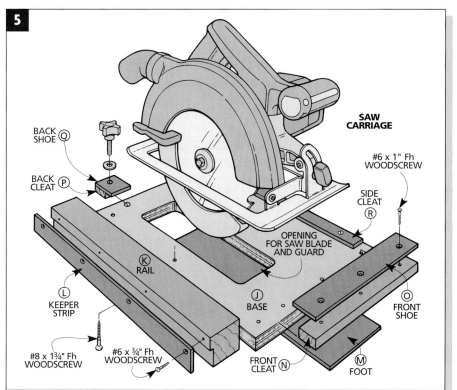

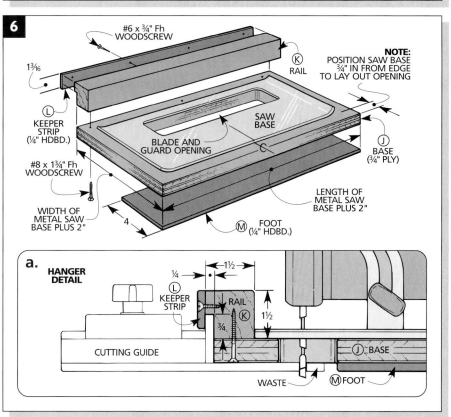

board foot (M) *(Fig. 6)*. The purpose of this foot is simple. Since one edge of the carriage rides on the cutting guide, the foot supports the opposite edge of the base and keeps the carriage level when making a cut.

To determine the foot's width, measure from the edge of the blade opening to the outside edge of the base *(Figs. 6 and 6a)*. In my case, this measurement was 4". The foot is the same length as the base.

Having the saw carriage locked to the cutting guide fence won't do you any good if the saw isn't properly secured to the carriage. So after gluing the foot in place, you can add brackets to hold the saw to the carriage.

FRONT BRACKET. The front of the saw is held in place with a two-part bracket. It's made up of a hardwood front cleat (N), and a hardboard shoe (O) that form a lip for the metal base of the saw to slide under *(Fig. 7)*. To make this work, the cleat is cut to match the height of the front edge of the saw base *(Fig. 7a)*.

Note: Since different brands of saws have different types of bases, you may have to make some modifications to the brackets. See the Shop Tip at right for some ways of adapting the brackets to different saws.

Once the front cleat and front shoe are cut to size, glue and screw them to the base (J).

BACK BRACKET. After attaching the front bracket, I added a small back bracket *(Figs. 7 and 7b)*. This bracket is also built up from a hardwood cleat (P) and a shoe (Q) made of hardboard. Here again, I cut the pieces to fit the base of my saw.

One difference with the back bracket is that it isn't permanently attached to the base like the front bracket. To make it easy to remove the saw, this bracket is held in place with a threaded knob that tightens into a T-nut in the base *(Fig. 7b)*.

When you're figuring out the location for the back bracket, it's a good idea to set the saw on the carriage. That way you can see exactly where you'll have enough clearance.

SIDE CLEAT. To complete the saw carriage, I added a side cleat (R). This is just a strip of hardboard that's glued and screwed to the base.

What you're after here is a snug fit against the saw base. So to help position the side cleat, set the saw in place and use the front and back brackets to clamp it down.

When all the pieces were assembled, I eased the sharp edges of the carriage and cutting guide. I used a chamfer bit in the router table where possible and sandpaper on the remaining spots.

REFERENCE EDGE. All that's left is to clamp the cutting guide to a bench and trim the base to final width. The edge that's cut provides a reference to indicate the path of the saw blade. This way, it's just a matter of positioning this edge on the layout line to set up a cut.

I found it easiest to fasten both sections of the cutting guide together and

then trim the full length of the edge with one pass.

When you're ready to use the jig, one thing to keep in mind is that not all saw blades are the same width. So when cutting your workpiece, use the same blade you used to trim the base.

SHOP TIP
Modifications

The shoes of different circular saws are not the same. To work around knobs and other items, you may need to customize the brackets to hold your saw in place.

Here, a notch had to be cut in the front bracket to make room for the bevel lock.

A thicker spacer allows the back cleat to accomodate the higher back end of this saw.

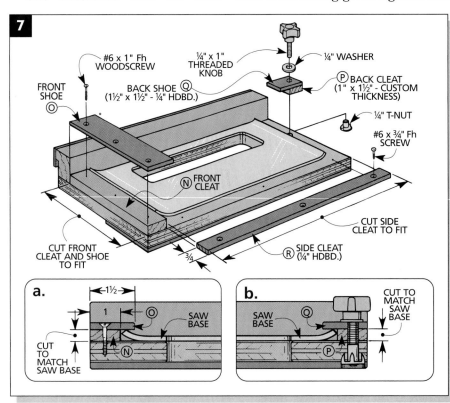

7

#6 x 1" Fh WOODSCREW

¼" x 1" THREADED KNOB

¼" WASHER

FRONT SHOE (O)

BACK SHOE (Q) (1½" x 1½" - ¼" HDBD.)

(P) BACK CLEAT (1" x 1½" - CUSTOM THICKNESS)

¼" T-NUT

#6 x ¾" Fh SCREW

(N) FRONT CLEAT

CUT FRONT CLEAT AND SHOE TO FIT

¾

CUT SIDE CLEAT TO FIT

(R) SIDE CLEAT (¼" HDBD.)

a. ←1½→
1
(O)
SAW BASE
CUT TO MATCH SAW BASE
(N)

b. SAW BASE
(Q)
CUT TO MATCH SAW BASE
(P)

WOODWORKER'S NOTEBOOK

Your circular saw isn't the only tool that can be made more accurate with the straight-edge guide. By building a base to carry your router, you can also cut perfectly straight dadoes and rabbets.

ROUTER CARRIAGE

Just because it was made to help your circular saw cut a straight line doesn't mean that's the only use for the straight-edge cutting guide. Routing straight dadoes and rabbets is automatic when you make a carriage for your router.

■ Like the saw carriage, the router carriage has a base that supports the tool. But to provide maximum depth adjustment for the bit, this base (S) is made from 1/4"-thick hardboard *(Fig. 1)*.

■ Here again, a rail (T) and a keeper strip (U) combine to make a groove that tracks the carriage on the fence. Only this time, you'll need to allow for the difference in thicknesses between the saw base and the router base. This is just a matter of making the rail taller (wider) and cutting the rabbet wider *(Fig. 1a)*.

■ As before, a hardboard foot (V) is glued to the bottom of the base to keep the carriage level.

To determine the width of the foot, hook the router carriage onto the fence of the cutting guide *(Fig. 1a)*. Then measure from the outside of the base (S) to the base of the cutting guide. Subtract 1/4" from this measurement to allow for clearance and cut the foot (V) to this width.

■ When mounting the router, don't forget to provide some knuckle room between the handles and the rail. The simplest way to do this is to mount the router so the handles are at a 45° angle to the rail *(Fig. 1)*.

■ To locate the holes for the bit and the mounting screws, it's easiest to remove the plastic base from the router and use it as a template.

Since the carriage base is likely thicker than the base of the router, drill counterbored shank holes for the mounting screws *(Fig. 1a)*.

■ Remember, the reference edge of the cutting guide is only accurate for the circular saw. To make a quick layout guide to use with the router, clamp the cutting guide to some scrap. Then mark the reference edge onto the scrap and rout a short dado. Then, use the measurement from the mark to the edge of the dado to position the cutting guide on your workpiece.

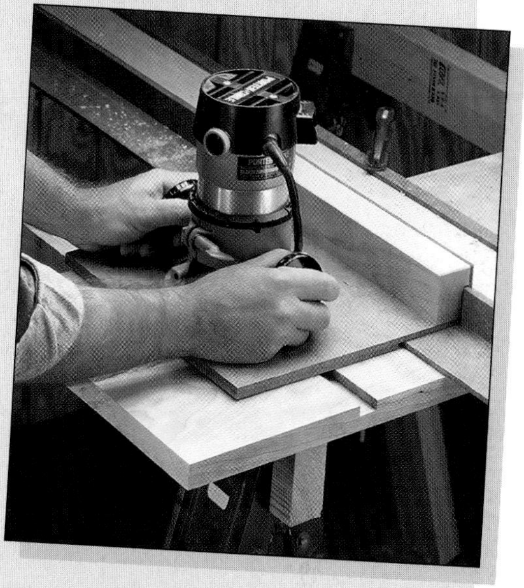

1

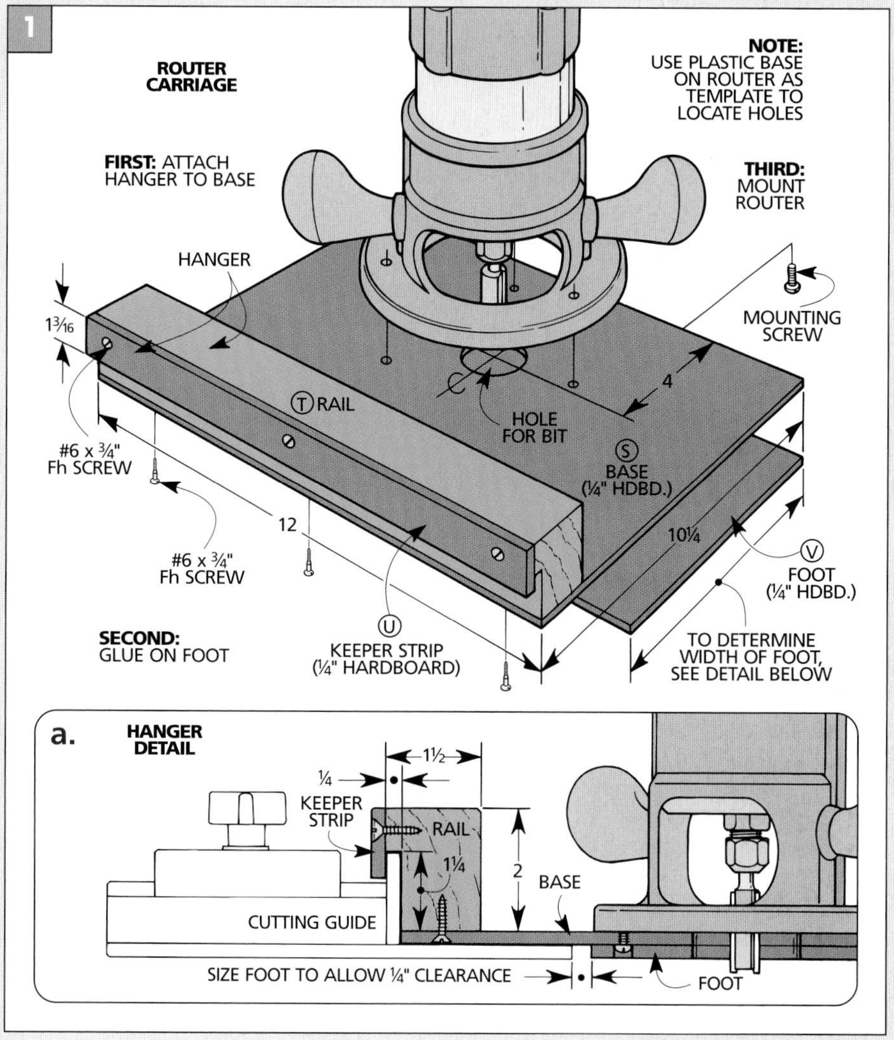

ROUTER CARRIAGE
NOTE: USE PLASTIC BASE ON ROUTER AS TEMPLATE TO LOCATE HOLES
FIRST: ATTACH HANGER TO BASE
THIRD: MOUNT ROUTER
HANGER
MOUNTING SCREW
1³⁄₁₆
4
Ⓣ RAIL
HOLE FOR BIT
Ⓢ BASE (¼" HDBD.)
#6 x ¾" Fh SCREW
12
10¼
#6 x ¾" Fh SCREW
Ⓥ FOOT (¼" HDBD.)
SECOND: GLUE ON FOOT
Ⓤ KEEPER STRIP (¼" HARDBOARD)
TO DETERMINE WIDTH OF FOOT, SEE DETAIL BELOW
a. HANGER DETAIL
1½
¼
KEEPER STRIP
RAIL
1¼
2
BASE
CUTTING GUIDE
SIZE FOOT TO ALLOW ¼" CLEARANCE
FOOT

MATERIALS LIST

NEW PARTS

S	Base (1)	1/4 hdbd. x 10 1/4 - 12
T	Rail (1)	1 1/2 x 2 - 12
U	Keeper Strip (1)	1/4 hdbd. x 1 3/16 - 12
V	Foot (1)	1/4 hdbd. x custom - 12

HARDWARE SUPPLIES

(6) No. 6 x 3/4" Fh woodscrews

Router Trammel

With this simple trammel, cutting perfect circles is as easy as switching on the router.
The sliding adjustment feature allows you to cut circles up to four feet in diameter.

You remember using a compass to draw circles in school. You'd clamp a pencil in one side of the compass, then stick the sharp point on the other side onto the paper. When you spun the compass around the sharp point, it drew a perfect circle.

That same idea is what makes this trammel work. Instead of a sharp point, however, the trammel rotates around a dowel pin in the center of the workpiece. And instead of drawing with a pencil, the trammel uses your router bit to cut a circle.

ADJUSTABLE. The trammel shown here can cut circles any size from 6½"

in diameter up to four feet in diameter. A sliding arm in the base sets the trammel for the size you need. Simply tightening a wing nut locks the sliding arm in place. (If you need circles larger than four feet, just make the trammel longer. If you need circles smaller than 6½", see the band saw circle jig on page 96.)

SIMPLE CONSTRUCTION. Whatever the length of the trammel, it won't take long to build. There are only three pieces, all cut from ¼" hardboard. (For tips on working with hardboard, see the Woodworker's Notebook on page 55.) The only hardware is a machine screw, a nut, a fender washer, and a wing nut.

USES. Even though it's a simple jig, the trammel can be used in a number of ways. Using a straight bit in the router, it's perfect for cutting out a circle as shown in the photo. Once the piece is cut to size, you can then round over the edges or add a decorative edge profile.

You can also use it to rout a circular groove into the surface of a workpiece. The groove can serve as an accent on its own or be filled with an inlay.

The trammel is also the ideal choice for cutting an arc. Instead of routing a full circle, simply clamp scrap blocks to the workpiece to stop the trammel at the beginning and end of the arc.

EXPLODED VIEW

OVERALL DIMENSIONS:
6W X 1¹¹/₁₆H X 24L

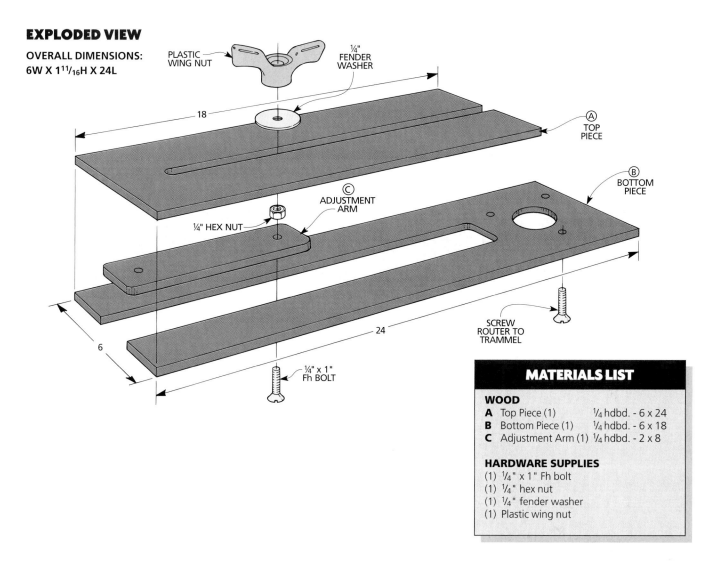

PLASTIC WING NUT

¼" FENDER WASHER

18

Ⓐ TOP PIECE

Ⓒ ADJUSTMENT ARM

¼" HEX NUT

Ⓑ BOTTOM PIECE

6

24

¼" x 1" Fh BOLT

SCREW ROUTER TO TRAMMEL

MATERIALS LIST

WOOD
A Top Piece (1)   ¼ hdbd. - 6 x 24
B Bottom Piece (1)   ¼ hdbd. - 6 x 18
C Adjustment Arm (1) ¼ hdbd. - 2 x 8

HARDWARE SUPPLIES
(1) ¼" x 1" Fh bolt
(1) ¼" hex nut
(1) ¼" fender washer
(1) Plastic wing nut

SHOP TIP .... Routing Direction

If you're cutting a circle from a larger workpiece, it doesn't matter which direction you run the trammel. Since the bit is surrounded by stock, the cut is always backed up by uncut wood and won't chip out (*Figs. 1 and 2*).

When routing an *outside* edge, direction should be a consideration. Typically, you would run the trammel in a counterclockwise direction (*Fig. 3*). This gives you the best control. But the cut isn't backed up, so it may chip out.

A way to get around this is to move the trammel clockwise (Fig. 4). "Backrouting" like this is not something you would do freehand, as the router would want to bounce along the edge. But with a trammel, the tool is anchored and you have more control.

The rotation of the bit will still cause the router to want to pull itself along. So keep a firm grip on it and make shallow passes.

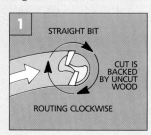

1 STRAIGHT BIT
CUT IS BACKED BY UNCUT WOOD
ROUTING CLOCKWISE

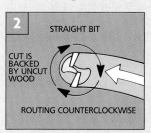

2 STRAIGHT BIT
CUT IS BACKED BY UNCUT WOOD
ROUTING COUNTERCLOCKWISE

3 EDGE ROUTING
ROUTER COUNTER-CLOCKWISE
NOTE: THERE MAY BE SOME CHIPOUT WHEN ROUTING COUNTERCLOCKWISE

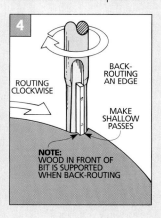

4 ROUTING CLOCKWISE
BACK-ROUTING AN EDGE
MAKE SHALLOW PASSES
NOTE: WOOD IN FRONT OF BIT IS SUPPORTED WHEN BACK-ROUTING

The trammel is easy to make. There are just two parts: a long base and a short adjustment arm.

BASE. The trammel base is made by gluing two pieces of $\frac{1}{4}$" tempered hardboard together *(Fig. 2)*.

The width of the top piece (A) and bottom piece (B) is determined by the size of your router base. Make these pieces just slightly larger than the base *(Fig. 1a)*. (In my case, this is 6".)

But the *length* of these pieces depends on the size of circle you want to rout. To rout circles up to four feet in diameter, I decided to make the bottom piece (B) 24" long.

To allow room for mounting the router, the top piece is cut 6" shorter than the bottom piece. (Here again, this depends on the size of your router base.) Cut both pieces to size. Then drill a hole in the bottom piece for the router bit to fit through *(Fig. 1a)*. An easy way to determine the location of this hole is to set your router base in place and trace the bit opening.

SLOTS. After cutting the top and bottom pieces to size, the next step is to cut slots down the center of each piece.

The bottom piece has a 2"-wide slot that holds the adjustment arm (added later). The top piece has a slot to allow a bolt to pass through to lock the adjustment arm in place *(Fig. 3)*.

To make the slots, first drill $\frac{5}{8}$"-dia. holes to locate the ends of each slot *(Figs. 1a and 2a)*. The slots are cut on the table saw. To make sure the edge of the slot lines up with the hole, lower the table saw blade just below the table surface. Set the base piece on the saw so the inside edge of the blade aligns with the edge of the hole. Then slide the rip fence next to the base piece.

When cutting the slots, stop the cut about $\frac{1}{2}$" before reaching these holes *(Fig. 1)*. This will prevent the waste piece from kicking back. Then finish the cut with a hand saw.

To complete the base after the slots are cut, simply glue the top and bottom pieces together *(Fig. 2)*.

ADJUSTMENT ARM. Next, an adjustment arm (C) is cut to fit the slot in the bottom piece *(Fig. 3)*. Sand a radius on each corner of the adjustment arm to match the rounded corners of the slot. Then drill a $\frac{1}{4}$"-dia. pivot hole near one end of the arm.

The adjustment arm is mounted to the base with a bolt and wing nut. So the bolt doesn't fall out, it's held in place with a hex nut. And a fender washer transfers pressure to the trammel when the wing nut is tightened down.

MOUNT ROUTER. All that's left to do is to mount the trammel base to your router. Use the base from your router to locate the screw holes *(Fig. 4)*. Then drill and countersink holes and screw the trammel to your router. ■

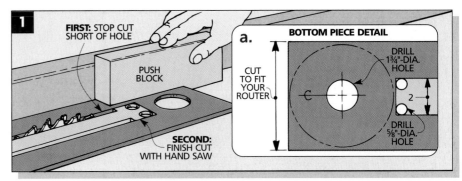

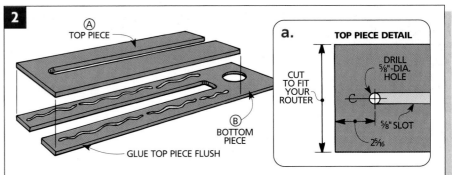

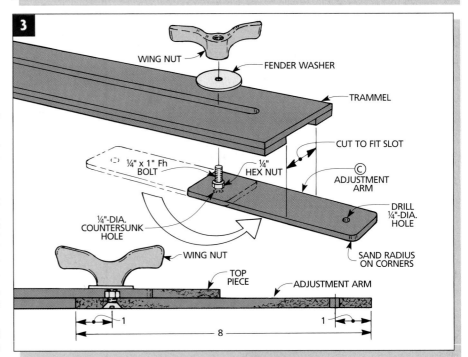

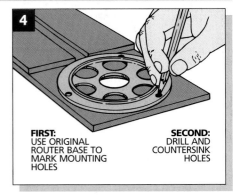

TECHNIQUE ...... *Using the Trammel*

Cutting circles with the router trammel is just about as easy as building it. The first step is to locate a pivot point for the trammel to rotate around. This pivot point is the center of the circle. So first, you need to find the center of your workpiece.

FINDING CENTER

There's no need to guess to find the center of a workpiece. Whether it's a square, a rectangle or a circle, finding the exact center is just a matter of drawing some straight lines.

SQUARES AND RECTANGLES. Finding the centerpoint of a square or rectangle is easy to do. Using a straightedge, simply connect the corners of the workpiece with diagonal lines. The lines intersect at the center of the workpiece.

CIRCLES. Finding the center of a circle takes a bit more work, but it's not that difficult. I use a simple jig and a framing square.

Make the jig from a piece of scrap *(Fig. 1)*. The length isn't critical, just as long as it's less than the diameter of the circle *(Fig. 2)*.

Drill a hole for a nail 1" from each end and centered on the width of the jig *(Fig. 1)*. It's important that these holes be straight up and down, so I use the drill press to do this. Next, mark the centerline of the jig's length as measured between the nails *(Fig. 1)*.

To use the jig, simply press the nails against the side of the circle (Step 1 in *Fig. 2*). Then align a square with the jig's centerline mark and draw a line along the edge of the square.

Now move the jig to a second location at about a right angle to the first. (This location can actually be anywhere on the circle, but having it at a right angle makes it easier to see the marks.) Align the square with the jig's centerline and draw a second line that intersects the first (Step 2 in *Fig. 2*). The lines intersect at the center of the circle.

PIVOT POINT

Once you've found the center of the workpiece, you have to fasten a pivot point at this location. There are two ways to fasten a pivot point to the workpiece. Which one you choose depends on whether you are routing from the back side of the workpiece (which will be hidden later), or from a good side.

BACK SIDE. When routing from a face that won't be seen, simply drill a ¼"-dia. hole at the center of the circle. (But don't drill through the workpiece.) Then insert a piece of dowel into the hole to serve as the pivot point *(Fig. 3)*. The hole in the trammel's adjustment arm then fits over the dowel.

GOOD SIDE. With the second method, you don't have to drill a hole. This makes it a better choice when you work from the good side of a workpiece. To make the pivot point, cut a 2"-square base from ¼" hardboard *(Fig. 4)*. Locate the centerpoint of the base and drill a ¼"-dia. hole through it.

Next, mark the center of the workpiece and put a short piece of double-sided carpet tape on either side of the "X" *(Fig. 4)*. (You need to be able to see the point where the lines cross.) Stick the base to the center of the workpiece so the hole is centered on the "X".

Then to serve as the pivot point, put a length of ¼" dowel into the hole in the base. Before you slip the adjustment arm onto the dowel, fasten an auxiliary ¼" hardboard base under the router to keep it level *(Fig. 4)*.

Finally, adjust the trammel arm, and rout the circle. For small circles, mount the arm so the pivot hole is near the router (refer to *Fig. 3* on previous page). For large circles, rotate it so the hole extends out the end of the base.

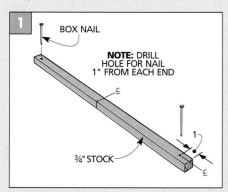

1

BOX NAIL

NOTE: DRILL HOLE FOR NAIL 1" FROM EACH END

¾" STOCK

1

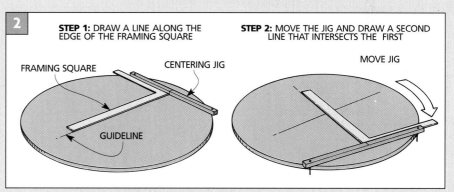

2

STEP 1: DRAW A LINE ALONG THE EDGE OF THE FRAMING SQUARE

FRAMING SQUARE

CENTERING JIG

GUIDELINE

STEP 2: MOVE THE JIG AND DRAW A SECOND LINE THAT INTERSECTS THE FIRST

MOVE JIG

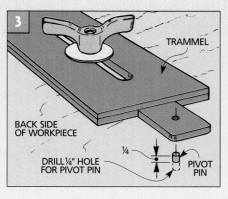

3

TRAMMEL

BACK SIDE OF WORKPIECE

¼

DRILL ¼" HOLE FOR PIVOT PIN

PIVOT PIN

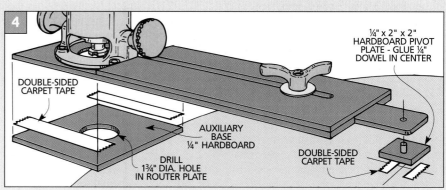

4

DOUBLE-SIDED CARPET TAPE

AUXILIARY BASE ¼" HARDBOARD

DRILL 1¾" DIA. HOLE IN ROUTER PLATE

¼" x 2" x 2" HARDBOARD PIVOT PLATE - GLUE ¼" DOWEL IN CENTER

DOUBLE-SIDED CARPET TAPE

Adjustable Dado Jig

For cutting snug-fitting dadoes exactly where you want them, it's hard to beat this jig.
It makes layout easy, and you can be cutting dadoes instead of fussing with measurements.

It's hard to decide what I like best about this jig. The fact that it allows me to rout perfect dadoes with pinpoint accuracy. Or how incredibly quick and easy it is to set up.

There's no more fiddling to position a straightedge just right so the bit cuts exactly where you want. And even if you need to make two passes (for a wide dado or a piece of plywood that's an odd thickness), there's no need to readjust the jig to sneak up on the final width.

TEMPLATE. The reason is simple. The jig can be easily adjusted to form an opening that's an exact template of the *width* of the dado.

Once you have set this opening, what you see is what you get when you rout the dado.

Note: You can use this jig to rout dadoes from 1/2" to 1 1/2" wide in workpieces up to 25" across.

ADJUSTMENTS. Setting the opening to the correct width is automatic. Just insert the piece that's going to fit in the dado and close the jig around it. Since the *thickness* of the workpiece is what determines the opening, you're guaranteed a tight fit.

Even easier than setting the width of the opening is transferring it to the workpiece. Simply place the jig on the

panel so the opening aligns with the desired location of the dado and clamp it in place. The jig even squares itself to the workpiece automatically.

MATERIALS. The jig is made of 1/4"-thick hardboard with a hardwood cleat at each end. For hardware, all you need are a few woodscrews, plus a couple of T-nuts, threaded knobs, and washers.

OTHER USES. Besides cutting regular dadoes or grooves in a workpiece, this jig can also be used for cutting stopped dadoes or grooves. Plus it's a big help when you need to cut a regular or stopped rabbet. Details on how to do this can be found on page 59.

EXPLODED VIEW

OVERALL DIMENSIONS:
10W X 30L X 2⁵/₁₆H

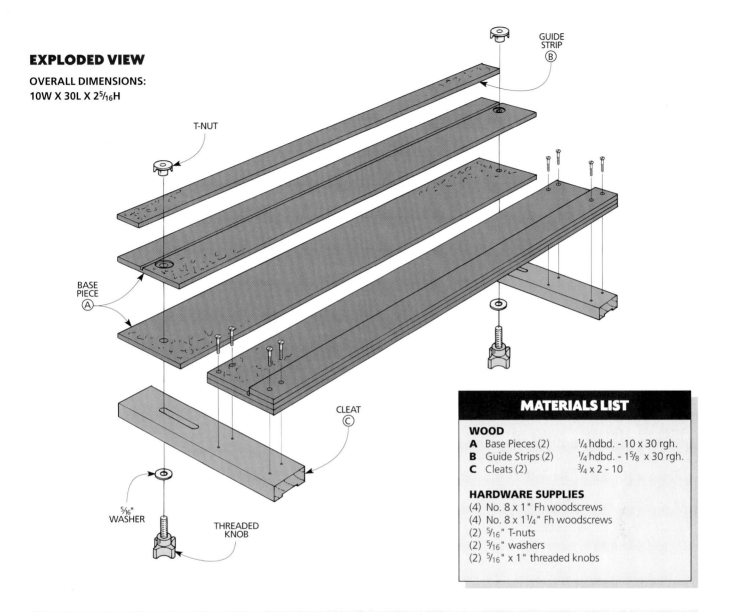

GUIDE
STRIP
Ⓑ

T-NUT

BASE
PIECE
Ⓐ

CLEAT
Ⓒ

⁵/₁₆"
WASHER

THREADED
KNOB

MATERIALS LIST		
WOOD		
A Base Pieces (2)	¼ hdbd. - 10 x 30 rgh.	
B Guide Strips (2)	¼ hdbd. - 1⅝ x 30 rgh.	
C Cleats (2)	¾ x 2 - 10	
HARDWARE SUPPLIES		
(4) No. 8 x 1 " Fh woodscrews		
(4) No. 8 x 1¼" Fh woodscrews		
(2) ⁵/₁₆" T-nuts		
(2) ⁵/₁₆" washers		
(2) ⁵/₁₆" x 1 " threaded knobs		

WOODWORKER'S NOTEBOOK

USING HARDBOARD

Hardboard is an excellent material to use when making jigs. It's made from finely ground wood and resins bonded together under heat and pressure. This makes it hard, dense, and extremely stable during changes in humidity. It also holds up well to wear.

You can find hardboard at most home centers and lumberyards in ⅛" and ¼" thicknesses. There are two types: standard and service-tempered. Tempered is better for jigs. It's harder and more resistant to moisture.

Look for hardboard that's smooth on both sides, instead of waffled on one side (see inset photo). The smooth faces provide better gluing surfaces. Plus it helps reduce friction when two parts of a jig have to slide against each other. If you do have to use "waffled" hardboard, try to place the smooth faces together where parts need to slide.

The base of the adjustable dado jig consists of two parts that work together to form a template of the dado. One part is fixed, and the other is adjustable.

Except for the fact that one part moves and the other doesn't, the two halves are the same. So it's easiest to build one large blank, then rip it into two equal parts.

BLANK. The blank starts out as two oversize base pieces (A) that act as a platform for the router *(Fig. 1)*. These are just pieces of ¼" hardboard held together with contact cement. When joining these pieces, the edges don't have to be perfectly aligned. They are all trimmed later.

GUIDE STRIPS. The router is tracked by a pair of hardboard guide strips (B) that are glued to the top base piece *(Fig. 1)*. Here again, don't worry about getting the guide strips and base pieces perfectly flush (although being close will save some work). The accuracy will be built in as you true up the base.

The first step in truing up the base is jointing one long edge. Then put the jointed edge against the rip fence of the table saw and rip the opposite edge. Once you have two "good" outside edges, you can cut the base to final length of 29".

Next, turn the base upside down and trim the *inside* edges of the guide strips — the edges that guide the base of the router. Removing a saw blade's width should be enough to give you a straight edge *(Fig. 2a)*. Trimming these edges also serves another purpose. By adjusting the height of the saw blade so it cuts ⅛" deep into the base piece, it creates a relief channel for sawdust *(Figs. 2a and 2b)*.

Next, to make two equal halves, just rip the base down the middle *(Fig. 2b)*.

REFERENCE EDGE. Now you can establish the reference edges of the base pieces by routing the waste off each half *(Fig. 3)*. Keep in mind that these edges are only a reference for your router and one particular bit. So use the same router and bit as the one you plan to use with the jig. (I used a ½" straight bit.)

Depending on the router you're using, the bit may not be centered in the router base. So to get an accurate reference edge, draw an arrow on the router base and always keep the arrow against the guide strips *(Fig. 3)*.

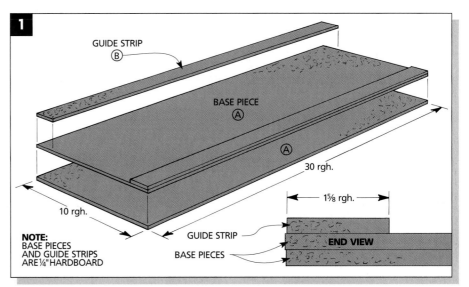

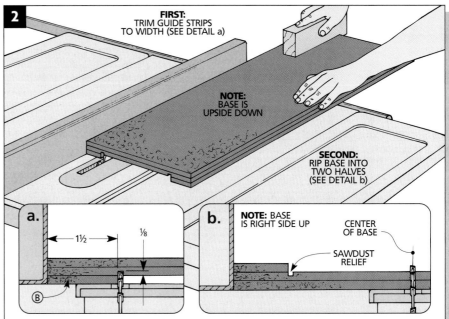

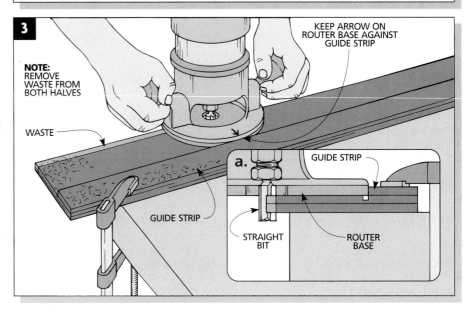

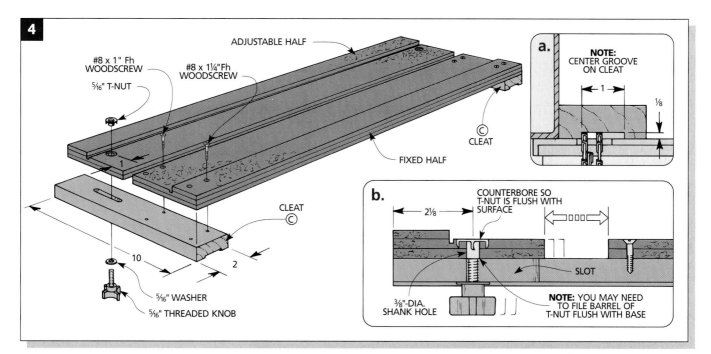

4

ADJUSTABLE HALF

#8 x 1" Fh WOODSCREW

#8 x 1¼"Fh WOODSCREW

⁵⁄₁₆" T-NUT

ⓒ CLEAT

FIXED HALF

CLEAT ⓒ

10

2

1

⁵⁄₁₆" WASHER

⁵⁄₁₆" THREADED KNOB

a.

NOTE: CENTER GROOVE ON CLEAT

1

⅛

b.

2⅛

COUNTERBORE SO T-NUT IS FLUSH WITH SURFACE

SLOT

⅜"-DIA. SHANK HOLE

NOTE: YOU MAY NEED TO FILE BARREL OF T-NUT FLUSH WITH BASE

CLEATS

With the base complete, the next step is to add two cleats. These cleats help square up the jig to the workpiece. And they let you adjust the opening to the desired width of the dado.

Each cleat (C) is made from a piece of ³⁄₄"-thick hardwood *(Fig. 4)*. (I used maple.) To provide a recess for a threaded knob and washer (installed later), cut a shallow groove down the length of each cleat *(Fig. 4a)*.

SLOTS. The next step is to cut a slot in each cleat. These slots allow you to slide the adjustable half of the base back and forth to change the width of the opening.

Before locating the slots, you'll need to first decide which half of the base is the adjustable part. Then drill a pair of counterbored shank holes for two T-nuts added later *(Figs. 4 and 4b)*. Now you can use these holes to locate the slots in the cleats.

This is just a matter of clamping the fixed half of the base to the cleats and butting the adjustable half against it *(Fig. 5)*. Make certain that the cleats are perfectly square to the fixed half of the base. Now mark one end of each slot through the holes, slide the adjustable half back so it's flush with the ends of the cleats, and mark the other end *(Fig. 5a)*.

After drilling starter holes at each end, I used a sabre saw with an edge guide to cut the slots.

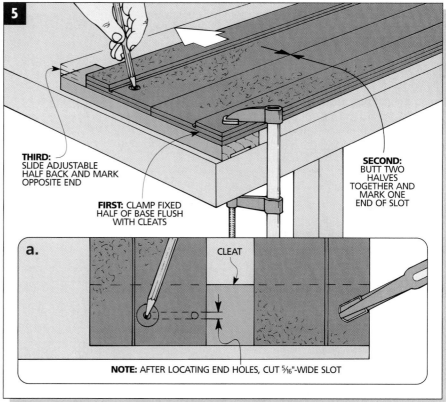

5

THIRD: SLIDE ADJUSTABLE HALF BACK AND MARK OPPOSITE END

FIRST: CLAMP FIXED HALF OF BASE FLUSH WITH CLEATS

SECOND: BUTT TWO HALVES TOGETHER AND MARK ONE END OF SLOT

a.

CLEAT

NOTE: AFTER LOCATING END HOLES, CUT ⁵⁄₁₆"-WIDE SLOT

ASSEMBLY. After cutting the slots, all that's left is to attach the two halves of the base to the cleats.

When attaching the fixed half, check that the cleats are 90° to the base. Then glue and screw them in place so the ends are flush with the edge of the base.

Before attaching the adjustable part of the base, drive a T-nut into each of the holes bored earlier *(Fig. 4b)*.

Now fasten the adjustable half of the base to the cleats with threaded knobs (or machine screws) that pass through the slots in the cleats and into the T-nuts *(Fig. 4)*.

One note on using and storing your jig: Be careful the guide strip edges don't get dinged. A gouge along the edge could cause the router to shift and mar the dado. ■

TECHNIQUE .... Using the Dado Jig

It's hard not to get spoiled when using this adjustable dado jig. A simple layout and a quick adjustment and you're ready to clamp the jig and rout the dado, see *Figs. 1* through *4* below.

Another nice thing about the jig is that it can be used almost any time you need to rout a straight line. On the opposite page are tips on using the jig to rout stopped dadoes and rabbets.

Typically when routing a dado, the hassle is trying to figure out where to position a guide for the router so the bit cuts exactly where you want.

With the adjustable dado jig, layout is simple. Just mark the position of one side of the dado *(Fig. 1)*. To make sure the jig gets lined up properly, I find it's helpful to mark an "X" in the waste area.

There's also no measuring needed to set the opening of the jig for the proper width. Simply use a piece of the stock

that will fit the dado *(Fig. 2)*. Place one face against the fixed edge of the base and slide the adjustable half against it. Then tighten down the adjustable half.

With the opening set, align the jig on the workpiece. To do this, press a cleat against the workpiece and align one reference edge with the layout line. Make sure the "X" is visible in the gap *(Fig. 3)*.

When clamping the jig, there are several options. A long workpiece can be supported on a pair of sawhorses, or extended over the edge of the bench as shown in the photo. But to provide clearance for the clamp heads when routing a small panel, you'll need to raise the work off the bench with a scrap piece.

After you've set the bit to the proper depth, you're ready to rout. One thing to be aware of is that when you make the first cuts with the jig, you'll have to rout through the cleat. So start the cut with the router bit sitting outside of the cleat. Then rout in a clockwise direction *(Fig. 4)*. Keep the same point on the router base against the guide strip.

If the dado is wider than your bit, place the router against the other guide strip and rout the other side.

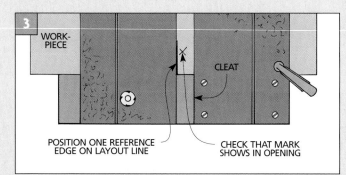

Lay out one side. *Using a try square, lay out one side of the dado. This line doesn't have to extend across the full width of the workpiece. To ensure that you rout on the correct side of the line, mark an 'x' to show the waste area.*

Set width. *To set the width of the opening, insert the piece that will fit in the finished dado snug against the fixed side of the base. Then slide the adjustable half of the jig against the other face and tighten the knob to lock the guide in place.*

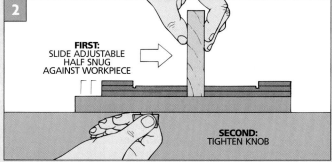

Clamp down. *Press a cleat against one edge of the workpiece to square up the jig. Then clamp the jig in place so one reference edge is on the layout line and the 'x' indicating the waste area shows in the opening.*

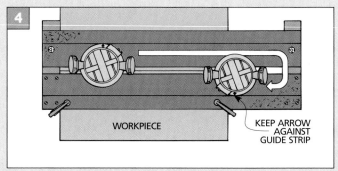

Rout clockwise. *After adjusting the depth of cut, rout in a clockwise direction. Keep the router pressed firmly against the guide strip. For a consistent cut, always keep the arrow on the router base pointing to the guide strips.*

STOPPED DADOES

When a dado stops short of either edge of a workpiece, it's referred to as a "stopped dado." These are used in places where you don't want the end of the dado to cut through the edge of the workpiece *(Fig. 5)*. And cutting a stopped dado with the adjustable dado jig is not much different from cutting a regular dado.

The first part of the layout and setup is the same. Mark one side of the dado on the workpiece, set the width of the jig opening, and clamp the jig to the workpiece. But before starting to rout the dado, you need to provide a way to stop the router at the end of the cut.

STOP BLOCK. This is done by fastening a stop block across the base of the jig *(Fig. 5)*. The stop block is just a piece of scrap held in place with double-sided carpet tape.

To determine the location of the stop block, first mark the end of the dado on the workpiece. Then position the router so the cutting edge of the bit just

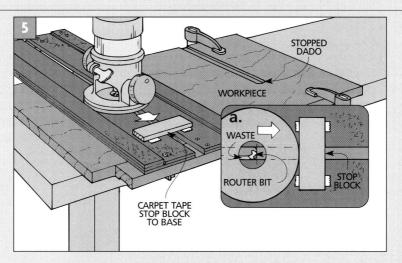

touches the line *(Fig. 5a)*. Now, place one edge of the stop block against the router base and press it in place.

BLIND DADO. A dado that is stopped at *both* ends is called a "blind dado." To make this cut, all you have to do is fasten a second stop block to mark the other end of the cut.

When routing a blind dado, use a plunge router. Or tip a standard router, then lower the bit into the workpiece. Keep a firm grip on the router, as the bit may want to "grab" the wood and try to pull the router along. Hold the router base against a stop block to steady the tool as you lower it into the cut.

RABBETS

Rabbets can be cut a number of ways. To quickly cut a rabbet, you can use special rabbeting bits for the router. These have a bearing on the bottom that guides the bit along the edge of a workpiece. The only drawbacks are that you're limited to the width of the bit and you can't cut rabbets wider than ³/₄".

If you need a wider rabbet, you can always set up a dado blade in the table saw, but this can take some time.

With the dado jig, you get the best of both methods. You can quickly rout rabbets any width you need.

Mark the edge of the rabbet on the workpiece as if you were laying out a dado. But before clamping the jig in place, there's one more thing to do.

If you position the jig on the workpiece now, the unsupported side would sag. This would cause the bit to cut deeper at the outside of the rabbet. To prevent this, slide a piece of scrap the same thickness as the workpiece under the outside edge of the jig *(Fig. 6)*. Now you can align the jig with the layout line and clamp it in place.

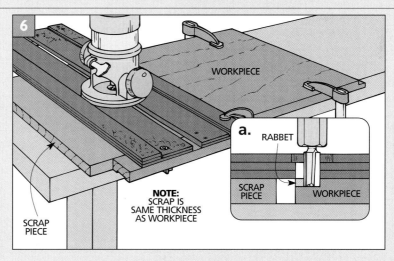

When cutting a rabbet, it's not necessary to align the outside half of the jig precisely. What you want here is to position this half of the jig so the router bit will cut either exactly on or just outside the edge of the workpiece *(Fig. 6a)*.

If you have an extra-wide rabbet that exceeds the width of the jig, simply start at the layout line, and move the jig when you've cut its full width.

STOPPED RABBET. Cutting a stopped rabbet is also a snap with the adjustable dado jig. Just like cutting a stopped dado, you need to position a stop block across the base before making the cut.

For a rabbet that is stopped at both ends, you may want to set the adjustable fence away from the edge of the workpiece. This will let you move the bit *into* the cut without having to tip the router.

Raised Panel Jig

Adding raised panels to a project can give it that extra touch of character. With this jig, you can add that beautiful feature to your projects without having to buy expensive panel-raising bits.

Making raised panels for doors causes mixed emotions for me. On the one hand, I love the look of craftsmanship they can give a project. But when it comes to actually making them, my enthusiasm seems to fade a little. That's because raising panels seems to involve one of two things. Either tilting the blade on my table saw, then trying to steady a tall workpiece on edge, or buying expensive panel-raising bits to use on the router table. I couldn't help but think there had to be another way.

RAISING PANELS. "Raising" a panel is a bit of a misleading term. You're not really raising a panel in the center of the workpiece. You're actually lowering the surface around the sides. So what you need is a way to remove the waste along the outside edges.

ROUTER. This jig allows me to cut away that waste a little at a time using a common straight bit in the router. And since the workpiece lies flat on the jig instead of standing on edge (as on the table saw), it's also easier to control it.

ANGLE. The principle of the jig is simple. The router is suspended at an angle over the workpiece. Then the panel is passed under the router. Between passes, the router is moved up the jig slightly. Gradually a beveled border is formed around the edges of the panel, "raising" a field in the center.

CURVED PANELS. This jig was originally designed to rout square or rectangular pieces. And it does that very well. But after working with it, I found that a simple modification allowed me to rout curved raised panels as well. For details on doing this, see the Woodworker's Notebook on page 65.

MATERIALS. The base of the jig is ³/₄" plywood. The other parts are ¹/₄" hardboard and ³/₄"-thick hardwood. All the hardware should be readily available at most hardware stores or home centers.

EXPLODED VIEW

OVERALL DIMENSIONS:
24W X 24L X 3½H

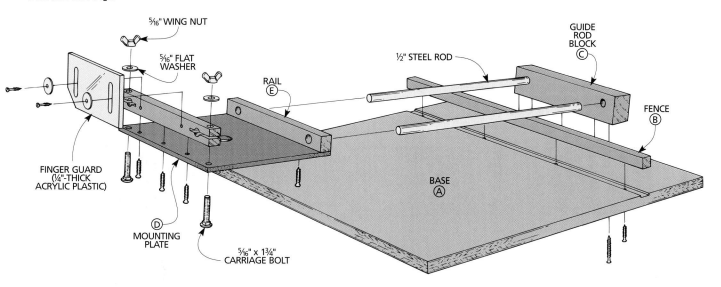

⁵⁄₁₆" WING NUT

⁵⁄₁₆" FLAT WASHER

½" STEEL ROD

GUIDE ROD BLOCK
Ⓒ

RAIL
Ⓔ

FENCE
Ⓑ

FINGER GUARD
(¼"-THICK ACRYLIC PLASTIC)

MOUNTING PLATE
Ⓓ

⁵⁄₁₆" x 1¾" CARRIAGE BOLT

BASE
Ⓐ

MATERIALS LIST

WOOD

A	Base (1)	¾ ply - 24 x 24
B	Fence (1)	¾ x ¾ - 24
C	Guide Rod Block (1)	1½ x 2½ rough - 10
D	Mounting Plate (1)	¼ hdbd.* - 8½ x 10
E	Rails (2)	¾ x 1 - 10

*Option: Use clear acrylic (see box below)

HARDWARE SUPPLIES
(2) ½" x 16" steel rods
(10) No. 8 x 1" Fh woodscrews

(5) No. 8 x 2" Fh woodscrews
(2) ⁵⁄₁₆" x 1¾" carriage bolts
(2) ⁵⁄₁₆" flat washers
(2) ⁵⁄₁₆" wing nuts
(2) No. 10 x ¾" Rh screws
(2) ⁵⁄₃₂" x ⅞" fender washers
(1 piece) ¼" acrylic plastic - 3" x 6"

SHOP TIP .... *Clear Router Base*

Hardboard is a good choice for an auxiliary router base. It's stiff enough and there's usually some scrap the right size in the shop.

But there are times when you need to be able to see the workpiece right around the bit. In these cases, I make a base from transparent acrylic plastic (see photo below left).

A clear base is helpful on the raised panel jig when cutting curved borders. When you rout a curved panel, you need to be able to see where the bit contacts the workpiece as you pivot it under the router (see photo below right).

A sabre saw with a fine-tooth blade works well for cutting ¼"-thick acrylic. Ease the sharp edges with a light sanding.

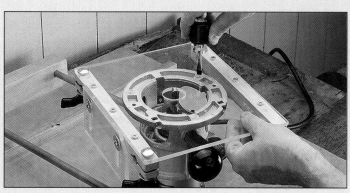

PLATFORM

The foundation of the jig is a smooth and sturdy base, so that's where I started working.

BASE. It's important that the base be smooth so the panels will slide easily across it. I found a good piece of plywood in my scrap bin. Once I had the stock, I began by cutting the plywood base (A) to size *(Fig. 1)*. The base can be as big as you like. It just needs to be large enough to support the workpiece. In my case, the base is 24" square.

FENCE. After the base is cut to size, a hardwood fence is installed. The first step is to cut a shallow dado in the base to accept the fence (B) *(Fig. 1)*. Then sneak up on the final width of the fence to get a snug fit in the dado.

The fence is screwed (but not glued) into the dado *(Fig. 1a)*. The fence is not glued in because if a curved panel is routed, the fence needs to be removed and replaced with a "pin." (For more on making curved raised panels, see the Woodworker's Notebook on page 65.)

CARRIAGE ASSEMBLY

The heart of the jig is the carriage assembly. This assembly suspends the router at an angle over the workpiece. Since the router is tilted, an ordinary straight bit can be used to rout the angled border.

GUIDE RODS. The router is mounted to a sliding platform (built later). The platform is held at an angle over the base by a pair of guide rods *(Fig. 1)*. These are 16" lengths cut from a 1/2"-dia. smooth steel rod available at most hardware stores.

GUIDE ROD BLOCK. The rods are supported by a 1 1/2"-thick guide rod block (C) *(Fig. 2)*. I made this block by gluing two pieces of 3/4"-thick stock together. Then two holes centered 7 1/2" apart are drilled to accept the ends of the guide rods *(Fig. 2)*. These holes do not go all the way through the block, but stop short of the far side *(Fig. 2a)*. **Note:** Be precise with the placement of these holes. Later, you'll have to match other holes to them when making the rails.

The trick to making the jig work is to tilt the rods at a slight angle. This angle eventually determines the angle of the border on the raised panel. To create the angle, the bottom edge of the block is ripped at a bevel to leave a 2"-wide

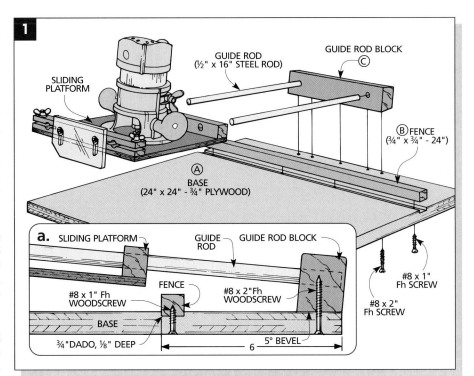

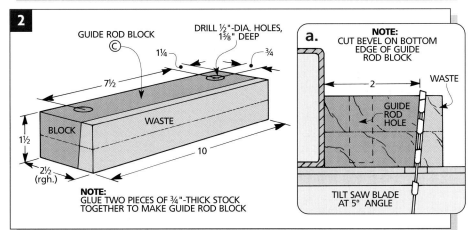

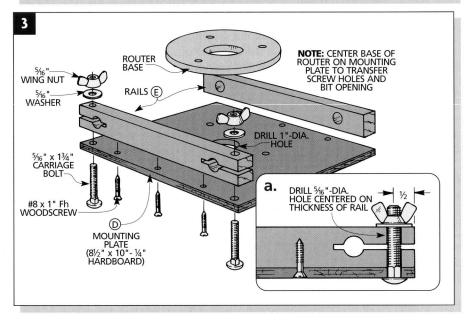

block. Then the guide rod block is glued and screwed to the base with the bevel down *(Fig. 1a)*.

Note: The 5° bevel I cut makes a panel with a wide border. For a narrower border, use a steeper bevel.

Before fastening the guide rods into the guide rod block, I ground a slight taper on each end of each rod. This made it easier to insert them into the block. The tapers on the opposite end make it easier to place the router assembly on the rods.

To finish the carriage assembly, use epoxy glue to secure the rods into the guide rod block.

SLIDING PLATFORM

With the rods in place, the next step is to add a sliding platform. The platform carries the router up and down the guide rods to increase the width of the border. It consists of three parts: a mounting plate for the router to sit on, a pair of rails that slide on the guide rods, and a finger guard *(Figs. 3 and 6)*.

MOUNTING PLATE. The mounting plate (D) is a piece of $1/4$" hardboard (or acrylic plastic) that replaces the original router base *(Fig. 3)*. To help locate the mounting holes and the opening for the bit, remove the plastic base from your router and use it as a template *(Fig. 3)*. (To prevent the base from moving, I use carpet tape to hold it in place while tracing the holes.)

RAILS. After marking and drilling the holes, a pair of hardwood rails (E) is added *(Fig. 3)*. Holes at each end of the rails fit over the guide rods and allow the platform to slide back and forth. To keep the platform from binding, the holes need to align with the guide rods and with each other. To do this, I taped

the rails together with double-sided tape and then centered the holes $7^1/2$" apart *(Fig. 4)*. Then I sanded the holes a touch oversize so the rails would slide easily on the rods.

Before attaching the rails to the platform, cut a kerf at each end of one rail *(Fig. 5)*. Later, this rail acts as part of a clamping system that locks the platform in place. After cutting the kerfs, the rails are glued and screwed to the mounting plate *(Fig. 3)*.

CLAMP. Now the clamping system can be completed with two carriage bolts that pass through holes drilled in the ends of the kerfed rail *(Fig. 3a)*. By tightening wing nuts on the bolts, the kerfed ends of the rail pinch against the guide rods and lock the platform in place. (See the Shop Tip at right for a way to drill these holes in the rail.)

FINGER GUARD. The last step is to add a finger guard. The guard is a piece of $1/4$"-thick acrylic plastic that's screwed *loosely* to the front rail *(Fig. 6)*. Two slots and a beveled bottom corner allow the guard to "ride up" on top of the workpiece as it's passed under the router. Sand the sharp edges before attaching the guard to the rail.

Before using the jig, apply a light

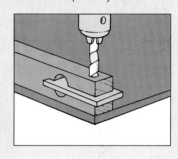
coat of wax to the rods to make the platform slide smoothly. But go easy. The platform is supposed to stay put when the bolts are tightened. ■

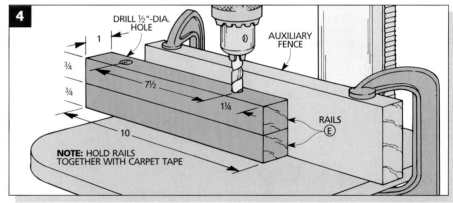

4 DRILL $1/2$"-DIA. HOLE — AUXILIARY FENCE — 1 — $3/4$ — $3/4$ — $7^1/2$ — $1^1/4$ — RAILS (E) — 10 — **NOTE:** HOLD RAILS TOGETHER WITH CARPET TAPE

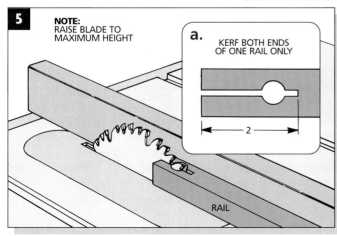

5 **NOTE:** RAISE BLADE TO MAXIMUM HEIGHT — **a.** KERF BOTH ENDS OF ONE RAIL ONLY — 2 — RAIL

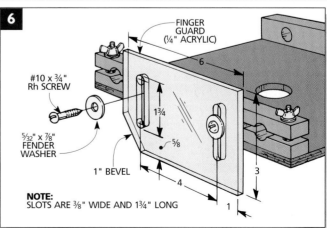

6 FINGER GUARD ($1/4$" ACRYLIC) — 6 — #10 x $3/4$" Rh SCREW — $1^3/4$ — $5/32$" x $7/8$" FENDER WASHER — $5/8$ — 1" BEVEL — 4 — 3 — 1 — **NOTE:** SLOTS ARE $3/8$" WIDE AND $1^3/4$" LONG

TECHNIQUE .... Making Raised Panels

One way to turn an ordinary project into something special is with a raised panel door or drawer. Making these panels is simple using a router and the raised panel jig.

RABBET. Since most panels are surrounded by a frame, first fit the panel to the frame. This requires cutting rabbets on both sides of the panel *(Fig. 1)*. The rabbets form a tongue that fits into a groove in the frame *(Fig. 1a)*.

Before routing the border of the panel, there are two things to consider: grain direction and feed direction.

GRAIN DIRECTION. To reduce the amount of chipout, the ends (or end grain) of the panel are routed first. Then, any chipout can be cleaned up by routing the sides (or edge grain).

FEED DIRECTION. For each pass, the panel is fed from *left to right*. This way, the clockwise rotation of the bit pulls the panel against the fence.

SET-UP. After mounting the router to the platform, the shoulder of the rabbet is used as a guide to position the router bit *(Fig. 2a)*. Since this first cut may be fairly deep, make a shallow pass followed by a pass at full depth.

WIDTH OF BORDER. When the first cut is completed around the entire panel, the width of the border can be increased. To do this, slide the platform up the guide rods, tighten the clamps, and make another pass around each edge. Then just repeat the process until the border is the desired width *(Fig. 3)*.

Then clean up the border and square the shoulder using a beveled sanding block *(Fig. 4)*.

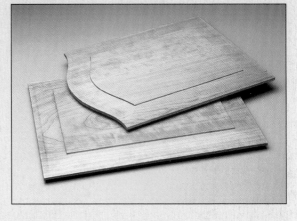

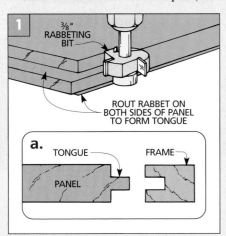

1 3/8" RABBETING BIT

ROUT RABBET ON BOTH SIDES OF PANEL TO FORM TONGUE

a. TONGUE — FRAME

PANEL

Form tongue. First, rabbet both sides of the panel to form a tongue that fits the groove in the frame.

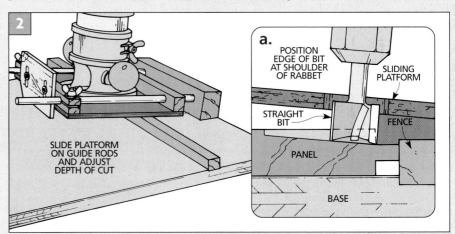

2 SLIDE PLATFORM ON GUIDE RODS AND ADJUST DEPTH OF CUT

a. POSITION EDGE OF BIT AT SHOULDER OF RABBET

SLIDING PLATFORM

STRAIGHT BIT

FENCE

PANEL

BASE

Set router. After mounting the router on the sliding platform, position the platform so the edge of the bit is at the shoulder of the rabbet. On this first cut, it may be necessary to take two shallow passes instead of one deep pass.

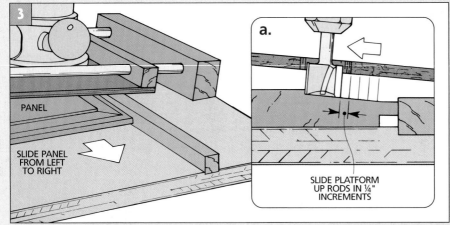

3 PANEL

SLIDE PANEL FROM LEFT TO RIGHT

a. SLIDE PLATFORM UP RODS IN 1/4" INCREMENTS

Routing. Make the first pass by sliding the panel from left to right. Make a pass on all sides. Then complete the border by making a series of passes (again on all sides), moving the sliding platform in 1/4" increments between each pass.

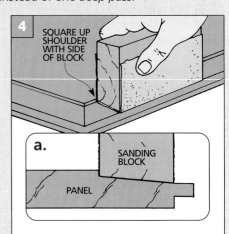

4 SQUARE UP SHOULDER WITH SIDE OF BLOCK

a. SANDING BLOCK

PANEL

Sanding. Clean up any router marks with a sanding block beveled to match the slope of the border.

WOODWORKER'S NOTEBOOK

You're not limited to just routing square or rectangular panels with this jig. With a simple modification and some practice, you can add the elegant look of curved raised panels to your projects.

CURVED RAISED PANELS

■ The beauty of this raised panel jig is it can also be used to rout curved panels. When doing this, the curved edge is routed first, for two reasons. First, the curved edge is usually in end grain. Second, the width of the borders on the straight edges depends on the width of the border on the curved edge.

■ It's much easier to rout a curved panel if you can see the workpiece as it passes under the router. To make a platform with a see-through base, refer to the Shop Tip on page 61.

■ Since the curved edge of the panel doesn't conform to the straight line of the fence, the fence is replaced with a rub block (F) *(Fig. 1)*. This is just a short piece of ³⁄₄"-dia. dowel. The dowel is screwed in a hole that's centered on the dado in the base *(Fig. 1a)*.

■ Once the rub block is in place, set up the jig the same as for routing a straight edge as shown on the previous page. Then you can start routing the curved end of the panel.

There is a different technique to feeding a curved panel through the jig. To maintain a consistent width on the profile, the panel must be pivoted as it is fed under the bit *(Fig. 2)*.

First, draw a reference line on the front center of the rub block *(Fig. 2)*. Then as you move the workpiece through the jig, keep the edge perpendicular to that line. To do this, start with the panel parallel to the outside edges of the platform. As you slide the panel, swing the right side up *(Fig. 2)*. Then as the midpoint of the panel approaches the rub block, start to swing the left side up. At the end of the cut, the panel sides should again be parallel with the sides of the platform.

Ideally, you should end up with a consistent width across the entire border. If it varies, an additional pass or two is all it should take to even it up.

Getting the hang of this pivoting motion may take some practice, so it's a good idea to cut a few extra blanks.

■ Once the curved portion is cut to width, complete the rest of the raised panel. To do this, simply replace the rub block with the fence *(Fig. 3)*. Then rout along the straight edges to create a border the same width as the curved border *(Fig. 3a)*.

■ Finally, clean up the beveled edges with a sanding block. The curved edges can be sanded by hand.

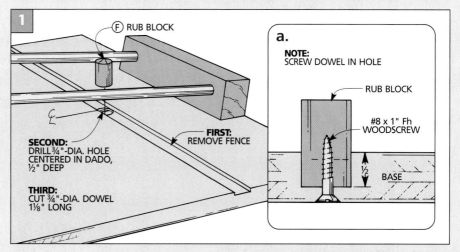

1

Ⓕ RUB BLOCK

SECOND:
DRILL ³⁄₄"-DIA. HOLE CENTERED IN DADO, ½" DEEP

THIRD:
CUT ³⁄₄"-DIA. DOWEL 1⅛" LONG

FIRST:
REMOVE FENCE

a.
NOTE:
SCREW DOWEL IN HOLE

RUB BLOCK

#8 x 1" Fh WOODSCREW

BASE

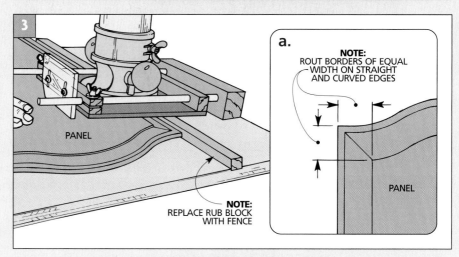

2

FIRST:
ROUT TONGUE ON ALL FOUR EDGES

SECOND:
ROUT CURVED END OF PANEL

RUB BLOCK

ROUTER BIT

SLIDE PANEL FROM LEFT TO RIGHT

FOR CONSISTENT WIDTH, PIVOT PANEL TO MAINTAIN CONTACT WITH FRONT CENTER POINT OF RUB BLOCK

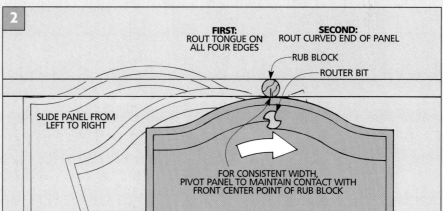

3

PANEL

NOTE:
REPLACE RUB BLOCK WITH FENCE

a.
NOTE:
ROUT BORDERS OF EQUAL WIDTH ON STRAIGHT AND CURVED EDGES

PANEL

Dovetail Jig

The beauty, symmetry and strength of dovetail joints can give a project that extra touch of class. And once you've built this jig, adding perfect dovetails to a project becomes quick and easy.

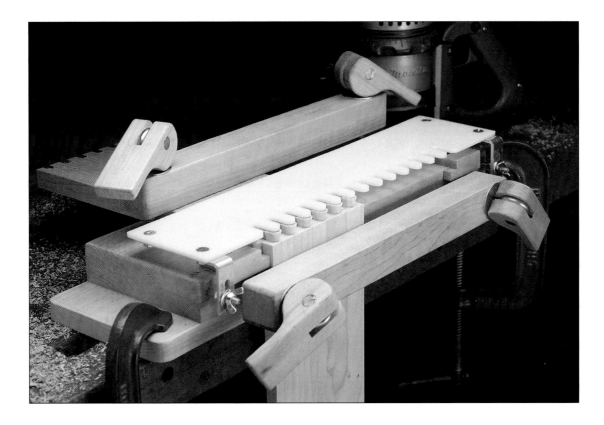

Tight-fitting dovetails make a statement. They say quality, craftsmanship and pride. In addition to the beauty they add to a project, they also provide strength.

Unfortunately, too many woodworkers never try their hand at dovetails because they look intimidating. With this jig, however, cutting professional-looking, half-blind dovetails is as easy as running your router.

CLAMPING. I've used other dovetail jigs and one problem I've had is keeping the parts clamped securely. If a workpiece shifts even slightly while you're cutting, the joint won't fit together properly, if at all.

CAMS. To solve this problem, this jig provides plenty of clamping power. It uses cams. With just a twist and a push,

they can apply considerable pressure. They also release quickly, so it's easier to move pieces in and out if you're making a number of joints.

PRESSURE BARS. The cams press down on the ends of a pressure bar, which then clamps the workpiece to the jig. With all that pressure building up, you need strong bars that won't bend. I built up 1½"-thick blanks from hard maple to make the bars.

COMB. The key to this jig is the "comb" on the top. The mating pieces of the drawer are clamped into the top and front of the jig under the comb. Then when cutting the joint, a dovetail bit sticks through a bushing mounted in the router base. This bushing rubs along the comb, guiding the bit as it cuts the dovetails.

The comb for this jig is designed to cut ½" dovetails. To do this, you'll need a ½" dovetail bit and a 7/16" guide bushing to fit your router.

But there's also a way to modify the jig that allows you to cut ¼" dovetails. The Woodworker's Notebook on page 70 shows you how to do this.

TROUBLESHOOTING. Getting a joint that's a picture-perfect fit does involve a bit of trial and error. Tips for getting the best fit are on page 74.

MATERIALS. All you need to make this jig is some standard off-the-shelf hardware, five board feet of hardwood, and a piece of ¼" hardboard to make the comb template. (A hardware kit is available that includes a ready-made plastic comb like the one in the photo. See Sources on page 126.)

EXPLODED VIEW

OVERALL DIMENSIONS:
9⅞W X 22L X 6⅜H

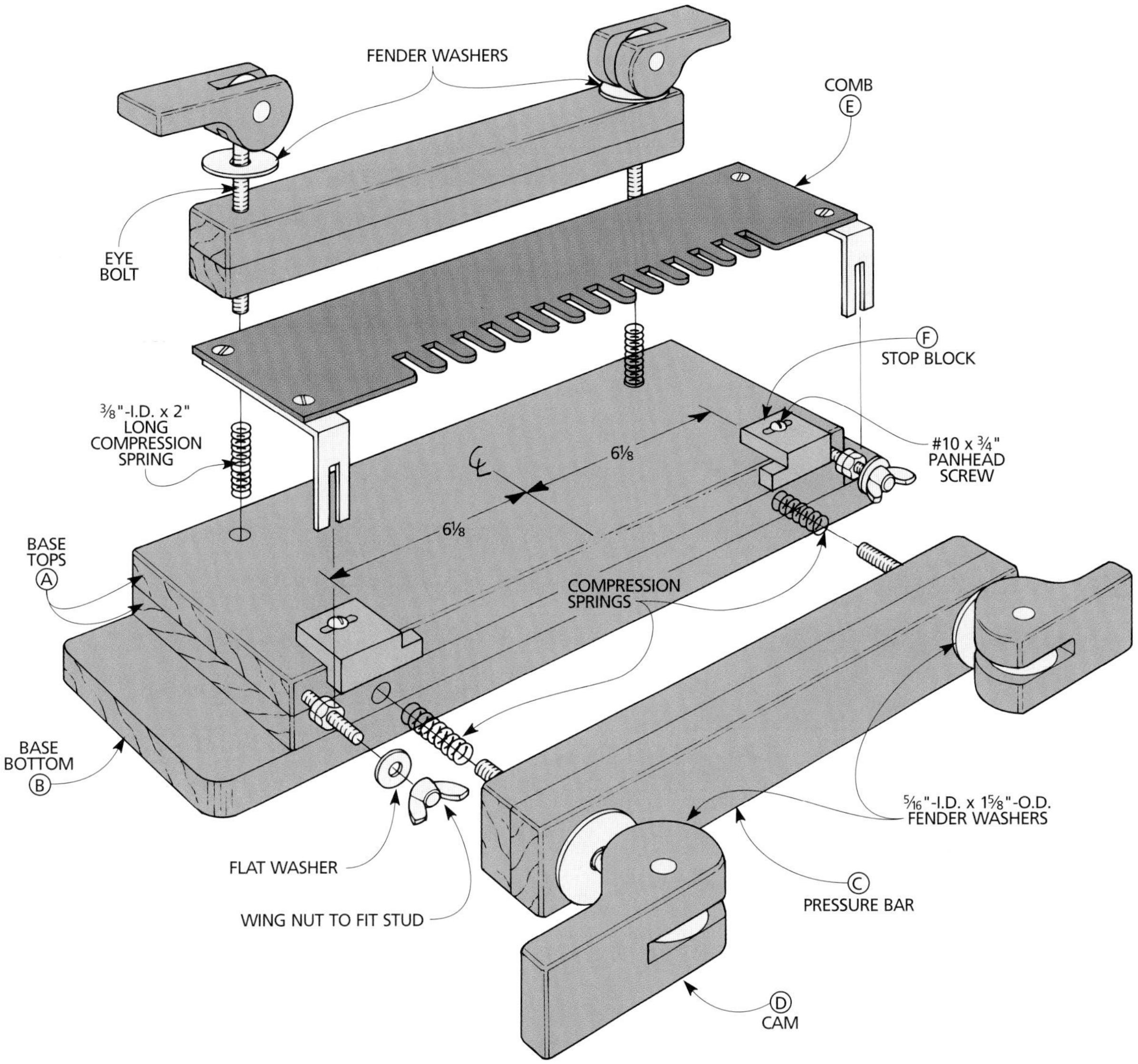
FENDER WASHERS
COMB
E
EYE BOLT
F
STOP BLOCK
⅜"-I.D. x 2" LONG COMPRESSION SPRING
6⅛
6⅛
#10 x ¾" PANHEAD SCREW
BASE TOPS
A
COMPRESSION SPRINGS
BASE BOTTOM
B
5⁄16"-I.D. x 1⅝"-O.D. FENDER WASHERS
FLAT WASHER
WING NUT TO FIT STUD
C
PRESSURE BAR
D
CAM

MATERIALS LIST

WOOD

- **A** Base Tops (2) — ¾ x 6 - 18
- **B** Base Bottom (1) — ¾ x 6 - 22
- **C** Pressure Bars (2) — 1½ x 1½ - 13
- **D** Cams (4) — 1½ x 1½ - 3⅞
- **E** Comb (1) — ¼ hdbd. - 4 x 24 rough
- **F** Stop Blocks (2) — ¾ x 2½ - 2 3⁄16

HARDWARE SUPPLIES

- (4) 5⁄16"-inside diameter threaded inserts
- (4) 5⁄16" x 5" eye bolts
- (1) ½" steel rod 12" long
- (2) 4" angle brackets
- (4) ¼" x ½" Fh machine screws
- (4) ¼" hex nuts
- (2) ¼" x 3" machine screws
- (4) ¼" hex nuts
- (2) ¼" flat washers
- (2) ¼" wing nuts
- (4) 5⁄16"-inside diameter fender washers
- (4) ⅜"-inside diameter x 2"-long compression springs
- (2) No. 10 x ¾" Ph woodscrews

The first step in making the jig is to build the base. It's built up from three pieces of $3/4$"-thick hardwood. It's important to use a tight-grained hardwood such as maple. The threaded inserts need something to really "bite" into so they won't pull out.

GLUE UP BASE. I began by cutting two base top pieces (A) to rough dimensions of $6^1/2$" wide and 19" long and laminating the pieces together face-to-face. After this blank is dry, cut it to a finished length of 18" *(Fig. 1)*.

Next, I cut a base bottom piece (B) from $3/4$"-thick stock to a rough width of $6^1/2$" and finished length of 22". Then glue this piece onto the bottom of the top blank so there are 2" wings overhanging on each end. (The wings are used for clamping the jig down to a bench or table.)

CUT TO WIDTH. Once the base is assembled, trim it down to a finished width of 6" *(Fig. 1)*. When trimming the front edge, make sure it's exactly 90° to the top of the base.

DRILL HOLES. After the base block was trimmed, I drilled six holes in it for parts that are added later. First, drill two $1/8$"-dia. pilot holes in the top, $1/2$" from the front edge *(Fig. 1)*. These are for the screws that hold the stop blocks.

The other four holes are for the threaded inserts that will accept eye bolts for the cams (refer to *Fig. 6*).

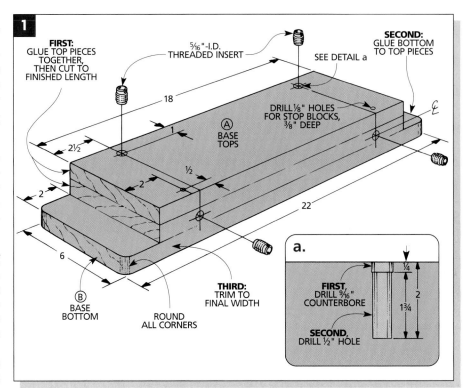

However, before drilling the holes for the inserts, I counterbored $9/16$"-dia. holes $1/4$" deep to make a space for the springs that hold the pressure bars away from the jig *(Fig. 1a)*.

Next, I drilled a $1/2$"-dia. hole centered in each counterbore to accept the threaded insert *(Fig. 1a)*. This hole has to be 2" deep so the eye bolt can be screwed all the way through the insert.

Note: Most $5/16$" (inside diameter) threaded inserts tighten into a $1/2$"-dia. hole, but some require a smaller diameter hole. Drill the holes to match the specific inserts you have.

MOUNT INSERTS. After the holes are drilled, tighten the inserts down so they're set $1/4$" below the surface of the base (the top of the insert should be flush with the bottom of the counterbore). See the Shop Tip below for one way to do this.

SHOP TIP .... Installing Inserts

To install the four threaded inserts into the base of the dovetail jig, I made a simple driver.

First, I tightened two nuts against each other on a $5/16$" bolt (see drawing). Then I screwed an insert onto the bolt snug against the nuts. I also rubbed some candle wax on the threads of the insert to lubricate it. (Paste wax or car wax will also work.)

Use some extra care when you start the insert into the wood. Make sure it's straight up and down.

Otherwise, the insert might not seat properly or deeply enough.

Next, I tightened down the bolt with a socket wrench until the top of the insert was flush with the bottom of the counterbore (see detail in drawing).

Once the insert is in place, that's where you want it to stay as you remove the bolt. So first, loosen the top nut on the driver a turn or two, then gently back the bolt (along with the bottom nut) out of the insert.

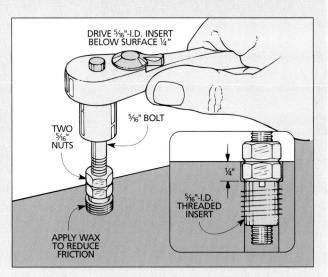

When all four of the threaded inserts were screwed in place, I began work on the pressure bars and cams. These pieces are cut from three blanks that start out 2" wide and 17" long *(Fig. 2)*. (**Note**: These blanks can be built up from two pieces of $3/4$"-thick stock or one piece of $13/4$"-thick stock — just so they're about $11/2$" to $13/4$" thick.)

PRESSURE BARS. To make the two pressure bars (C), cut two of the blanks square ($11/2$" x $11/2$") and to a finished length of 15". Then drill a $3/8$"-dia. hole 1" from each end *(Fig. 2)*. The eye bolts used in the cams pass through these holes when the jig is assembled.

CAMS. The four whistle-shaped cams (D) can be cut from the third blank. I started by squaring up one edge of the blank and then cut it in half lengthwise *(Fig. 3)*. This makes it easier to cut the slots in the cams later.

LAY OUT CAMS. Next, I made a poster board pattern of a cam *(Fig. 3)*. To achieve the gradual tightening action of the cam, the rounded bottom is made from two different radii ($7/8$" and 1"). These radii start at two different center points ($1/8$" apart), and intersect at the bottom. This increasing radius creates the cam action that exerts gradually increasing pressure on the bar.

After transferring the pattern to each workpiece, I drilled a $1/2$"-diameter hole centered on the 1" radius centerpoint in each cam *(Fig. 3)*. This hole accepts the axle pins added later (refer to *Fig. 6*).

CUT SLOT. Before cutting the cams to final shape, cut a $5/16$"-wide slot through each end of the cam blanks to accept the eye bolts. I did this by standing the piece up on end on the table saw and backing it with a 2x4 block to steady it during the cut *(Fig. 4)*.

Cut a $13/4$"-deep slot centered on each end (Step 1 in *Fig. 4a*). To widen the slot to $5/16$", move the rip fence slightly away from the blade and repeat the cut. Then turn the piece around so the opposite face is against the fence and make another cut. Continue moving the fence slightly and cutting on opposite sides (Step 2 in *Fig. 4a*) until the $5/16$" eye bolt slides into the slot.

CUT TO SHAPE. Once the eye bolt fits the slots, I cut each cam from the blanks with the band saw. Then I sanded them to final shape. While you're at it, slightly soften all of the sharp edges to make the

cams easier on your hands when using the jig *(Fig. 5)*.

EYE BOLT. The eye bolt is just a standard $5/16$" x 5" eye bolt purchased from a hardware store. After using the jig for a while, I discovered that the eye section started to uncurl when extreme pressure was applied to the cam. To prevent this, I had it welded shut *(Fig. 6)*.

CUT AXLE PIN. Next, I cut a piece of $1/2$" rod to act as an axle pin through the eye bolt *(Fig. 6)*. I cut this from a long rod. You can also cut the pin from the unthreaded section of a $1/2$" bolt. If the pin fits loosely in the cam, use a dab of epoxy toward each end to hold it. Just be careful not to get any on the eye bolt.

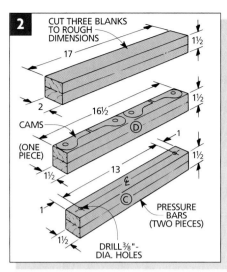

CUT THREE BLANKS TO ROUGH DIMENSIONS

17 · $11/2$

2 · $161/2$ · $11/2$ · 1

CAMS (ONE PIECE) · $11/2$ · 13 · $11/2$

1 · C · PRESSURE BARS (TWO PIECES)

$11/2$ · DRILL $3/8$"-DIA. HOLES

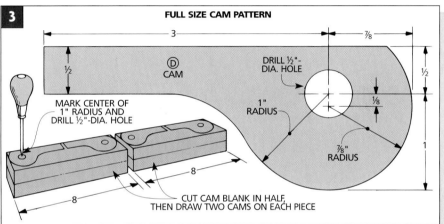

FULL SIZE CAM PATTERN

3 · $7/8$

$1/2$ · D CAM · DRILL $1/2$"-DIA. HOLE · $1/2$

MARK CENTER OF 1" RADIUS AND DRILL $1/2$"-DIA. HOLE · 1" RADIUS · $1/8$ · 1

$7/8$" RADIUS

8 · 8 · CUT CAM BLANK IN HALF, THEN DRAW TWO CAMS ON EACH PIECE

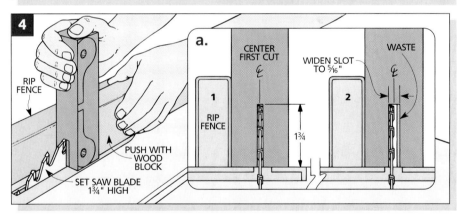

a.

RIP FENCE · PUSH WITH WOOD BLOCK · SET SAW BLADE $13/4$" HIGH

1 RIP FENCE · CENTER FIRST CUT · WIDEN SLOT TO $5/16$" · WASTE · 2 · $13/4$

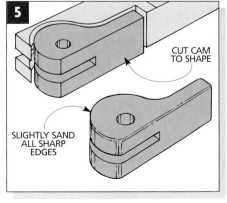

CUT CAM TO SHAPE

SLIGHTLY SAND ALL SHARP EDGES

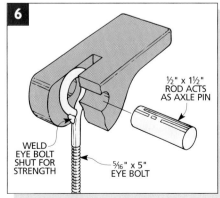

WELD EYE BOLT SHUT FOR STRENGTH · $1/2$" x $11/2$" ROD ACTS AS AXLE PIN · $5/16$" x 5" EYE BOLT

TEMPLATE

Next, I began work on the "comb" template that guides the router. This template must be extremely accurate or the dovetail joint won't fit together correctly. The most accurate way to cut the comb is to use an indexing jig.

CUT NOTCHES. Start by cutting a piece of $1/4$" hardboard for the comb *(Fig. 7)*. The next step is cutting the notches. These notches have to be exactly $7/16$" wide since a router guide bushing with a $7/16$" outside diameter is used with the jig.

After setting a dado blade to the correct width, raise the blade 1" high. Then screw a tall auxiliary fence to the miter gauge *(Fig. 8)*. Stand the hardboard on edge and cut a notch 6" from one end.

INDEXING KEY. Now glue an indexing key into the notch in the fence *(Fig. 9)*. Then, screw the fence to the miter gauge so the key is *exactly* $7/16$" from the blade.

When the jig is set up, place the notch in the comb over the key and cut a second notch *(Fig. 9)*. Move the new notch over the key and repeat the steps until fourteen notches are cut *(Fig. 10)*. The distance from the first notch to the last should be $11^{13}/16$" *(Fig. 7)*.

Once the notches are cut, file the front end of each pin round *(Fig. 11)*.

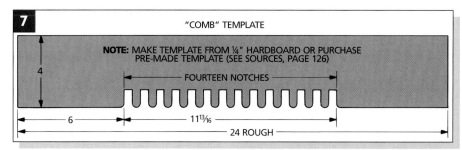

7 "COMB" TEMPLATE

NOTE: MAKE TEMPLATE FROM 1/4" HARDBOARD OR PURCHASE PRE-MADE TEMPLATE (SEE SOURCES, PAGE 126)

4

FOURTEEN NOTCHES

6 — 11¹³⁄₁₆ — 24 ROUGH

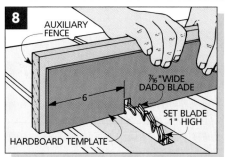

8 AUXILIARY FENCE · 7/16" WIDE DADO BLADE · SET BLADE 1" HIGH · HARDBOARD TEMPLATE · 6

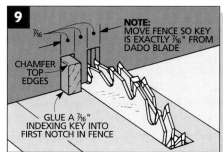

9 7/16 · NOTE: MOVE FENCE SO KEY IS EXACTLY 7/16" FROM DADO BLADE · CHAMFER TOP EDGES · GLUE A 7/16" INDEXING KEY INTO FIRST NOTCH IN FENCE

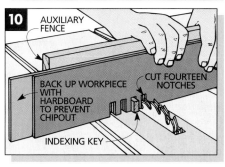

10 AUXILIARY FENCE · BACK UP WORKPIECE WITH HARDBOARD TO PREVENT CHIPOUT · CUT FOURTEEN NOTCHES · INDEXING KEY

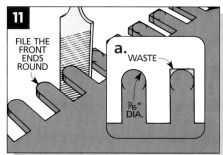

11 FILE THE FRONT ENDS ROUND · **a.** WASTE · 7/16" DIA.

CUT TO LENGTH. Next, center the comb's middle pin on the length of the base *(Fig. 12)*. Then cut the template the same length as the top of the base.

WOODWORKER'S NOTEBOOK

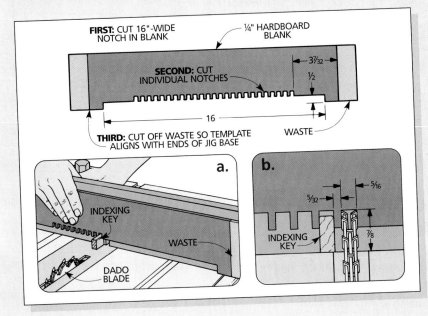

FIRST: CUT 16"-WIDE NOTCH IN BLANK

1/4" HARDBOARD BLANK

SECOND: CUT INDIVIDUAL NOTCHES

3⁷⁄₃₂ · ½

16

THIRD: CUT OFF WASTE SO TEMPLATE ALIGNS WITH ENDS OF JIG BASE

WASTE

a. INDEXING KEY · WASTE · DADO BLADE

b. INDEXING KEY · 5/32 · 5/16 · 7/8

¼" DOVETAILS

- To cut $1/4$" dovetails with the jig, make a template with the notches set back $1/2$" from the edge. Start by cutting a wide notch along the front edge of the blank.
- Center the blank against the base and mark the ends of the base onto the blank. Then measure for the position of the first notch.
- To cut the notches in the comb, make an indexing jig *(Detail a)*. Cut a $5/16$"-wide dado $7/8$" deep in an auxiliary fence *(Detail b)*.
- Glue a $5/16$"-thick indexing key in the auxiliary fence and set the key $5/32$" from the blade *(Detail b)*.
- Cut the notches along the blank, then trim the blank to length.
- Use a $1/4$" dovetail bit with a $5/16$" guide bushing when routing the joint.

BRACKETS. The template is attached to the block with angle brackets made from steel corner brackets *(Fig. 13)*. Start by hacksawing one "leg" on each bracket to 2" long *(Fig. 13)*. Then cut a slot up from the cut-off end. You will probably be cutting up through a mounting hole, so make the slot width the same as the diameter of the hole.

After the slots are cut, fasten the brackets to the comb, flush with the outside edges *(Fig. 14)*.

STUDS. Next, two studs are mounted in the base block to hold and position the brackets. To do this, position the template flush with the ends of the block and mark the slot positions on the block *(Fig. 14)*.

The studs are created by tightening two machine screws into the block and then cutting off their heads (Stud Detail in *Fig. 14*). The diameter of the studs should match the slots in the brackets.

Note: Before tightening the screw into the block, thread on two nuts to act as stops (Stud Detail in *Fig. 14*).

STOP BLOCKS

All that's left are the stop blocks that position the workpieces on the jig.

RABBET. Start by cutting a blank for the stop blocks *(Fig. 15)*. Then cut a wide rabbet along one edge (Steps 1 and 2 in *Fig. 15a*). Next, cut the blank to finished width (Step 3 in *Fig. 15a*).

END NOTCH. When cutting dovetails, the two workpieces have to be offset $7/16$" from each other. To allow for this offset, cut notches at both ends of the stop block to produce $7/16$"-long fingers *(Fig. 16)*. Check the length against the comb template — the finger should be exactly as long as the width of a pin on the comb.

ADJUSTMENT SLOT. To make the blocks adjustable, I cut screw slots by drilling a series of holes *(Fig. 17)*. Then cut a stop block off each end.

FINAL ASSEMBLY

After the stop blocks are made, you can assemble all the pieces (see Exploded View on page 67). To start, screw the stop blocks down with sheet metal screws so the shoulder of each stop block is $6\frac{1}{8}$" from the center of the jig. Then add the springs, bars, and cams. And finally, secure the template to the studs with washers and wing nuts. ∎

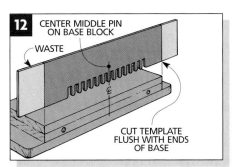

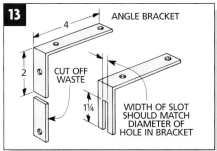

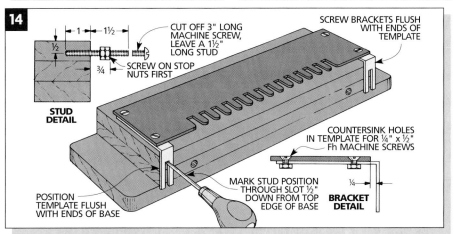

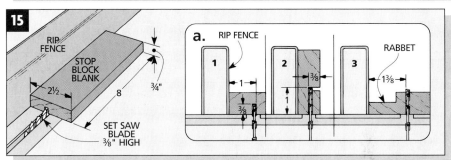

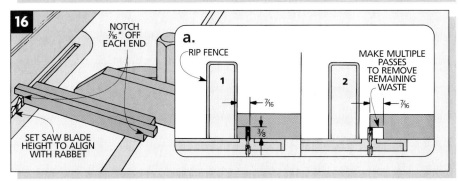

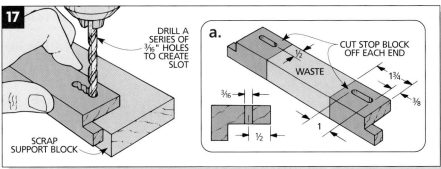

TECHNIQUE ..... *Using the Dovetail Jig*

Cutting tight dovetail joints with a router and template is easy — but it requires a little planning ahead. It's best to plan the dimensions of the cabinet to accommodate drawers that are joined with router-cut dovetails.

DRAWER WIDTH. The reason is that the width (height) of the drawer has to be a multiple of $7/8$" (see drawing at right). This makes a symmetrical joint, with a half pin on both the top and bottom edges.

Note: These instructions are for flush-front drawers. See page 75 for details on making overlay (rabbeted-front) drawers.

LABEL PIECES. Once all the pieces are cut to finished size, lay them out on the bench with the inside faces up. Label each piece and the bottom edge of each piece, and number the matching corners *(Step 1)*.

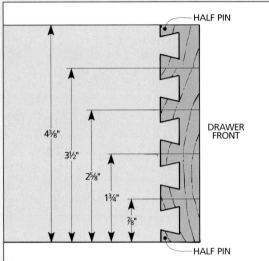

- HALF PIN
- DRAWER FRONT
- $4\frac{3}{8}$"
- $3\frac{1}{2}$"
- $2\frac{5}{8}$"
- $1\frac{3}{4}$"
- $\frac{7}{8}$"
- HALF PIN

ALIGNMENT. Setting up the jig takes some trial and error, so don't start with the finished pieces. Work with scrap that's the same thickness and width as the drawer pieces.

MOUNT PIECES. Placing the pieces in the jig can be a little confusing because it's opposite from the way the drawer is assembled. Start by placing a test drawer side under the front pressure bar and a test drawer top under the top pressure bar. The insides should be facing out *(Step 2)*. (That's why the labeling for the drawer pieces is on the inside face.) Press the bottom edges tight against the left-hand stop block.

After the drawer front is clamped down, reposition the drawer side so its end is level with the drawer front *(Step 3)*.

ADJUST STOP BLOCK. When pressed against the stop block, the bottom edge of the drawer side should be centered on the first notch of the template *(Step 4)*.

ADJUST TEMPLATE. Next, you may need to adjust the "comb" template so

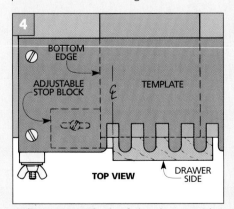

Label Pieces. *Lay out the drawer pieces on a bench, insides facing up. Label all pieces and the matching corners.*

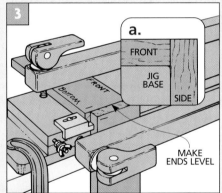

Insert Pieces. *Clamp a drawer side under the front bar. Clamp a drawer front on top tight to the side.*

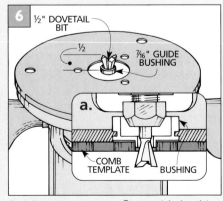

Reposition Side. *Reposition the drawer side piece so it is perfectly flush with the top of the drawer front.*

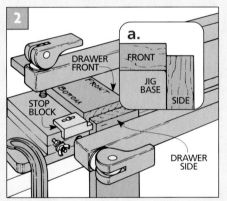

Adjust Stop Block. *If the drawer side's bottom edge isn't centered on the first notch, adjust the stop block.*

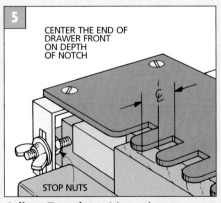

Adjust Template. *Move the stop nuts so the end of the drawer front is centered on the depth of the notch.*

Set Router. *Mount a $7/16$" guide bushing in the router. Raise the $1/2$" dovetail bit $1/2$" above the base to start.*

the end of the drawer front is centered on the end of the notch *(Step 5)*. The location of the stop nuts on the studs may take some adjustment. Then hold the template down on the drawer front and tighten the wing nuts.

ROUTER SETUP. Mount a $^{7}/_{16}$"-dia. guide bushing in the router *(Step 6)*.

Next, chuck a $^{1}/_{2}$" dovetail bit in the router, making sure the bit is centered in the collar of the guide bushing. If it's not, adjust the router's plastic base slightly. I start with the bit $^{1}/_{2}$" deep (from the base), but this may vary.

ROUTING THE PIECES. To prevent chipout, start by making a light scoring pass from right to left *(Step 7)*.

Then gently move the router in and out of the fingers, moving from left to right *(Step 8)*. You should be able to feel the guide bushing stop at the back of each notch. Before removing the pieces from the jig, check that you've routed each socket evenly *(Step 9)*.

ROUTING REMAINING JOINTS. At this point, you've routed the joint at the left front corner of the drawer. (It's marked No. 1 in *Step 1*.) Next rout the right rear corner joint (marked No. 3) using the same procedure.

The other two joints (Nos. 2 and 4) are routed with the pieces tight against the stop block on the *right* side of the jig. Again, always clamp the drawer side to the front of the jig, with the inside of

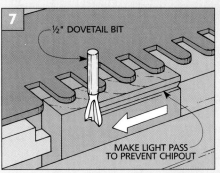

Scoring Pass. *Score a light pass from right to left to establish the shoulder line and prevent chipout.*

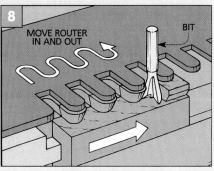

Rout Dovetails. *Move the router left to right, in and out of the comb. Press the bushing to the back of each notch.*

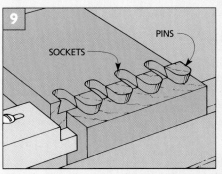

Check Cut. *Remove the template and check that all sockets and pins are uniform. Remove the pieces and test fit.*

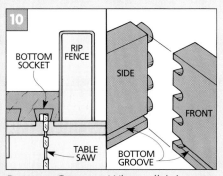

Bottom Groove. *When all joints are done, cut a groove centered in the bottom socket for the drawer bottom.*

the pieces facing out and the bottom edges against the stops.

When routing on the right side, follow the same procedure. Make a light pass from right to left and then

move the router in and out of the notches from left to right.

BOTTOM GROOVE. When all the joints are routed, cut the grooves for the drawer bottom *(Step 10)*.

SHOP TIP .... Depth Setting Gauge

Once you have the bit set to cut a nice, tight joint, it's worth taking a few minutes to make a simple depth-setting gauge. Then you can easily reset the bit the next time you want to cut dovetails.

I started with a long hardwood scrap *(Fig. 1)*. (It's cut to length later.) To provide clearance for the bushing collar, cut a $^{3}/_{4}$"-wide dado across the block *(Fig. 1a)*.

Next, clamp the piece in a vise and rout an

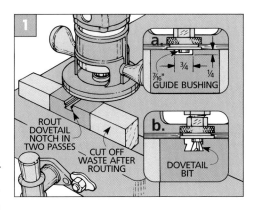

oversized dovetail-shaped notch across it *(Figs. 1 and 1b)*. To do this, run the bushing against the left shoulder of the dado and then back out along the dado's

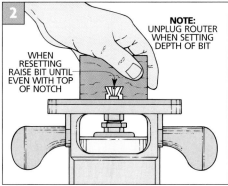

right shoulder *(Fig. 1b)*.

Now whenever you need to set up your router for dovetails, use the gauge to reset the height of the bit *(Fig. 2)*.

Setting up to make router-cut dovetails involves fiddling around with trial pieces and readjusting parts of the jig to get a joint with a perfect fit. Here's how to solve the most common problems with fit.

TOO LOOSE. If the pieces wiggle around when they're put together, the depth of cut is too shallow (see left photo below). *Increase* the depth of cut about 1/32" and try again.

TOO TIGHT. If a trial cut is so tight that the pieces can't be tapped together, the router bit is too deep. *Decrease* the depth of cut about 1/32".

TOO DEEP. If the pins on the drawer sides go too far into the sockets on the drawer front, the sockets are too deep (see center photo). To correct this, move the template toward you by turning the stop nuts on the studs counterclockwise. (Be sure to adjust the nuts on both ends of the jig.)

Note: You may want the pins to be recessed from the ends of the sockets about 1/32". This helps when sanding the joints flush later.

TOO SHALLOW. If the pins don't go far enough into the sockets, move the template away from you by turning the stop nuts clockwise.

OFFSET. Sometimes the top of the drawer front doesn't align with the top edge of the side (see right photo).

If both the top and bottom edges are offset equal amounts, a couple of things could be wrong. First, the edges of both pieces may not have been tight against the stop block.

Second, the offset on the stop block may not be exactly 7/16". If it's a little less than that, you might try adding a layer or two of masking tape to the "finger" on the stop block.

Note: The end of the stop block should be centered on the first notch of

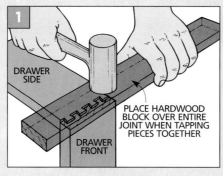

PLACE HARDWOOD BLOCK OVER ENTIRE JOINT WHEN TAPPING PIECES TOGETHER
DRAWER SIDE
DRAWER FRONT

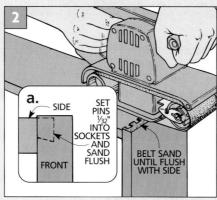

a. SIDE — SET PINS 1/32" INTO SOCKETS AND SAND FLUSH
FRONT
BELT SAND UNTIL FLUSH WITH SIDE

the template. If it's not, the top edges of the two pieces will be aligned, but the joint won't be symmetrical on the top and bottom edges.

OTHER PROBLEMS. Most other problems are usually caused by the pieces not being clamped down in the jig so they are flush across the top, or because they move out of position as they're being routed.

GLUING

How much glue should be applied to a dovetail joint? And where should you put it — on the pins or in the sockets?

TIGHT JOINT. If the joint fits tightly, I usually squirt just one dot of glue on the back side of each pin. Then when the pin seats in the socket, the glue oozes

around the pin and the socket.

LOOSE JOINT. If the joint is a little loose, you may need to brush the glue all the way around the pins and also in the sockets. The problem is that there are a lot of surfaces to cover and the glue can start setting up before you get the drawer assembled. It's a good idea to have some help to spread the glue quickly.

ASSEMBLY

A good fit should take some light tapping to get the joint together.

However, even with light tapping, it's best to apply even pressure across the whole joint to prevent the pins from splitting out. Place a block of hardwood over all the pins on the drawer side and then tap until the pins are seated in the bottom of the sockets *(Fig. 1)*.

NO CLAMPS. One advantage of tight fitting joints is that you won't need clamps to hold the drawer together while the glue dries. (Clamps can sometimes pull the drawer out of square or cause it to rack.) Just check the drawer for square as soon as the joints are tapped home. Then allow the drawer to dry on a flat surface.

SANDING SMOOTH

Since I know the joint may not be perfect, I plan the fit of the joint so it has to be sanded down exactly smooth.

DRAWER ENDS. If the joint is cut so the pins are deep, then you only have to sand the ends of the sockets (the ends of the drawer front and back) *(Fig. 2)*. So cut the joint so the pins sit about 1/32" too deep in the sockets *(Fig. 2a)*.

I account for this when measuring and cutting the drawer front and back by adding 1/16" to their lengths.

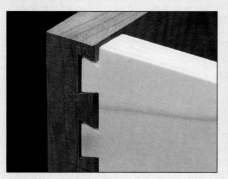

Making dovetail joints for an overlay drawer is a little different from routing a flush-front drawer. You have to take into consideration the rabbetted lip around the drawer front.

LAYOUT. When you lay out the pieces, the width of the drawer's back and sides has to equal the *shoulder-to-shoulder* width of the drawer front instead of the overall width *(Step 1)*. And the length of the back equals the shoulder-to-shoulder length of the front, not the overall length. (I cut the rabbets before routing the joint.)

Note: Again, it's best if the cabinet is designed so the width of the drawer back and sides is a multiple of ⁷⁄₈".

SPACER. When clamping the drawer front to the jig, you have to take the rabbet into consideration. To position the shoulder correctly, I put a spacer between the drawer front and the stop block *(Step 2)*.

To determine the thickness of this spacer, subtract the width of the rabbet from ⁷⁄₈". For a ³⁄₈" rabbet, then, you need a ¹⁄₂" spacer *(Step 2)*.

END ALIGNMENT. On the drawer front, the shoulder of the rabbet (not the end of the piece) has to be aligned with the front of the jig *(Step 2a)*. To set this up, cut a matching rabbet in a piece of scrap and clamp it under the front pressure bar *(Step 3)*. Then bring the drawer front up tight against the rabbet in the scrap.

ROUTING SIDES. After routing the drawer front *(Step 4)*, replace it with a piece of scrap *(Step 5)*. Then bring the drawer side up tight against the front of the jig and the scrap. Since the side piece doesn't have a rabbet in it, you can rout it without a spacer.

BACK CORNERS. The back corners (where the drawer back meets the sides) are cut with the flush dovetail technique as shown on pages 72-73.

BOTTOM GROOVE. The rabbet also has to be considered when locating the groove for the bottom. To do this, I make a low fence for the table saw that fits into the rabbet *(Step 6)*. Use the fence when cutting the groove in the side and back pieces as well *(Step 7)*. Then all the grooves will line up with each other.

Finally, check the fit of each joint as it is cut *(Step 8)*.

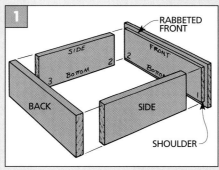

Layout. *Width of sides and back must equal front shoulder-to-shoulder width.*

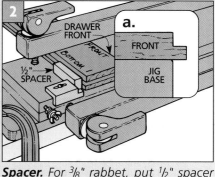

Spacer. *For ³⁄₈" rabbet, put ¹⁄₂" spacer between stop block and drawer front.*

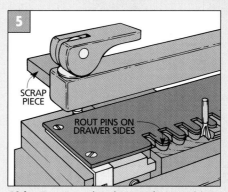

Rabbeted Scrap. *A rabbeted scrap in front positions the drawer front on top.*

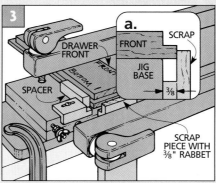

Cut Joint. *Cut sockets from left to right. Push bushing to the back of each notch.*

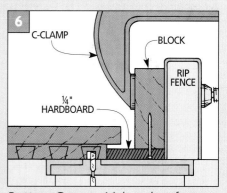

Side. *Scrap under the top bar positions the drawer side before cutting the pins.*

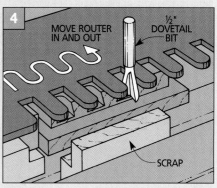

Bottom Groove. *Make a low fence to help position the groove in a socket.*

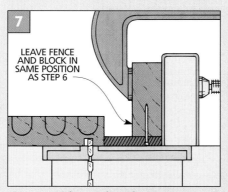

Groove Sides and Back. *Cut grooves in side and back pieces using low fence.*

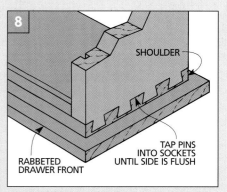

Assemble. *Tap the front joint together and check for a snug fit.*

Machine Tool Jigs

Whether you're after precision drilling, sharpening, or crosscutting or need custom-tailored circles, tapers, tenons or box joints, look no further. These shop-built fixtures add accuracy and convenience to your machine tools to make the most of your shop time.

Miter Gauge Fence

An auxiliary miter gauge fence helps support a workpiece when crosscutting on the table saw. This version adds accuracy and consistency with a built-in stop block and tape measure.

L ike many woodworkers, I attach an auxiliary fence to the miter gauge when crosscutting a board on the table saw. This provides more support for the workpiece than the miter gauge by itself.

But what I like best about an auxiliary fence is you can clamp a stop block to it and cut several pieces to the same length. The only problem is it can be a bit frustrating to clamp the block *exactly* where you want it.

To set up repeat cuts quickly and accurately, I made a miter gauge fence with a built-in, movable stop block. A measuring tape attached to the back of the fence makes it easy to position the

stop block accurately (see inset photo). Adding a hairline indicator made out of clear acrylic plastic makes it easy to lock the stop block at an *exact* spot on the measuring tape.

MITER CUTS. With a slight modification, the miter gauge fence can also be used for 45° miter cuts. The fence itself doesn't change — only the way it's positioned on your gauge.

This positioning is shown in the Woodworker's Notebook on page 81.

MATERIALS AND HARDWARE. The main parts of the project (the fence and stop block) are both built from hardwood,

although you have options for how thick you want to make the fence (see page 80 for details).

A simple toilet bolt and plastic knob allow the stop block to slide along the fence The fence is attached to your miter gauge with threaded inserts and machine screws, and the indicator is attached to the stop block with sheet-metal screws.

EXPLODED VIEW

OVERALL DIMENSIONS:
$1^7/_8$T X 26L X $4^1/_4$H

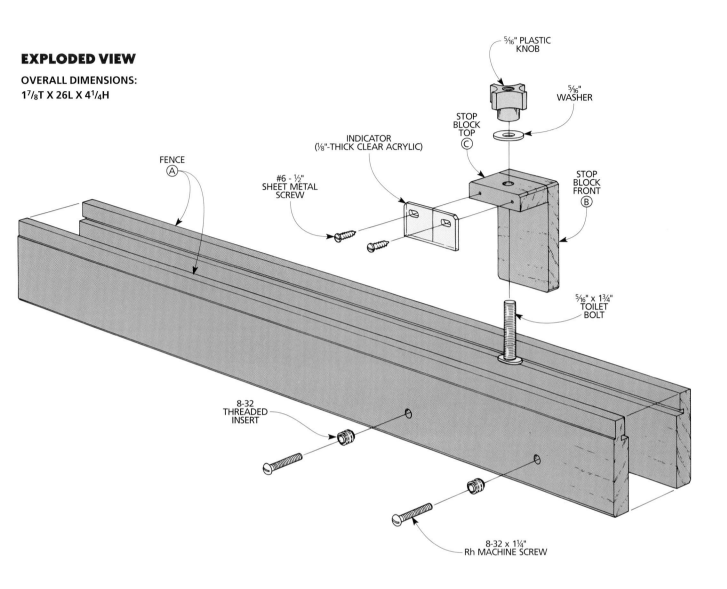

$5/_{16}$" PLASTIC KNOB

$5/_{16}$" WASHER

STOP BLOCK TOP ©

INDICATOR ($^1/_8$"-THICK CLEAR ACRYLIC)

FENCE Ⓐ

#6 - $^1/_2$" SHEET METAL SCREW

STOP BLOCK FRONT Ⓑ

$5/_{16}$" x $1^3/_4$" TOILET BOLT

8-32 THREADED INSERT

8-32 x $1^1/_4$" Rh MACHINE SCREW

SHOP TIP . . . . . *Self-Adhesive Rule*

The miter gauge fence has a self-adhesive rule for added convenience.

This measuring tape comes in versions that read from right-to-left (as shown in photo) or left-to-right. It is available through mail order catalogs.

The rule is included in the hardware kit for this fence, and for the Band Saw Circle Jig on page 96. See page 126 for more information.

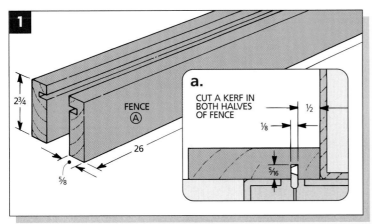

1

$2\frac{3}{4}$

FENCE
Ⓐ

26

$\frac{5}{8}$

a.
CUT A KERF IN
BOTH HALVES
OF FENCE

$\frac{1}{2}$

$\frac{1}{8}$

$\frac{5}{16}$

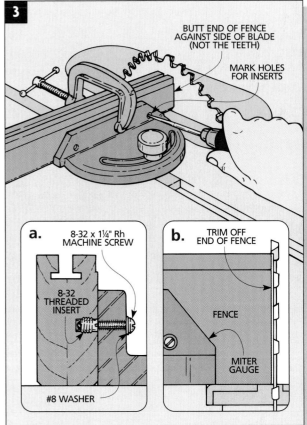

3

BUTT END OF FENCE
AGAINST SIDE OF BLADE
(NOT THE TEETH)

MARK HOLES
FOR INSERTS

a.
8-32 x 1¼" Rh
MACHINE SCREW

8-32
THREADED
INSERT

#8 WASHER

b.
TRIM OFF
END OF FENCE

FENCE

MITER
GAUGE

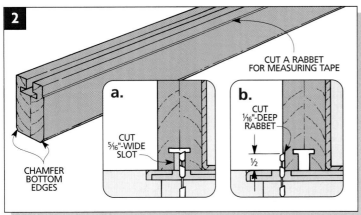

2

CUT A RABBET
FOR MEASURING TAPE

a.
CUT
$\frac{5}{16}$"-WIDE
SLOT

b.
CUT
$\frac{1}{16}$"-DEEP
RABBET

$\frac{1}{2}$

CHAMFER
BOTTOM
EDGES

FENCE

The fence (A) consists of two pieces of $\frac{5}{8}$"-thick hardwood *(Fig. 1)*. Although the fence can be as long as you want, make sure it's not so long that it's awkward to use. (I cut each piece 26" long.)

Note: The reason I made the fence from two pieces of $\frac{5}{8}$"-thick hardwood was so it would be relatively light and easy to handle. However, if you don't have a way of planing stock down to that thickness (or if you prefer a thicker, heavier miter gauge fence), you could use two pieces of $\frac{3}{4}$"-thick hardwood. If you do, just remember to build the top of the stop block (see opposite page) to width to fit.

T-SLOT. To allow the stop block to slide back and forth, there's a T-slot in the top of the fence.

The bottom part of this slot is cut *before* gluing the fence pieces together. To do this, cut matching $\frac{1}{8}$" kerfs in both fence pieces ($\frac{1}{2}$" from the top) using the table saw *(Fig. 1a)*. Then glue the fence pieces together. To keep the kerfs aligned when gluing, see the Shop Tip box at right.

When the glue dries, the T-slot can be completed by cutting a $\frac{5}{16}$"-wide slot, centered in the edge of the fence *(Figs. 2 and 2a)*.

Next, cut a shallow rabbet for the measuring tape (added later) *(Fig. 2b)*, and chamfer the bottom edges of the fence for sawdust relief.

ATTACH FENCE. The fence is held in place with machine screws that pass through the head of the miter gauge and into threaded inserts in the back of the fence *(Fig. 3a)*.

The location of the holes for these inserts determines the position of the fence on the miter gauge. I wanted the end of the fence to be right up against the blade. This requires shaving off just a bit of the fence *after* it's attached to the miter gauge.

Start by placing the miter gauge in the slot in the saw table. Then, with the fence clamped to the miter gauge so the end butts against the side of the blade (not the teeth), mark the location of the holes *(Fig. 3)*.

Now it's just a matter of drilling the holes and installing the threaded inserts. After attaching the fence, trim off the end *(Fig. 3b)*.

To reposition the fence for 45° cuts, see the Woodworker's Notebook on the opposite page.

SHOP TIP
Aligning Kerfs

When gluing together the two halves of the fence, it's important that the kerfs (cut to form the bottom part of the T-slot) align.

So instead of just lining up the outside edges of the two fence halves, I also used a waxed "key" to align the kerfs. (The wax keeps the key from being glued in.)

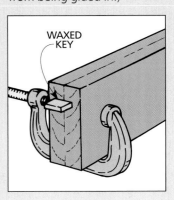

WAXED
KEY

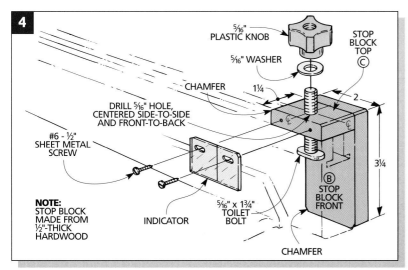

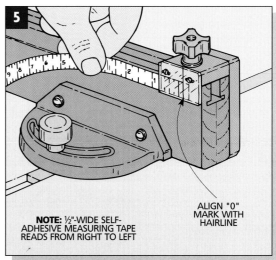

STOP BLOCK & TAPE

The next step is to add the stop block. It's made from two 1/2"-thick pieces of hardwood that are glued together in an L-shape (note grain direction in Exploded View). Both pieces are 2" long *(Fig. 4)*.

The 3¼"-high front (B) hangs in front of the fence and acts as the "stop."

Note: The bottom corners are chamfered for sawdust relief.

The top (C) is cut to width to match the thickness of the fence (1¼").

Drill a hole centered in the top (C) to hold the stop block's locking mechanism, a simple toilet bolt *(Fig. 4)*. When you tighten a knob on the end of the bolt, the head pinches against the T-slot and locks the stop block in place.

To position the stop block accurately, I added an indicator (see the Shop Tip box at right).

INSTALL TAPE. The next step is to install the measuring tape. Note: Because I place the miter gauge on the *left* side of the blade, I used a self-adhesive measuring tape that reads from

right to left (see Sources on page 126).

To install the tape, lock the stop block flush with the end of the fence *(Fig. 5)*. Then slide the tape under the indicator so the "0" mark aligns with the hairline and press it in place.

FINE TUNING. After trimming off the excess tape, the last step is to "fine tune" the indicator. Make a test cut, and compare the length of the piece with the position of the hairline. If necessary, loosen the screws and adjust the indicator. ∎

SHOP TIP . . . . Indicator

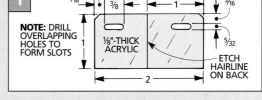

I made an indicator from a piece of 1/8"-thick acrylic *(Fig. 1)*.

The indicator has a "hairline" etched in the back side with a utility knife. To make the line easier to see, fill it in with a permanent marker and wipe off the excess *(Fig. 2)*.

To attach the indicator and allow it to be adjusted later, there are two slots near the top *(Fig. 1)*. (I made

these small slots by drilling a series of overlapping holes.)

Then, after screwing it in place, I sanded chamfers on the top edges of the indicator and stop block.

WOODWORKER'S NOTEBOOK

45° MITER CUTS

To keep the fence close to the saw blade when making a 45° cut, you'll need to reposition the fence on the miter gauge.

This requires adding another pair of threaded inserts. To locate the holes for these inserts, first remove the fence and tilt the miter gauge to 45° (see drawing at right).

Next, position the fence so the back corner is 1/16" away from the blade, and make a new set of marks for the holes.

Then install the threaded inserts and reattach the fence.

Note: Since the tape is set up for 90° cuts, it won't provide accurate readings when making 45° cuts.

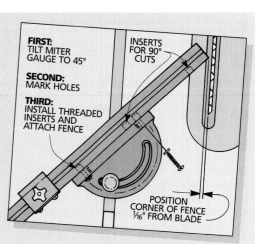

Drill Press Table & Fence

You don't have to settle for the small metal table that came with your drill press. For woodworkers, this auxiliary table with a fence and a removable insert makes it easy to handle large workpieces.

've often wondered why tool manufacturers don't design drill presses for woodworkers. The problem is the table. Drill press tables are almost always too small, hard to clamp onto, and don't work well with a fence.

TABLE. The first improvement I would make is a large auxiliary table. So I built the one in the photo, which is much larger than the metal drill press table it's attached to. It offers plenty of support for long pieces.

This table is made up of two layers. To add rigidity, there's a layer of ply-wood on the bottom. A top layer of hardboard is added to create a flat, durable work surface.

INSERT. There's also another advantage to this double-layered table. The top layer has a removable center piece (insert). It's beveled, along with the inside edges of the top, so it stays in place and keeps sawdust from building up beneath it.

When this insert gets chewed up with use, it can be simply slid in or out to expose a "fresh" drilling surface, or replaced with a new insert.

You can also make extra hardboard inserts of varying sizes for use with a drum sander (see the Woodworker's Notebook on page 85).

FENCE. The table also lays the groundwork for an adjustable fence, which is the second addition I like to see on a drill press table. To position the fence quickly and accurately, it slides along two T-shaped slots in the table. And a toilet bolt locks it in place.

MATERIALS. The base and fence are made of $3/4$"-thick plywood, while the top and inserts are $1/4$" hardboard.

EXPLODED VIEW

OVERALL DIMENSIONS:
30L X 12D X 4H

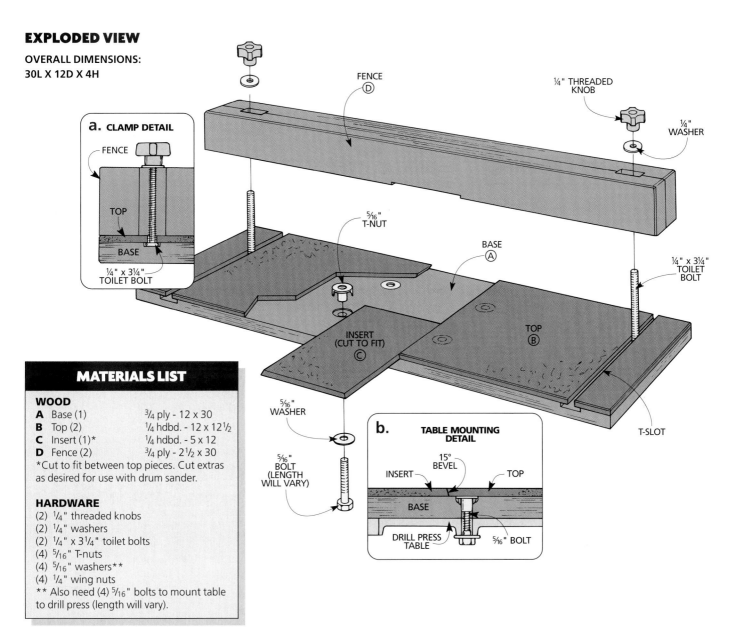

a. CLAMP DETAIL

FENCE
TOP
BASE
¼" x 3¼" TOILET BOLT

FENCE ⒟

¼" THREADED KNOB

¼" WASHER

⁵⁄₁₆" T-NUT

BASE Ⓐ

¼" x 3¼" TOILET BOLT

INSERT (CUT TO FIT) Ⓒ

TOP Ⓑ

T-SLOT

⁵⁄₁₆" WASHER

⁵⁄₁₆" BOLT (LENGTH WILL VARY)

b. TABLE MOUNTING DETAIL

INSERT
15° BEVEL
TOP
BASE
DRILL PRESS TABLE
⁵⁄₁₆" BOLT

MATERIALS LIST

WOOD
A	Base (1)	¾ ply - 12 x 30
B	Top (2)	¼ hdbd. - 12 x 12½
C	Insert (1)*	¼ hdbd. - 5 x 12
D	Fence (2)	¾ ply - 2½ x 30

*Cut to fit between top pieces. Cut extras as desired for use with drum sander.

HARDWARE
(2) ¼" threaded knobs
(2) ¼" washers
(2) ¼" x 3¼" toilet bolts
(4) ⁵⁄₁₆" T-nuts
(4) ⁵⁄₁₆" washers**
(4) ¼" wing nuts
** Also need (4) ⁵⁄₁₆" bolts to mount table to drill press (length will vary).

WOODWORKER'S NOTEBOOK

PLYWOOD FOR JIGS

A question that comes up often is what material to use to make jigs. Most of my jigs are made out of plywood. It's flat, consistent in thickness, and dimensionally stable — ideal for jigs.

SOFTWOOD PLYWOOD. But not all plywood is the same. Softwood plywood (see top board in photo) has voids in the inner plies, and knots and defects on the face veneers, making it undesirable for making jigs.

HARDWOOD PLYWOOD. A better choice is hardwood plywood, which comes in veneer core, fiber core and lumber core (see middle three boards). Hardwood plywood (like birch or maple) is clean and relatively void-free.

BALTIC BIRCH PLYWOOD. The best plywood to use for building jigs is Baltic birch plywood (see bottom board). This imported product has many thin, consistent layers of veneer. This makes it virtually void-free, and the edges are clean enough to use as a finished edge

on some projects. You'll find the slight extra cost more than offset by the higher quality.

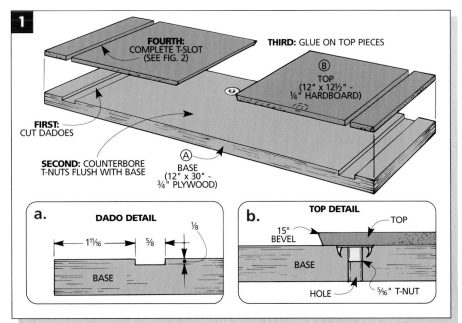

1

FOURTH: COMPLETE T-SLOT (SEE FIG. 2)

THIRD: GLUE ON TOP PIECES

Ⓑ TOP (12" x 12½" - ¼" HARDBOARD)

FIRST: CUT DADOES

SECOND: COUNTERBORE T-NUTS FLUSH WITH BASE

Ⓐ BASE (12" x 30" - ¾" PLYWOOD)

a. DADO DETAIL

1¹¹⁄₁₆ ⅝ ⅛

BASE

b. TOP DETAIL

15° BEVEL TOP

BASE

HOLE ⁵⁄₁₆" T-NUT

2

AUXILIARY FENCE

BASE

TOP

NOTE: DADO IN TOP IS CENTERED OVER DADO IN BASE (SEE DETAIL a)

a. ⁵⁄₁₆

Ⓐ Ⓑ

DADO BLADE

The table is the main part of this project. So I decided to build it first, and then build the fence to fit.

BASE. I started on the table by making the plywood base (A) *(Fig. 1)*. To form the first half of the T-slots, you'll need to cut two ⅝" dadoes in the base *(Fig. 1a)*. Later, each of these dadoes will accept the head of a toilet bolt that guides the fence in the slot.

INSTALL T-NUTS. The next step is to install the four T-nuts that will be used later to attach the base to the metal drill press table.

To locate the holes for these T-nuts, start by setting the base on your metal drill press table. Then, after marking the location of the holes from underneath the table, drill counterbored shank holes and install the T-nuts *(Fig. 1b)*.

TOP. Now you can concentrate on the top of the table. It consists of two top pieces (B) and the insert (C) (refer to the Exploded View on page 83).

Note: It's best to cut the top pieces oversize and trim them flush later.

To hold the insert in place, I made a dovetail-shaped opening in the top of the table. This opening is formed by cutting a bevel on the inside edge *only* of the top pieces *(Fig. 1b)*. I found that a 15° bevel works well for this project.

To prevent the insert from binding,

SHOP TIP . . . . *Gluing Up Table*

The trick to gluing up the drill press table is making sure the inside edges of the top pieces are *parallel*.

The insert itself might cause the top pieces to "ride up" over the bevel. So I used a thick spacer

(see drawing). It's square to ensure correct spacing. I also used wood strips for clamping to distribute

clamping pressure evenly. When the glue dries, trim the edges of the top pieces flush with the base.

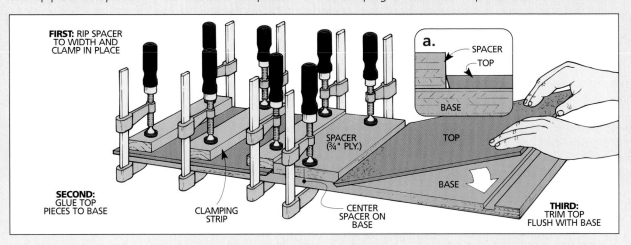

FIRST: RIP SPACER TO WIDTH AND CLAMP IN PLACE

a. SPACER TOP

BASE

SECOND: GLUE TOP PIECES TO BASE

CLAMPING STRIP

SPACER (¾" PLY.)

CENTER SPACER ON BASE

TOP

BASE

THIRD: TRIM TOP FLUSH WITH BASE

the beveled edges of the top pieces need to be parallel to each other. A simple way to do this is to use a spacer when gluing on the top pieces (see the Shop Tip box on the opposite page).

After gluing up the top and trimming the edges flush, you can complete the second half of each T-slot. This is just a matter of cutting narrow ($5/16"$) dadoes in the top pieces, centered on the dadoes in the base (*Figs. 2 and 2a*).

Now all that's left is to cut an insert (C) to fit the opening in the table. To do this, you'll need to bevel both edges of the insert at the same angle that you beveled the top pieces (B).

While you're at it, it's a good idea to make several inserts so you'll have a few spares. You can also make inserts specially designed for use with a drum sander (see the Woodworker's Notebook below).

FENCE

After attaching the drill press table to the original metal table with bolts (refer to detail 'b' in the Exploded View), the next step is to add the fence.

The thing I like best about this fence is you can adjust it without having to coax first one end and then the other. The reason has to do with a thin slot, cut near each end of the fence. These slots form openings for the toilet bolts that guide the fence.

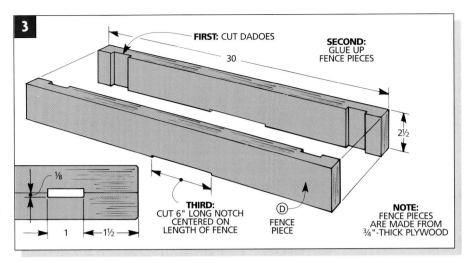

3 FIRST: CUT DADOES   30   **SECOND:** GLUE UP FENCE PIECES   2½

$1/8$ 1   1½

THIRD: CUT 6" LONG NOTCH CENTERED ON LENGTH OF FENCE   D   FENCE PIECE   **NOTE:** FENCE PIECES ARE MADE FROM ¾"-THICK PLYWOOD

Why not just drill holes for the bolts? After all, it would be significantly quicker. The only problem is if you don't move both ends of the fence the same amount when making an adjustment, the bolts would jam in the holes and cause the fence to bind.

So I decided to cut slots to allow more room for error. There's clearance between the bolt and the ends of the slot, so even if both ends of the fence aren't perfectly aligned, it still slides nice and smooth.

FENCE PIECES. To make the fence, start by cutting two fence pieces (D) (*Fig. 3*). The slot for the toilet bolts is formed by first cutting a pair of dadoes in each fence piece, then gluing the pieces together.

Note: Refer to the Shop Tip box on page 80 for help with aligning the two fence pieces while gluing.

NOTCH. Before installing the fence on the table, I cut a shallow notch in the bottom edge. In use, this notch straddles the insert in the table (*Fig. 3* and the Exploded View).

This way, when the fence is tightened down, it won't apply pressure on the insert. So you'll still be able to slide the insert in or out.

ATTACH FENCE. Now all that's left is to attach the fence to the table. After slipping the toilet bolts in place, set the fence down over them.

Tightening knobs or wing nuts on the ends of the bolts locks the fence in place. (I used plastic star knobs.) ■

WOODWORKER'S NOTEBOOK

DRUM SANDER INSERTS

One of the advantages to having a removable insert plate is that you can make additional inserts for use with a drum sander.

"Burying" a drum sander partially in the table allows you to sand the entire edge of a piece. It also allows you to raise and lower the drum for more even sandpaper wear.

CUT TO SIZE. First, cut to size as many inserts as you think you'll need.

Then, to allow you to drill through the table, position the table on top of a couple of spacers so the insert opening is centered, and lock it in place.

DRILL HOLES. Next, you can slide the inserts into the table and drill a hole for

each drum sander. I made each of mine $1/4"$ larger in diameter than the drum sander it's intended for. This allows $1/8"$ clearance all around. For example, a 2" drum sander would require a $2\frac{1}{4}"$ hole.

Note: If you don't have the right size bits, consider using a hole saw or an adjustable circle cutter (sometimes called a "fly cutter").

SMALL TO LARGE. Cut the hole for the smallest sander first, then work up to the largest. That way, after you drill the

largest hole, you can drill the same size hole through the plywood base for the sander to lower into.

Bevel Grinding Jig

Without the right support or the proper angle, a bench grinder can quickly ruin a chisel or plane iron. This jig makes it easy to grind perfect bevels on your valuable tools.

The first step toward getting a razor sharp edge on a tool (like a chisel or a plane iron) is to grind the correct bevel. A bench grinder can do this very quickly — sometimes a little too quickly.

A grinder cuts so fast — and removes so much material — that if the tool isn't held at the correct angle, or if it remains in one spot too long, the bevel can be ruined.

FEATURES. To solve this problem, I built a bevel grinding jig. This jig is designed to hold the tool at the correct angle while you slide it across the grinding wheel. It even has a built-in

"stop" to set the angle and to prevent you from grinding too far.

TWO PARTS. The jig is made in two separate parts: a cradle (with a stop bar) and a carriage assembly.

The cradle supports the carriage assembly, which in turn holds the tool you're grinding.

MATERIALS AND HARDWARE. The cradle and stop bar are made entirely from ³/₄"-thick stock, while the carriage assembly is built from ¹/₄", ³/₄" and 1¹/₂"-thick stock. Any hardwood will work, and you might already have enough scrap wood in your shop to build the jig.

The woodscrews, carriage bolts, eye bolts and wing nuts needed to assemble the jig should be readily available at a local hardware store or home center. You will also need a ¹/₂"-diameter, 16"-long steel rod.

GRINDING TECHNIQUES. Step-by-step instructions on how to use this bevel grinding jig are shown on page 89.

But using a grinder is only part of the process. So immediately following the jig instructions is a special section on what to do *after* you have used the jig to grind a bevel. With the proper techniques, you can bring your chisels and plane irons to a razor-sharp edge.

EXPLODED VIEW

OVERALL DIMENSIONS:
4W X 16L X 7½H

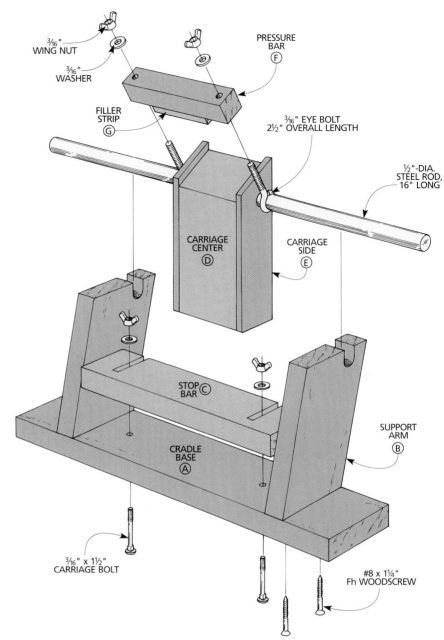

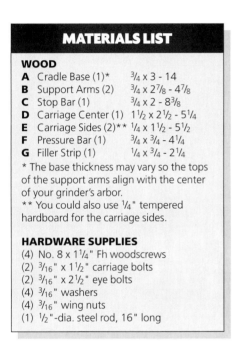

MATERIALS LIST

WOOD

A	Cradle Base (1)*	¾ x 3 - 14
B	Support Arms (2)	¾ x 2⅞ - 4⅞
C	Stop Bar (1)	¾ x 2 - 8⅜
D	Carriage Center (1)	1½ x 2½ - 5¼
E	Carriage Sides (2)**	¼ x 1½ - 5½
F	Pressure Bar (1)	¾ x ¾ - 4¼
G	Filler Strip (1)	¼ x ¾ - 2¼

* The base thickness may vary so the tops of the support arms align with the center of your grinder's arbor.
** You could also use ¼" tempered hardboard for the carriage sides.

HARDWARE SUPPLIES

(4) No. 8 x 1¼" Fh woodscrews
(2) ³⁄₁₆" x 1½" carriage bolts
(2) ³⁄₁₆" x 2½" eye bolts
(4) ³⁄₁₆" washers
(4) ³⁄₁₆" wing nuts
(1) ½"-dia. steel rod, 16" long

CRADLE

To make the cradle, first cut a base (A) to size *(Fig. 1)*. Drill two counterbore holes to accept a stop bar (built later) *(Fig. 1a)*.

Attached to the base are two support arms (B). To get the carriage (and tool) close to the grinding wheel, the ends of the support arms are angled *(Fig. 1)*.

Note: The tops of the arms should align with the center of your grinder's arbor, so the base's thickness may vary.

Cut notches in the top ends of the support arms to hold the carriage assembly rod *(Fig. 1a)*. After the notches are cut, screw the support arms to the base. You can use the steel rod to keep them aligned.

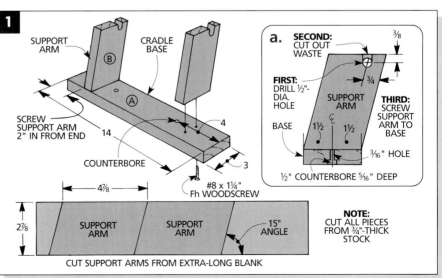

STOP BAR

The next part to make is the stop bar (C). This adjusts the angle of the carriage (and thus the grinding angle).

Cut this bar to fit between the support arms with a small amount of clearance. Two adjustment slots will be added so the stop bar can slide onto a pair of carriage bolts *(Fig. 2)*. Cut the slots so they align with the holes already drilled in the base.

Slide the stop bar onto the base with the carriage bolts fitting in the slots, and tighten down the assembly with washers and wing nuts *(Fig. 2a)*.

CARRIAGE ASSEMBLY

The carriage assembly is the heart of this jig. It holds the tool in the correct position for bevel grinding. And it also slides side-to-side, allowing you to grind a consistent bevel all across the end of the tool.

Four parts make up the carriage assembly: the carriage block, the support rod, and the pressure bar.

CARRIAGE BLOCK. The carriage block is built up from three pieces: a carriage center (D) and two carriage sides (E) *(Fig. 3)*.

The side pieces are glued to the center piece so they extend $1/4$" above the center piece. This creates a lip to position the tool against.

SUPPORT ROD. After gluing up the carriage block, the next step is to drill a hole in the block to insert the steel support rod *(Fig. 3)*.

This round rod rests in the notched support arms and allows the carriage block to pivot so you can gently tip the end of the tool against the grinding wheel (see photo on page 86).

PRESSURE BAR. To hold the tool to the carriage block, I attached a pressure bar (F) *(Fig. 4)*.

This bar has a filler strip (G) attached to the bottom. The purpose of this filler strip is to fit between the extended sides of the carriage block and put pressure directly on the tool you're grinding (refer to the Technique on the opposite page).

The pressure bar is clamped down to the carriage block with a couple of eye bolts and wing nuts *(Fig. 4a)*. These eye bolts slide over the support rod. (For hardware information, see sources on page 126.)

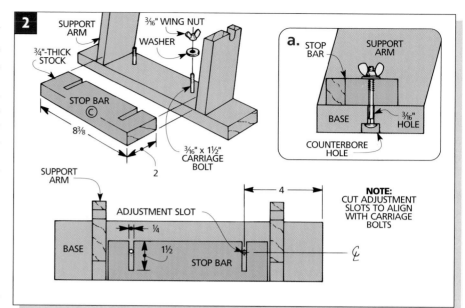

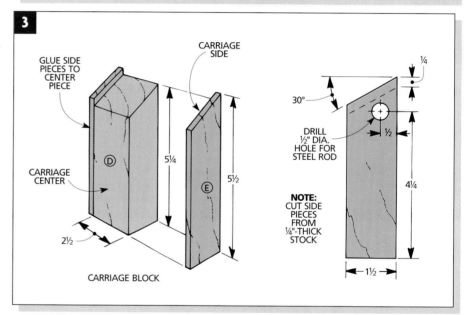

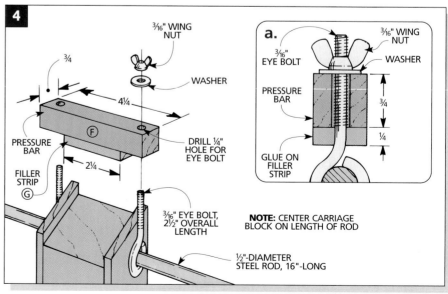

Setting up the grinding jig starts with getting the jig in the proper position relative to the grinding wheel.

To do this, first center the cradle in front of the grinding wheel, and remove the stop bar from the cradle base *(Fig. 1)*. Then clamp the cradle so the carriage block is approximately ¹/₂" away from the wheel.

Once the jig is positioned, slip the plane blade under the pressure bar, and snug the bar against it *(Fig. 2)*. Now adjust both the angle of the carriage block and the position of the blade to get the desired angle.

When the angle is set, tighten the stop bar against the bottom end of the carriage block *(Fig. 3)*.

To grind the bevel, tip the blade into the grinding wheel while moving the carriage from side to side.

Then, once you have ground the bevel, follow the tips shown below to hone the bevel.

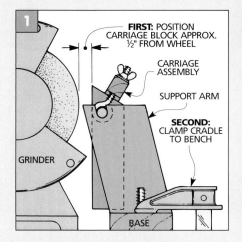

1 **FIRST:** POSITION CARRIAGE BLOCK APPROX. ¹/₂" FROM WHEEL — CARRIAGE ASSEMBLY — SUPPORT ARM — **SECOND:** CLAMP CRADLE TO BENCH — GRINDER — BASE

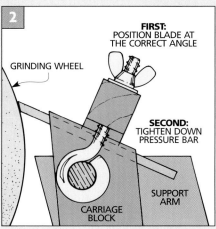

2 **FIRST:** POSITION BLADE AT THE CORRECT ANGLE — GRINDING WHEEL — **SECOND:** TIGHTEN DOWN PRESSURE BAR — CARRIAGE BLOCK — SUPPORT ARM

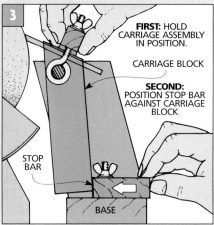

3 **FIRST:** HOLD CARRIAGE ASSEMBLY IN POSITION. — CARRIAGE BLOCK — **SECOND:** POSITION STOP BAR AGAINST CARRIAGE BLOCK — STOP BAR — BASE

HONING THE BEVEL

Before leaving the grinding wheel altogether, you should take a moment to check that the cutting edge of your chisel (or plane blade) is square to the side of the tool *(Fig. 4)*. If it isn't, it's just a matter of adjusting the angle of the carriage and re-grinding the bevel.

When you've finished grinding the bevel, you'll notice that the grinding wheel raised a burr along the back of the cutting edge.

So the first step in honing is to remove that burr. To do this, I like to use a 1000-grit Japanese waterstone (a "medium" grit stone) *(Fig. 5)*. Just stroke the back of the last inch of the chisel flat on the sharpening stone. Waterstones cut very fast, and the 1000-grit stone will hone the surface to a near mirror finish.

Finally, it's important to hone the cutting edge. The grinding wheel leaves grooves that create a ragged cutting edge that feels sharp. But it doesn't stay sharp because the points on that ragged edge break off easily. The more they break, the more ragged the edge becomes, making it duller faster.

To hone the cutting edge, place the hollow ground bevel on the stone so both the front and back edges touch the stone *(Fig. 6)*. Then gently push the bevel over the stone. You can push from end to end, or make little arcs. Just do what is easiest for you to keep both the front and back edges of the bevel on the stone.

Hone until the grinding marks along the cutting edge disappear.

4 END OF CHISEL SHOULD BE SQUARE TO SIDE

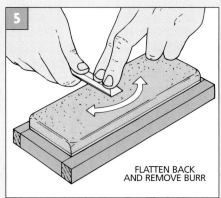

5 FLATTEN BACK AND REMOVE BURR

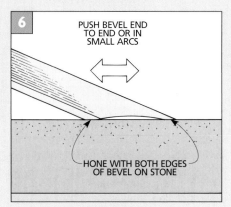

6 PUSH BEVEL END TO END OR IN SMALL ARCS — HONE WITH BOTH EDGES OF BEVEL ON STONE

Sliding Crosscut Box

Crosscutting wide panels on a table saw can be difficult using your miter gauge by itself. This versatile sliding crosscut box makes straight and angled cuts easy, safe, and accurate.

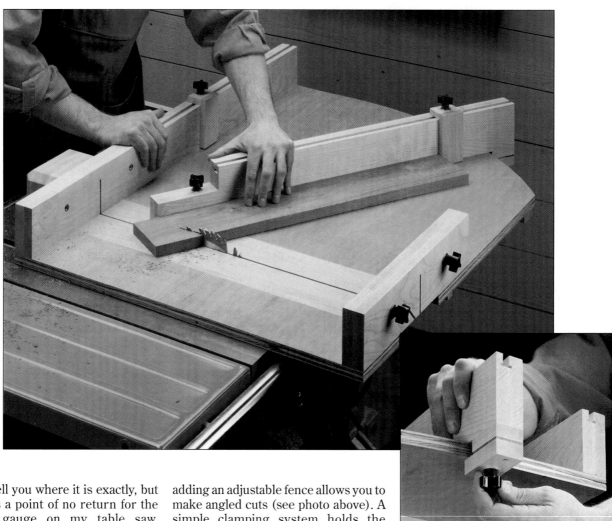

I can't tell you where it is exactly, but there's a point of no return for the miter gauge on my table saw. Especially when I pull it back to crosscut a wide panel.

It's the point where the head starts to wobble because the runner isn't fully supported in the miter gauge slot. And that lack of support makes it almost impossible to crosscut a wide panel safely and accurately.

That's why I built this sliding crosscut box. With the workpiece resting on a large platform that slides across the saw table, it's easy to crosscut panels up to 24" wide. And

adding an adjustable fence allows you to make angled cuts (see photo above). A simple clamping system holds the adjustable fence in place at the desired angle (see inset photo).

STOPS. Whether you make straight or angled cuts, sometimes you need a number of pieces that are identical in length. To ensure accuracy, a pair of stops that slide in T-shaped slots in the fences can be locked tightly in place.

INSERTS. In addition to the stop blocks, this sliding crosscut box has two "zero-clearance" inserts that prevent chipout on the bottom of a workpiece. To make this work for both 90° and 45°

cuts, it's just a matter of removing one insert and replacing it with another.

SAFETY. Finally, a pair of wood blocks work together to stop the crosscut box at the end of a cut. This "buries" the blade in a thick block to prevent the blade from being exposed.

MATERIALS AND HARDWARE. All of the main parts for this project are built from hardwood and plywood, and the knobs, threaded inserts, toilet bolts and screws should be readily available.

EXPLODED VIEW

OVERALL DIMENSIONS:
40½"W X 32¼"D X 6H

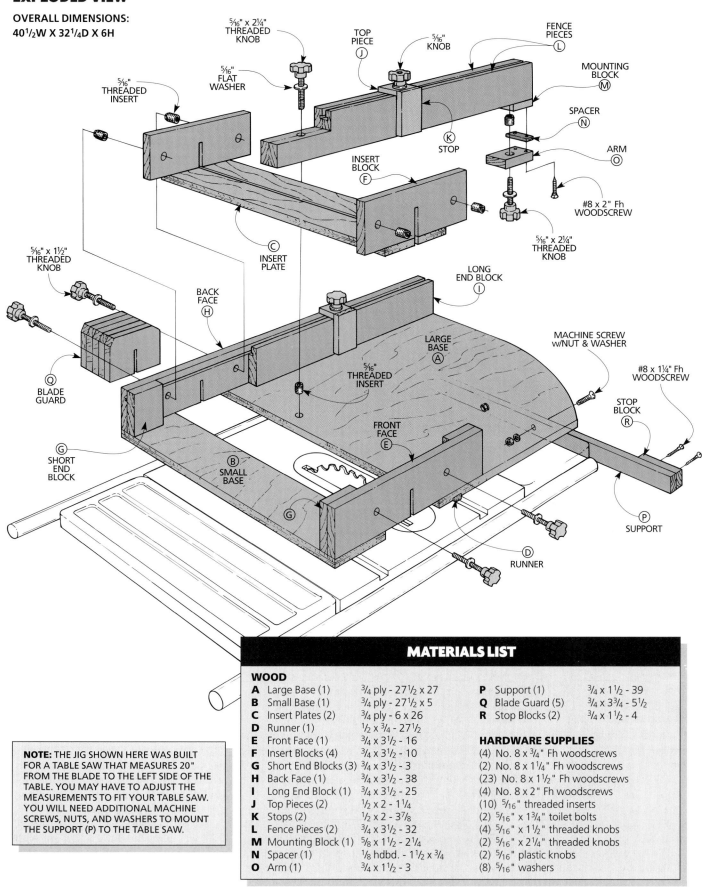

NOTE: THE JIG SHOWN HERE WAS BUILT FOR A TABLE SAW THAT MEASURES 20" FROM THE BLADE TO THE LEFT SIDE OF THE TABLE. YOU MAY HAVE TO ADJUST THE MEASUREMENTS TO FIT YOUR TABLE SAW. YOU WILL NEED ADDITIONAL MACHINE SCREWS, NUTS, AND WASHERS TO MOUNT THE SUPPORT (P) TO THE TABLE SAW.

MATERIALS LIST

WOOD

A	Large Base (1)	¾ ply - 27½ x 27
B	Small Base (1)	¾ ply - 27½ x 5
C	Insert Plates (2)	¾ ply - 6 x 26
D	Runner (1)	½ x ¾ - 27½
E	Front Face (1)	¾ x 3½ - 16
F	Insert Blocks (4)	¾ x 3½ - 10
G	Short End Blocks (3)	¾ x 3½ - 3
H	Back Face (1)	¾ x 3½ - 38
I	Long End Block (1)	¾ x 3½ - 25
J	Top Pieces (2)	½ x 2 - 1¼
K	Stops (2)	½ x 2 - 3⅞
L	Fence Pieces (2)	¾ x 3½ - 32
M	Mounting Block (1)	⅝ x 1½ - 2¼
N	Spacer (1)	⅛ hdbd. - 1½ x ¾
O	Arm (1)	¾ x 1½ - 3

P	Support (1)	¾ x 1½ - 39
Q	Blade Guard (5)	¾ x 3¾ - 5½
R	Stop Blocks (2)	¾ x 1½ - 4

HARDWARE SUPPLIES

(4) No. 8 x ¾" Fh woodscrews
(2) No. 8 x 1¼" Fh woodscrews
(23) No. 8 x 1½" Fh woodscrews
(4) No. 8 x 2" Fh woodscrews
(10) ⁵⁄₁₆" threaded inserts
(2) ⁵⁄₁₆" x 1¾" toilet bolts
(4) ⁵⁄₁₆" x 1½" threaded knobs
(2) ⁵⁄₁₆" x 2¼" threaded knobs
(2) ⁵⁄₁₆" plastic knobs
(8) ⁵⁄₁₆" washers

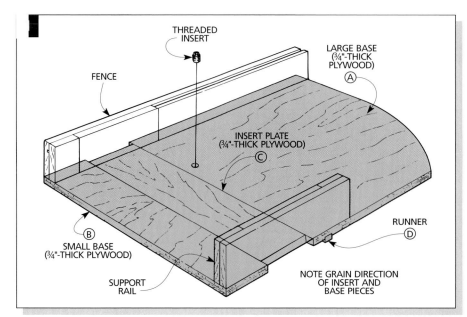

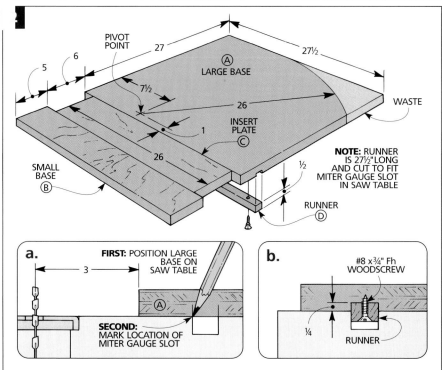

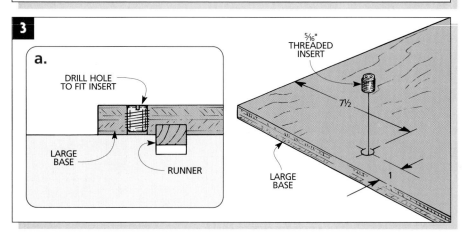

BASE

I began work on the sliding crosscut box by building the plywood base. This base will serve as the platform that carries the workpiece through the table saw blade.

The base is made up of three parts: a large base (A), a small base (B), and a removeable insert plate (C) that is sandwiched in between the large and small base pieces *(Figs. 1 and 2)*.

Note: To make straight and beveled cuts, I made two insert plates (see the Shop Tip box on the opposite page).

CURVE. To keep the adjustable fence (added later on) from binding, there's a curve cut on the outside corner of the large base piece *(Fig. 2)*. This requires establishing a pivot point for the fence, then cutting the curved shape and sanding it smooth.

RUNNER. The base is guided by a hardwood runner that slides in the miter gauge slot. To produce accurate cuts you'll need to make sure this slot is parallel to the blade.

The runner fits in a dado cut in the bottom of the base. When laying out the location of this dado, the idea is to have the blade cut through the center of the insert plate.

To do this, place the base piece on the saw table 3" away (half the width of the insert) from the center of the blade *(Fig. 2a)*. Then mark the location of the dado by using the slot as a reference.

Before cutting the dado, it's best to have the runner (D) in hand. It's a piece of hardwood (maple) cut to fit the miter gauge slot so it slides smoothly without any "play" *(Fig. 2b)*.

THREADED INSERT. After cutting the dado and screwing the runner in place, all that's left is to install a threaded insert *(Fig. 3)*. It fits in a hole that's drilled at the pivot point for the adjustable fence.

FIXED FENCE & SUPPORT RAIL

The base is held together with two parts. A fixed fence runs across the back edge and supports the workpiece as you make a cut *(Fig. 4)*. And a support rail adds rigidity to the front.

POCKET. To slip the inserts in and out of the sliding table, the fence and support rail each have a "pocket" that's built up from $3/4$"-thick hardwood blocks (maple).

To form the pocket in the support rail, cut a front face (E) to length *(Fig. 5)*. Then an insert block (F) is sandwiched between two short end blocks (G).

Except for its size, the fence isn't all that different. But here, there's a long back face (H). And another insert block (F) fits between the short end block (G) and a long end block (I).

T-SLOT. Before assembling all these pieces, a T-shaped slot is cut in the fence for a toilet bolt that lets you adjust the stop block (added later).

Making this slot is simple. First, cut a shallow groove in the back face (H) and a deeper groove in the long end block (I) *(Fig. 5a)*. Then rabbet the top edge of the long end block.

ASSEMBLY. To assemble the fence and support rail, the end blocks only are glued in place. (I used the insert blocks as spacers.) When the glue dries, the fence is screwed (not glued) to the base pieces so it's square to the blade and flush with the back edge. And the support rail is screwed flush with the front edge.

INSERTS. At this point, the insert plates (B) and insert blocks (F) can be screwed together to form the inserts (see Shop Tip box below). They're held in place with knobs that tighten into threaded inserts *(Figs. 4 and 5)*.

STOP BLOCKS. All that's left is to add a stop block. It consists of a top piece (J) and a stop (K) glued together in an L-shape *(Fig. 6)*. Tightening a knob on a toilet bolt that passes through the top piece holds the stop block in place.

Note: You'll need another stop block for the adjustable fence (see page 94).

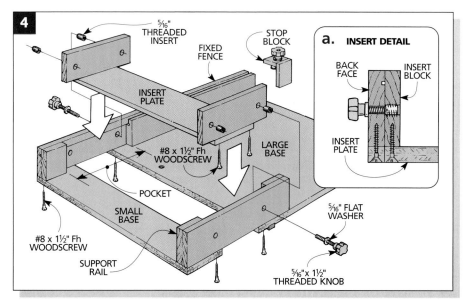

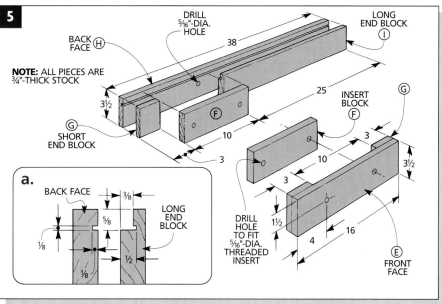

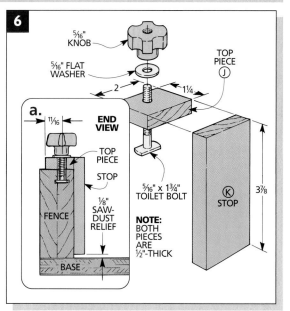

SHOP TIP . . . . . . *Two Inserts*

When I was making the insert for the sliding crosscut box, I decided to take a little extra time to make two, each for a different cutting angle.

The standard insert (see top insert in photo at right) is used for 90° cuts, while the alternate insert (see bottom) is used for 45° bevel cuts. Matching cuts should be made in the front face (E) (see photo on page 90).

Having different pre-made inserts like these helps to reduce chipout on the bottom of a workpiece.

ADJUSTABLE FENCE

At this point, there are only two things left to add to complete the crosscut box: an adustable fence for making angled cuts, and a stop system. I started with the adjustable fence (*Fig. 7* and the photo above).

T-SLOT. Like the fixed fence, a T-slot for a stop block runs along the top edge of the adjustable fence.

First cut two ³/₄"-thick fence pieces (L) to size. Then a T-slot is cut in the top of the adjustable fence the same way — and the same size — as the one in the fixed fence (*Figs. 8 and 8a*).

NOTCH. Once the fence is glued up, a notch is cut at one end. To provide a pivot point that lets you swing the fence to the desired angle, a knob passes through a hole drilled in the notch and into the threaded insert installed earlier (*Fig. 7a*). Tightening (or loosening) the knob lets you attach (or remove) the fence.

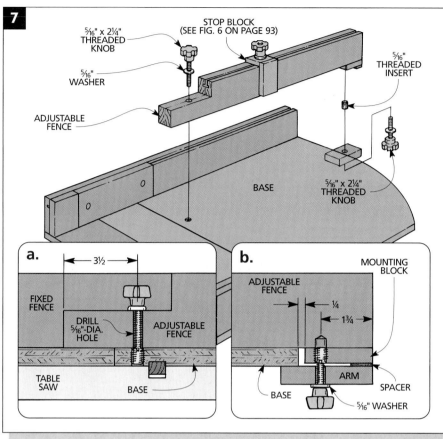

CLAMP. Now you can add the clamp. It consists of three parts: a mounting block and arm made of hardwood, and a hardboard spacer in between (*Fig. 7b*).

Note that the mounting block on this clamp is thinner than the base. This way, the spacer creates a small gap that allows the arm to pinch against the base of the crosscut box when you tighten the clamp.

To provide this clamping pressure, the mounting block (M) and spacer (N) are first glued in place (*Fig. 9*). After installing a threaded insert in the mounting block and attaching the arm (O) with screws, a simple knob can be used to tighten the clamp (*Fig. 7b*).

Finally, it's just a matter of adding a second stop block for the adjustable fence (*Fig. 7*).

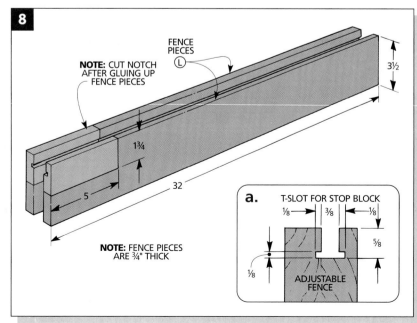

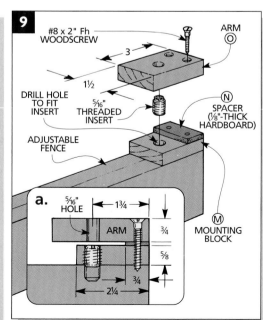

STOP SYSTEM

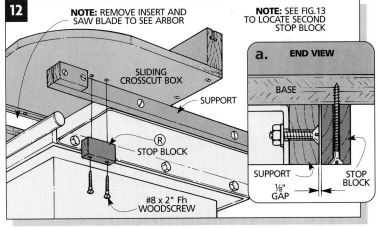

All that's left to complete the crosscut box is to add the stop system. Besides supporting the box, it covers the exposed part of the blade that passes through the fixed fence at the end of a cut.

The stop system has three parts: a support, a blade guard, and a pair of stop blocks (*Figs. 10, 11* and photo above).

SUPPORT. The support (P) is a long strip of wood that attaches to the extension wing of the table saw (*Fig. 10*). It prevents the box from tipping at the beginning and end of a cut.

To determine the length of the support, measure the depth of the saw table and add 12". (This gives you 6" of support at each end.) Cut the support to length and bolt it flush with the top of the saw table (*Fig. 10a*). Note: If your saw doesn't have pre-drilled holes, you will have to drill holes for the bolts.

BLADE GUARD. Now you can add the blade guard (Q) (*Fig. 11*). It's a thick block that's made by gluing up five pieces of 3/4"-thick hardwood. In use, the part of the blade that cuts through the back of the fence is "buried" in this block at the end of a cut.

Before attaching the guard, I cut 1/2"-wide chamfers on all the outside edges. Then the blade guard is glued in place so it's centered behind the insert.

STOP BLOCKS. The last thing to do is to add two stop blocks (R). These blocks prevent the blade from cutting through the blade guard by creating a positive stop at the end of a cut. One block is glued and screwed to the end of the support (*Fig. 10*). The other block attaches to the bottom of the crosscut box (*Fig. 12*).

To determine the location of this block, position the crosscut box on the saw so the front of the fence is centered over the saw arbor (*Fig. 13*). Then glue and screw it in place. Note: A 1/8" gap between the block and support keeps the table from binding (*Fig. 12a*). ∎

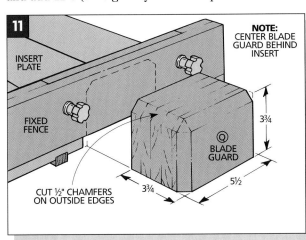

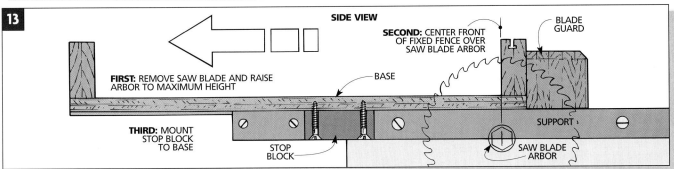

Band Saw Circle Jig

You can take all the guesswork out of cutting circles on the band saw with this convenient jig.
An adjustable rail and a built-in measuring tape allow you to cut circles quickly and accurately.

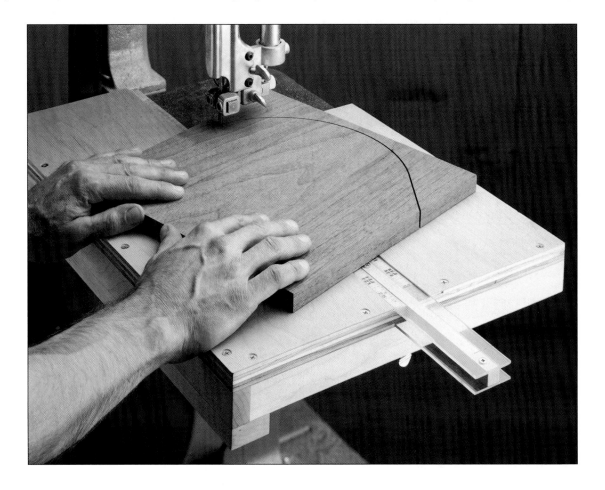

One of the easiest ways to make a perfect circle is to cut it on a band saw. All it takes is a pin to spin the workpiece on.

The problem is accurately positioning the pin to get the correct size circle. To solve this, we designed a circle cutting jig that allows you to quickly set up for an exact cut without measuring or marking.

There are only two main parts to this jig: a "split" base, and an adjustable rail (refer to the Exploded View on the opposite page).

EASY TO USE. The jig makes it very easy to cut circles, taking all the guess-

work out of sizing. First, the base serves as a carriage for the workpiece. This setup allows you to slide both the workpiece and the jig into the saw blade as you start the cut.

Then a cleat on the front of the jig catches the saw table and locks the jig in place, with the pin automatically aligned to the saw blade. All you have to do then is set the adjustable rail for the exact size circle you want.

SIZES. The band saw circle jig is ideal for cutting circles anywhere from 2" to 48" in diameter.

Note: If you want to cut circles larger than 48" (or if you don't own a band

saw), you can build the Router Trammel on page 50 for use with a hand-held router. But you will need to modify the trammel for very large circles.

MATERIALS AND HARDWARE. The front and rear base of the jig are made from $^3/_4$" plywood, while the other wooden parts are $^3/_4$" and $^1/_2$" hardwood. The adjustable rail also requires two pieces of $^1/_8$"-thick acrylic plastic.

The woodscrews, thumbscrew, threaded insert and nail you need for assembly should be available at your local hardware store or home center. You will also need a self-adhesive left-to-right reading measuring tape.

EXPLODED VIEW

OVERALL DIMENSIONS:
2¹³/₁₆T X 15W X 21L

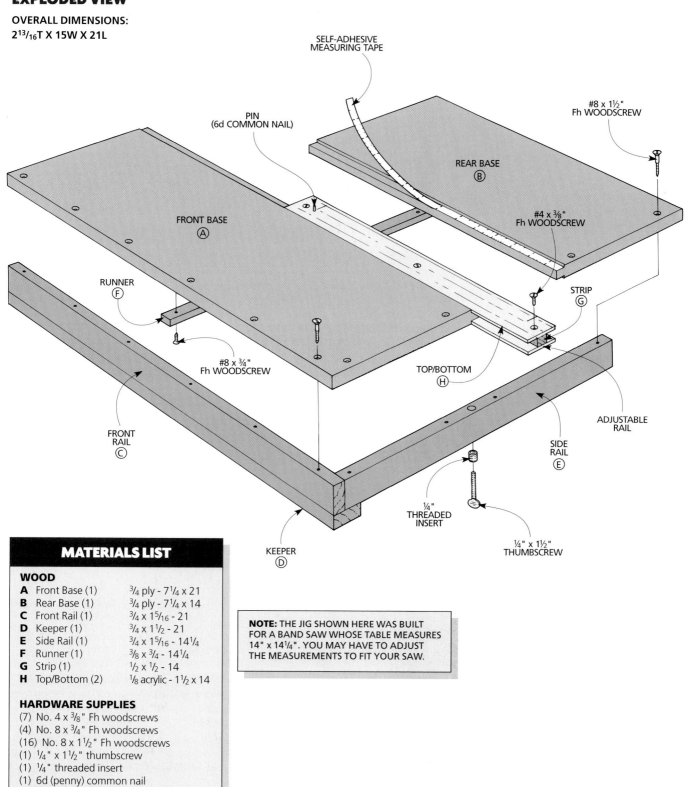

SELF-ADHESIVE
MEASURING TAPE

#8 x 1½"
Fh WOODSCREW

REAR BASE
Ⓑ

PIN
(6d COMMON NAIL)

FRONT BASE
Ⓐ

#4 x ³/₈"
Fh WOODSCREW

RUNNER
Ⓕ

STRIP
Ⓖ

#8 x ¾"
Fh WOODSCREW

TOP/BOTTOM
Ⓗ

FRONT
RAIL
Ⓒ

ADJUSTABLE
RAIL

SIDE
RAIL
Ⓔ

¼"
THREADED
INSERT

¼" x 1½"
THUMBSCREW

KEEPER
Ⓓ

MATERIALS LIST

WOOD

A	Front Base (1)	¾ ply - 7¼ x 21
B	Rear Base (1)	¾ ply - 7¼ x 14
C	Front Rail (1)	¾ x 1⁵/₁₆ - 21
D	Keeper (1)	¾ x 1½ - 21
E	Side Rail (1)	¾ x 1⁵/₁₆ - 14¼
F	Runner (1)	³/₈ x ¾ - 14¼
G	Strip (1)	½ x ½ - 14
H	Top/Bottom (2)	⅛ acrylic - 1½ x 14

HARDWARE SUPPLIES

(7) No. 4 x ³/₈" Fh woodscrews
(4) No. 8 x ¾" Fh woodscrews
(16) No. 8 x 1½" Fh woodscrews
(1) ¼" x 1½" thumbscrew
(1) ¼" threaded insert
(1) 6d (penny) common nail
(1) 48" L-R reading self-adhesive
measuring tape

NOTE: THE JIG SHOWN HERE WAS BUILT
FOR A BAND SAW WHOSE TABLE MEASURES
14" x 14¼". YOU MAY HAVE TO ADJUST
THE MEASUREMENTS TO FIT YOUR SAW.

I began work on the band saw circle jig by building the base. It's built to fit on your band saw table and hold the adjustable rail (built later). The base consists of a front base (A) and a rear base (B).

To make these, I started with two identical pieces *(Fig. 1)*. The size of the pieces depends on your saw.

To determine their width, measure from the teeth of the saw blade to the front edge of the table and add $1/2$" ($7^1/4$" in my case) *(Fig. 1)*.

Note: If your band saw has a rip fence, you'll need to measure from the front edge of the fence's rail.

To find their length, measure from the inside (throat) edge of the table to the saw blade and add 14" *(Fig. 1)*. (In my case, they're 21" long.)

TONGUE. The next step is to cut a tongue on each of the base pieces to accept the adjustable rail that's added later *(Fig. 1)*. This tongue is $1/2$" wide and $7/16$" thick and is centered on the thickness of each base piece *(Fig. 1a)*.

CLEAT. Before the base pieces can be joined together, there's one more thing to do — add an L-shaped cleat to the front base (A) *(Fig. 2)*.

The cleat consists of two pieces. A front rail (C) acts as a stop to automatically align the pin with the blade. And a keeper (D) forms a lip to catch the bottom of the table top.

Both pieces are the same length as the front base (21"). But their widths are different.

To determine the width (height) of the front rail (C), measure the thickness of your table top (or table top plus

fence rail, if your band saw has one) and add $1/16$" for clearance ($1^5/16$" in my case) *(Figs. 2a and 2b)*. The keeper (D) is easier — it's just $1^1/2$" wide.

After you've cut both these pieces to size, they can be screwed to the front base *(Fig. 2)*.

STRIP. With the cleat in place, the two halves of the base can be joined together. To create a uniform gap, I clamped a strip (G) between them *(Fig. 3)*. (It's just

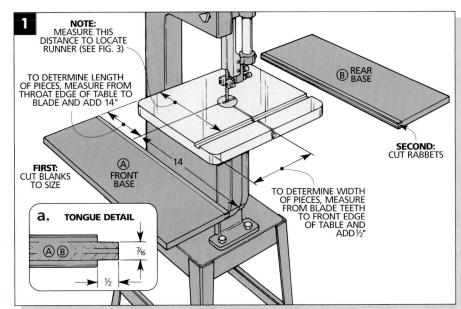

1

NOTE: MEASURE THIS DISTANCE TO LOCATE RUNNER (SEE FIG. 3)

TO DETERMINE LENGTH OF PIECES, MEASURE FROM THROAT EDGE OF TABLE TO BLADE AND ADD 14"

Ⓑ REAR BASE

FIRST: CUT BLANKS TO SIZE

Ⓐ FRONT BASE

14

SECOND: CUT RABBETS

TO DETERMINE WIDTH OF PIECES, MEASURE FROM BLADE TEETH TO FRONT EDGE OF TABLE AND ADD $1/2$"

a. TONGUE DETAIL

Ⓐ Ⓑ $7/16$ $1/2$

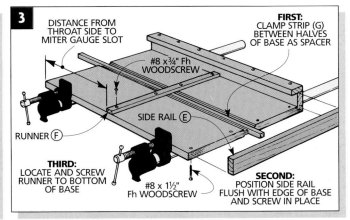

2

#8 x $1^1/2$" Fh WOODSCREW

Ⓐ FRONT BASE

NOTE: BOTH PIECES CUT FROM $3/4$"-THICK STOCK

NOTE: CUT FRONT RAIL AND KEEPER TO MATCH LENGTH OF BASE

FRONT RAIL Ⓒ

KEEPER Ⓓ

a. TABLE WITHOUT FENCE RAIL

MEASURE THICKNESS OF TABLE TOP AND ADD $1/16$"

$3/4$

$1^1/2$

b. TABLE WITH FENCE RAIL

MEASURE FROM TABLE TOP TO BOTTOM OF FENCE RAIL AND ADD $1/16$"

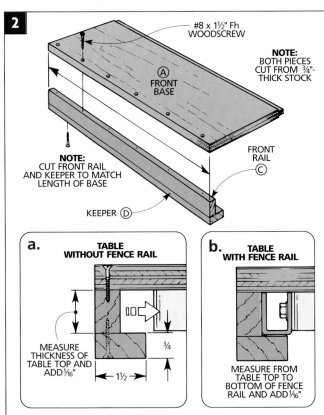

3

DISTANCE FROM THROAT SIDE TO MITER GAUGE SLOT

#8 x $3/4$" Fh WOODSCREW

FIRST: CLAMP STRIP (G) BETWEEN HALVES OF BASE AS SPACER

RUNNER Ⓕ

SIDE RAIL Ⓔ

THIRD: LOCATE AND SCREW RUNNER TO BOTTOM OF BASE

#8 x $1^1/2$" Fh WOODSCREW

SECOND: POSITION SIDE RAIL FLUSH WITH EDGE OF BASE AND SCREW IN PLACE

4

FIRST: REMOVE TEMPORARY SPACER

WASTE

SECOND: WITH RUNNER IN SLOT, PUSH FORWARD TO CUT REAR BASE TO LENGTH

a $1/2$" square piece of hardwood used as a temporary spacer.)

Note: Save this hardwood strip. You'll use it again later for the adjustable rail.

SIDE RAIL & RUNNER. The two halves of the base are connected with a side rail and a runner *(Fig. 3)*.

The side rail (E) adds strength to the jig. It's cut the same width as the front rail ($1^5/_{16}$") and screwed to the base flush with the edge.

The runner (F) allows you to quickly slip the jig in place and is cut to fit in the miter gauge slot on your band saw.

To locate the runner on the base, first measure in from the throat side of your saw table to the edge of the miter slot *(Figs. 1 and 3)*. Then transfer this line to the bottom of the jig and screw the runner in place.

To complete the base, all that's left is to remove the spacer and trim the rear base (B) to length *(Fig. 4)*.

Note: You don't need to measure or mark the length of the rear base. Just position the base on the saw table with the runner in the miter gauge slot, and push forward through the blade to trim off the right amount of material.

ADJUSTABLE RAIL

After trimming the rear base to size, you can begin working on the adjustable rail. This rail slides between the halves of the base so you can adjust the position of the pin *(Fig. 5)*.

The adjustable rail is shaped like an I-beam — a hardwood strip fits between a top and bottom of acrylic plastic.

STRIP. You've made the strip (G) already. It's the strip you used earlier as a spacer *(Fig. 5)*.

All that's left is to cut it to match the length of the rear base (14"). Then sand about $1/_{32}$" off the width and thickness. This ensures the rail will slide easily, and the top (added next) will be flush with the base.

TOP & BOTTOM. The $1/_8$"-thick top and bottom (H) are the same length as the strip (14") *(Fig. 6)*. As for their width, they're cut to slide in the rabbets in the base ($1^1/_2$").

Before you assemble the adjustable rail, scratch two indicator marks on the bottom face of the top piece *(Fig. 6a)*. (I used a scratch awl to scribe them.) These marks are used with the measuring tape (added later) to help you

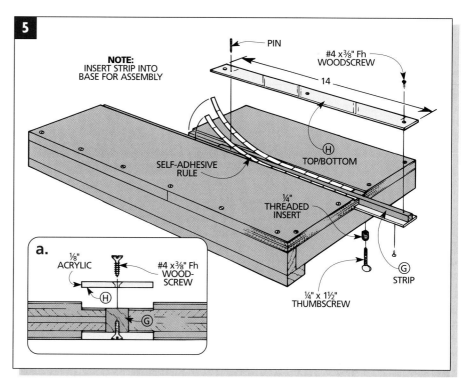

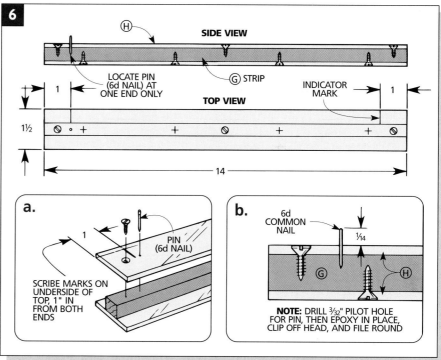

position the rail when setting up the jig.

ASSEMBLY. Now you can assemble the adjustable rail. The important thing here is to make sure all three parts of the rail are aligned parallel with each other so the rail won't bind in the base. So it's a good idea to screw the top and bottom to the strip while the strip is in place in the base *(Fig. 5)*.

PIN. To complete the adjustable rail, just add a pin for the workpiece to spin

on. This is a 6d (penny) common nail with the head cut off and filed to a slight crown *(Figs. 6a and 6b)*.

You want to make sure the pin is inserted perpendicular to the rail, so any workpiece you set on it will lie flat. So don't just nail the pin into the rail. Instead, pre-drill a $3/_{32}$" pilot hole through the top piece and into the strip. Then you can epoxy the pin in place and let it dry *(Fig. 6b)*.

LOCKING SYSTEM

With the adjustable rail complete, I added a simple locking system to hold the rail in place. This system is just a threaded insert and a thumbscrew (*Fig. 7*).

The $^1/_4$" threaded insert fits in a centered hole in the side rail (*Fig. 7*).

Note: Refer to the Shop Tip box on page 68 for more information on installing threaded inserts.

The $^1/_4$" x $1^1/_2$" thumbscrew then threads into the threaded insert to pinch the rail against the base (*Fig. 7a*). This locks the adjustable rail in place after you have positioned it.

FINISH

All that's left is to apply a finish to all the wooden parts of the jig.

Note: I used two coats of tung oil to finish this jig. This helps protect all of the wooden parts, and also creates a surface that the self-adhesive measuring tape (added next) will stick to.

ADDING THE TAPE

Once the finish has dried, you can add the measuring tape. I used a self-adhesive left-to-right reading tape. (For a complete hardware kit, see page 126.)

First, the measuring tape is cut into two separate pieces. Cut the tape at *exactly* the 13" mark (*Fig. 8*).

SMALL CIRCLE PIECE. The first piece (1"-13") goes in the rabbet in the rear base (B).

Butt the low end of this tape against the saw blade, make sure it lines up from end to end, and carefully secure it down (*Fig. 8a*).

This tape will be used when cutting small circles (2" to 26" diameter).

LARGE CIRCLE PIECE. The other piece (13"-24") fits in the rabbet in the front base (A).

To position this tape, align the low end with the 1" mark on the small circle tape (*Fig. 8a*). Again, carefully line it up from end to end and secure it.

This tape will be used when cutting larger circles (26" to 48" diameter).

ALIGNING RAIL. Now, the adjustable rail can be positioned accurately by simply aligning the indicator mark with the desired radius (half the diameter) of the circle you wish to cut (*Fig. 8b* and the photo above). ■

TAPE MEASURE. *The built-in tape measure on the band saw circle jig allows you to cut a circle to a specific size from an oversize blank. You don't have to cut the blank to size first. All you need to do is line up the indicator with a spot on the tape measure that is the same as the radius of the circle. The two pieces of tape allow you to cut small and large circles (see "Using the Circle Jig" on the opposite page).*

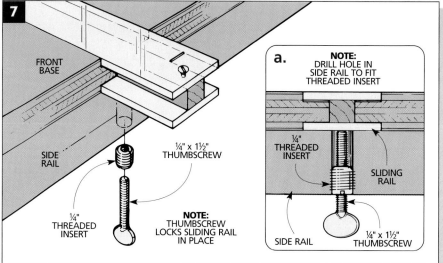

7

FRONT BASE

SIDE RAIL

$^1/_4$" THREADED INSERT

$^1/_4$" x $1^1/_2$" THUMBSCREW

NOTE: THUMBSCREW LOCKS SLIDING RAIL IN PLACE

a. **NOTE:** DRILL HOLE IN SIDE RAIL TO FIT THREADED INSERT

$^1/_4$" THREADED INSERT

SLIDING RAIL

SIDE RAIL

$^1/_4$" x $1^1/_2$" THUMBSCREW

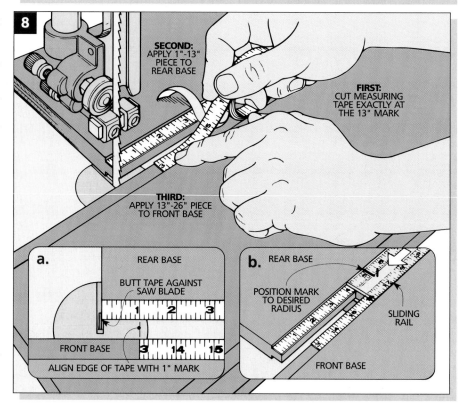

8

SECOND: APPLY 1"-13" PIECE TO REAR BASE

FIRST: CUT MEASURING TAPE EXACTLY AT THE 13" MARK

THIRD: APPLY 13"-26" PIECE TO FRONT BASE

a. REAR BASE

BUTT TAPE AGAINST SAW BLADE

FRONT BASE

ALIGN EDGE OF TAPE WITH 1" MARK

b. REAR BASE

POSITION MARK TO DESIRED RADIUS

SLIDING RAIL

FRONT BASE

TECHNIQUE .... *Using the Circle Jig*

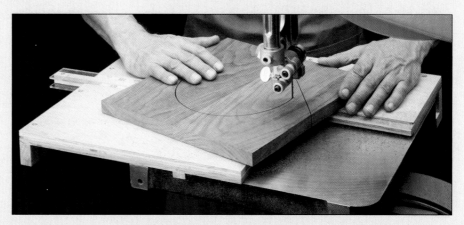

efore you actually set the adjustable rail and cut a circle using the jig, there are a few things to do to prepare the saw and workpiece.

ROUNDING BLADES. Since you're going to be cutting circles, you should consider preparing the band saw blade for rounded cuts. Turns can be tighter and smoother if you round the back of the blade. This keeps the back edge from catching on the side of the kerf.

To do this, hold a sharpening stone or file against the blade with the saw running. Then slowly roll it from one side (around the back edge) to the other side.

Safety Note: This can cause sparks. Clean the sawdust from the bottom of the saw *first* to avoid a fire.

DRILL HOLE. To prepare the workpiece, simply drill a hole for the pin (see drawing at right). This hole doesn't have to be centered, but you need enough room on all sides for the radius of the circle.

CUTTING. In use, the adjustable rail is inserted in the base so the pin end is closest to the saw blade. And to cut larger circles, the adjustable rail is turned around so the pin end is away from the saw blade.

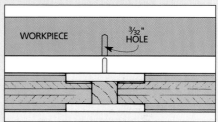

CUTTING SMALL CIRCLES

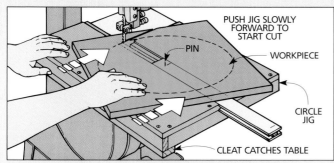

1 With the workpiece resting on the pin, turn on the band saw. Then slowly slide the jig forward. Hold the jig securely when the blade enters the workpiece. Continue pushing forward until the cleat catches the saw table.

2 Once the blade has entered the workpiece and the cleat is up against the table, cut the circle. Do this by slowly spinning the workpiece in a clockwise direction. Apply downward pressure on the workpiece for a smooth cut.

CUTTING LARGE CIRCLES

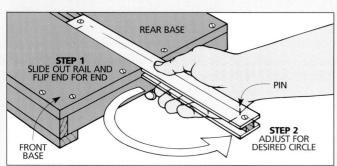

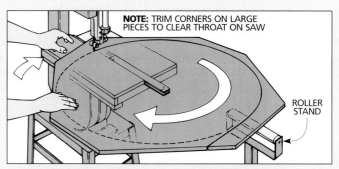

1 To cut larger circles (greater than 26" in diameter), remove the adjustable rail and flip it end for end. Then slip it into the base of the jig, and set it for the diameter of the circle you want.

2 To cut a larger circle, I use the same technique that's used for smaller circles. The only difference is I add extra support (like a roller stand) under the outside edge of the workpiece.

Taper Jig

Cutting different size tapers accurately and consistently is a cinch with this adjustable taper jig. And you can modify the jig for angled cuts or turn it into a straight-line ripping jig.

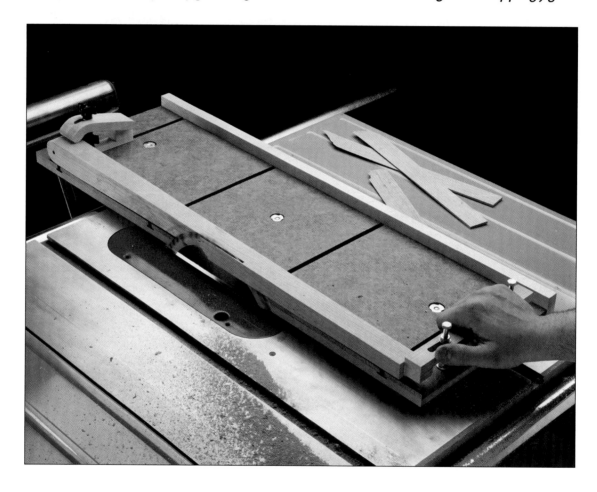

Sometimes a jig turns out even better than expected. Which is exactly what happened with this adjustable taper jig.

It started out quite simply — a platform that slides across the table saw and carries the workpiece past the blade. But it ended up as a jig that can do much more.

ADJUSTABLE. The first improvement was a built-in system that allows you to adjust the size of the taper on the leg you're building. It's really nothing more than a piece of hardwood and a steel pin (see Exploded View on opposite page).

But this system makes it easy to remove the exact amount of material you need to form the desired "footprint" on the bottom end of the leg.

And you don't need to do multiple setups. Once the jig is adjusted, you can cut four *identical* tapers in a matter of minutes — without changing the basic setup of the jig.

OTHER USES. As easy as it is to cut tapers, you'll probably use this jig just as often for another job. With two simple hold-downs clamping a workpiece securely in place, you can make long angled cuts safely and accurately.

And these same hold-downs can be used when ripping a straight edge on a piece of rough-sawn lumber. If the workpiece is particularly long (or wide), you can remove the adjustment system and the runner that rides in the miter gauge slot and use the rip fence.

MATERIALS. The top of the jig is made of 1/4" hardboard. I used 1/2"-thick medium-density fiberboard (MDF) for the bottom. But you could use plywood, which is more available than MDF. The rail, runner, and hold-down clamps are all made of hardwood.

Note: You can also purchase aluminum hold-down clamps. These are included with a complete hardware kit (see Sources on page 126).

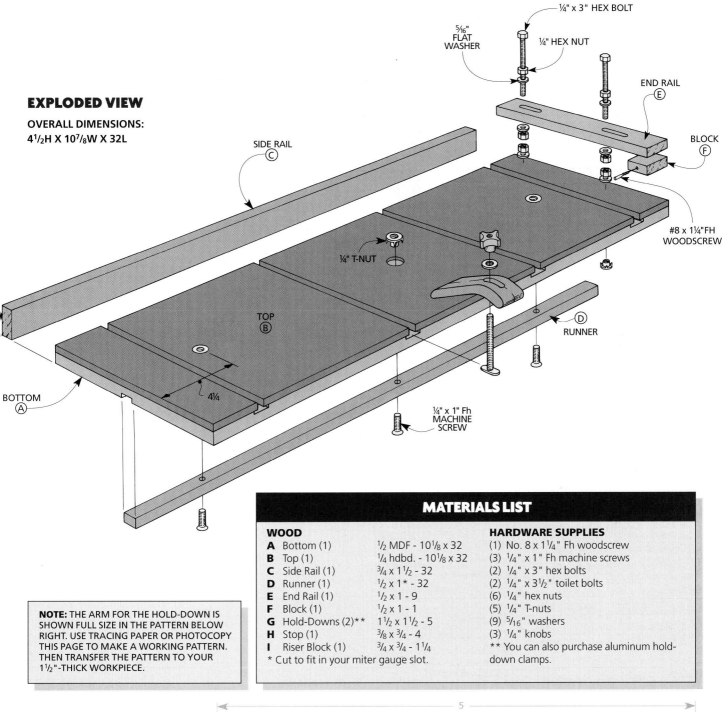

EXPLODED VIEW

OVERALL DIMENSIONS:
4$^1/_2$H X 10$^7/_8$W X 32L

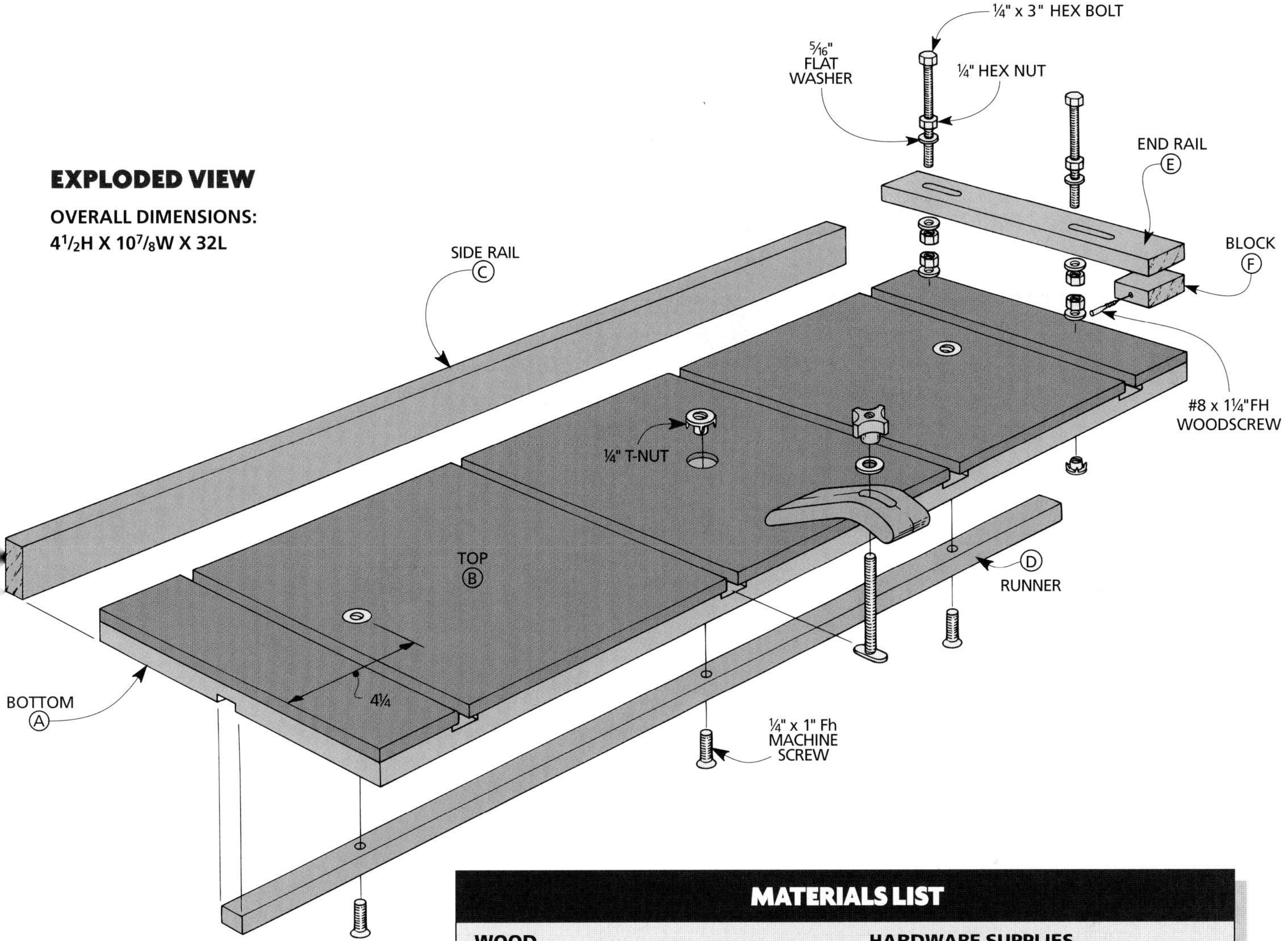

¼" x 3" HEX BOLT
5⁄16" FLAT WASHER
¼" HEX NUT
END RAIL (E)
BLOCK (F)
SIDE RAIL (C)
#8 x 1¼"FH WOODSCREW
¼" T-NUT
TOP (B)
(D) RUNNER
BOTTOM (A)
4¼
¼" x 1" Fh MACHINE SCREW

NOTE: THE ARM FOR THE HOLD-DOWN IS SHOWN FULL SIZE IN THE PATTERN BELOW RIGHT. USE TRACING PAPER OR PHOTOCOPY THIS PAGE TO MAKE A WORKING PATTERN. THEN TRANSFER THE PATTERN TO YOUR 1½"-THICK WORKPIECE.

MATERIALS LIST

WOOD

A	Bottom (1)	½ MDF - 10⅛ x 32
B	Top (1)	¼ hdbd. - 10⅛ x 32
C	Side Rail (1)	¾ x 1½ - 32
D	Runner (1)	½ x 1* - 32
E	End Rail (1)	½ x 1 - 9
F	Block (1)	½ x 1 - 1
G	Hold-Downs (2)**	1½ x 1½ - 5
H	Stop (1)	⅜ x ¾ - 4
I	Riser Block (1)	¾ x ¾ - 1¼

* Cut to fit in your miter gauge slot.

HARDWARE SUPPLIES

(1) No. 8 x 1¼" Fh woodscrew
(3) ¼" x 1" Fh machine screws
(2) ¼" x 3" hex bolts
(2) ¼" x 3½" toilet bolts
(6) ¼" hex nuts
(5) ¼" T-nuts
(9) 5⁄16" washers
(3) ¼" knobs
** You can also purchase aluminum hold-down clamps.

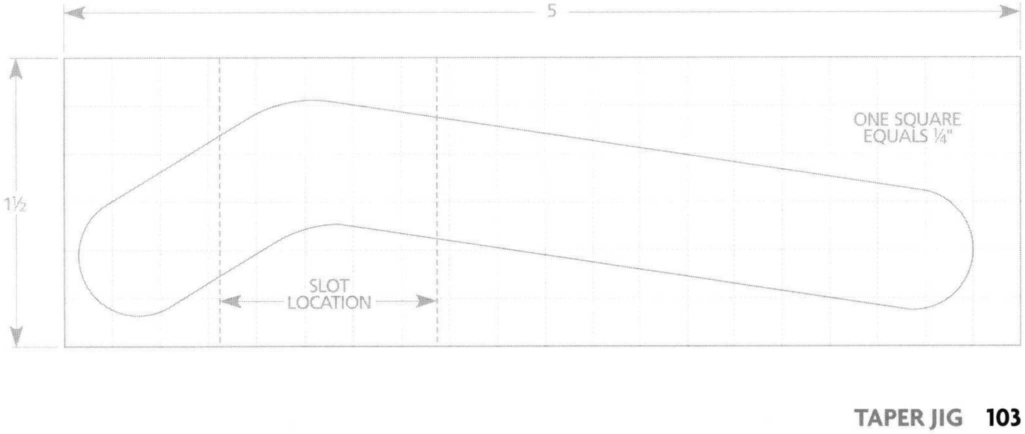

5
1½
ONE SQUARE EQUALS ¼"
SLOT LOCATION

The main part of this adjustable taper jig is a long platform with four T-shaped slots spaced out over its top. These T-slots serve as tracks for the adjustable hold-down clamps.

T-SLOTS. An easy way to form these T-slots is to make the platform out of two pieces, and cut part of the slot in each one.

The $1/2$"-thick bottom (A) is cut to size first. Next, four wide dadoes are cut in the top face of it to accept the head of a toilet bolt *(Figs. 1 and 1a)*. Then, after gluing on a hardboard top (B), complete the T-slots by cutting narrow dadoes for the shank of the bolt (refer to *Fig. 8* on page 106).

RAIL. To ensure that the platform remains flat after it's built, I added a hardwood rail (C) *(Fig. 2)*. It's simply glued to the edge of the platform.

RUNNER. The platform is guided by a $1/2$"-thick hardwood runner (D) that slides in the miter gauge slot of the saw table *(Fig. 2)*. To avoid any "play" in the platform, you want the runner to fit snug in the miter gauge slot, yet not so tight that it binds.

GROOVE. Once you're satisfied with the fit of the runner in the slot, the next step is to cut a groove in the bottom of the platform to accept the runner. Since the runner determines the position of the jig on the saw table, the location of this groove is important.

What you want is to locate the groove so that when you install the runner later, there will be some waste on the edge of the platform. (This waste will be trimmed off when you make your first pass.)

REFERENCE EDGE. At that point, the edge of the platform becomes a reference edge that indicates the path of the saw blade. So to make an accurate cut on a workpiece, all you'll need to do is align the layout marks with the reference edge.

THREE STEPS. An easy way to create this reference edge is to use a simple three-step process.

First, measure between the inside edge of the miter gauge slot and the outside edge of the saw blade *(Fig. 3)*.

This measurement is then transferred to the platform so you can cut the groove for the runner *(Fig. 4)*.

But before trimming the edge of the platform to make the reference edge *(Fig. 5)*, you'll need to attach the runner to the platform with machine screws and T-nuts *(Figs. 2 and 2a)*.

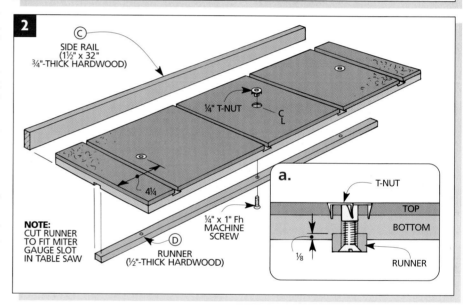

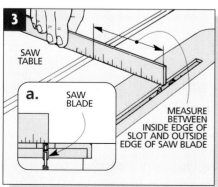

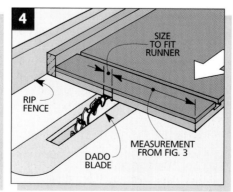

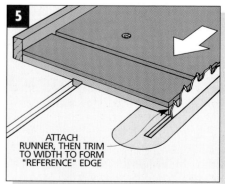

ADJUSTMENT BAR

The ingenious thing about this taper jig is the adjustment bar. It's nothing more than a slotted wood strip and a block with a metal pin *(Fig. 6)*. But it does two important things.

First, it makes it easy to adjust the size of the taper. Second, it provides a way to cut perfectly identical tapers.

SIZE. The secret is a pin that fits in a centered hole in the end of the leg you're tapering. This pin determines the position of the leg on the platform. By adjusting the bar, you can move the pin (and the leg) in two directions: side to side and up and down.

Say you want to cut a $1/4$" taper, for instance. Just slide the bar to the side so the leg overhangs the reference edge by $1/4$". To allow for pieces of different thicknesses, simply adjust the height of the bar.

IDENTICAL TAPERS. The pin also makes it easy to cut identical tapers without changing the setup of the jig. That's because it's centered on the end of the leg. Since the cut is referenced off a centerpoint, all you need to do is rotate the leg between each pass.

CONSTRUCTION. The adjustment bar is simple to make. After cutting the rail (E) to size, two slots are cut in it for hex bolts. This allows the side-to-side movement of the rail.

When the rail is complete, the block (F) is glued on.

To make the pin, drill a hole in the center of the block (F) and screw in a No. 8 x $1^1/2$" woodscrew just until the threads are buried. Then cut off the head *(Fig. 6a)*.

The adjustment bar is attached to the platform by means of the two hex bolts that thread into T-nuts *(Fig. 6b)*.

A pair of hex nuts "capture" the bar on the bolts. And tightening another single nut against the platform holds the bolts in place.

HOLD-DOWNS

All that's left is to add a pair of wooden hold-down clamps that hold workpieces flat, and a simple stop that's used with a hold-down to secure a tapered leg.

HOLD-DOWNS. Like the name implies, the hold-downs clamp work securely in place as you make a cut. By sliding them along the T-shaped slots in the platform, you can clamp different size pieces.

The unusual thing about the hold-downs is their angled shape *(Fig. 7* and the full-size pattern on page 103). This shape allows the long, straight end to rest on the platform and the short, angled end to apply pressure on top of the workpiece.

BLANK. Each hold-down (G) starts off as a $1^1/2$"-square blank *(Fig. 7)*. (I glued up two pieces of $3/4$"-thick maple.) Cut this blank to a rough length of 5".

Then transfer a pattern of the basic shape to the side. An easy way to transfer the pattern is to make a photocopy of the full-size pattern on page 103. Then fasten the pattern to the blank and cut around the shape.

Note: Before cutting the hold-down to shape, it's easiest to lay out and cut a slot for the toilet bolt *(Fig. 7)*. Then cut out the hold-down with a band saw or sabre saw.

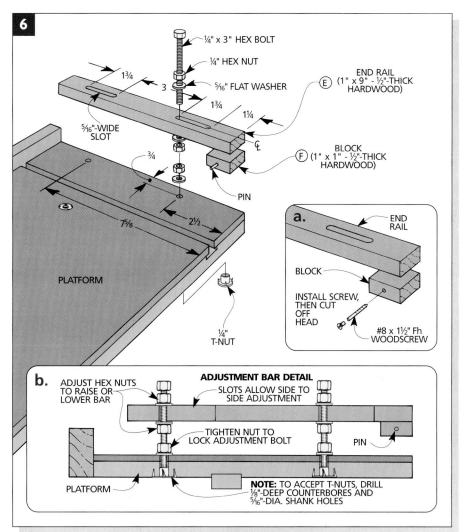

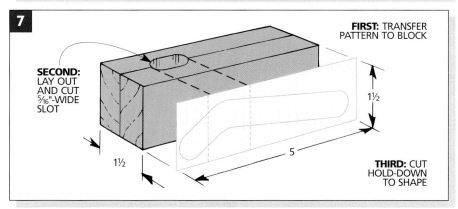

STOP & RISER BLOCK

When the hold-downs are completed, the clamping pressure is produced by tightening a plastic knob (and washer) on the end of a toilet bolt. This toilet bolt slides in the T-slot so you can clamp pieces of different widths *(Fig. 8)*.

The next step is to add a hardwood stop (H) *(Fig. 9)*. This is just a $^3/_8$"-thick strip with a curve sanded on one end.

In use, the curved end of this stop butts against the top (untapered) end of the leg (refer to Step 5 on the opposite page). This lets you reposition the leg at the same place between each pass.

The stop is locked in place by tightening a second knob toward the bottom of the toilet bolt *(Fig. 9)*.

To provide clearance for this knob when you use the hold-down and the stop together, you'll need to glue on a small hardwood riser block (I) *(Fig. 9)*.

The riser block acts as a platform for the "foot" of the hold-down to rest on during clamping (refer to Step 6 on the opposite page). ■

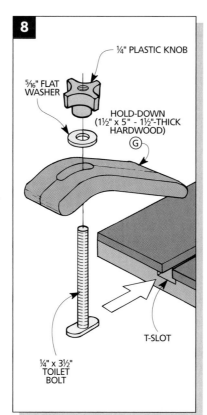

8

¼" PLASTIC KNOB

⁵/₁₆" FLAT WASHER

HOLD-DOWN (1½" x 5" - 1½"-THICK HARDWOOD)

Ⓖ

¼" x 3½" TOILET BOLT

T-SLOT

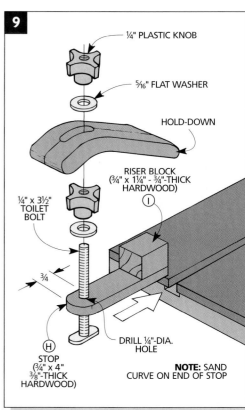

9

¼" PLASTIC KNOB

⁵/₁₆" FLAT WASHER

HOLD-DOWN

RISER BLOCK (¾" x 1¼" - ¾"-THICK HARDWOOD)

Ⓘ

¼" x 3½" TOILET BOLT

¾

Ⓗ

STOP (¾" x 4" ³/₈"-THICK HARDWOOD)

DRILL ¼"-DIA. HOLE

NOTE: SAND CURVE ON END OF STOP

WOODWORKER'S NOTEBOOK

ALTERNATE USES

In addition to cutting tapered legs quickly and accurately, the adjustable taper jig is useful for a couple of other applications as well. The two most obvious uses are angled cuts and straight-line ripping.

ANGLED CUTS. The taper jig can provide more stability and security for angled cuts than a miter gauge (see left photo below).

To make an angled cut using the taper jig, first slide two hold-downs into the middle two slots (or outer slots for a very long workpiece).

Mark a layout line on your workpiece where you want the angled cut. Then position the board with this layout mark aligned with the reference edge.

Tighten down the hold-downs, and slide the jig through the saw blade.

STRAIGHT-LINE RIPPING. Ripping a straight edge is similar to making an angled cut, with one key difference.

To rip a straight edge on a wide workpiece, remove the runner. This way, you can use the rip fence on your table saw to rip the workpiece.

Note: A simple version of a ripping jig with hold-downs is shown in the Woodworker's Notebook on page 25.

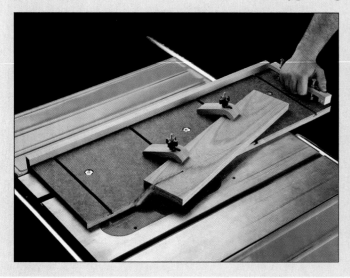

TECHNIQUE .... *Using the Taper Jig*

Once you are finished building the taper jig, using it is fairly straightforward. As long as everything is positioned and tightened down properly, you should be able to taper all four sides of a leg quickly and accurately.

Some taper jigs require several setups to cut a single leg, because they are designed to position the leg from it's outside edges. This jig is different, because it's designed so you can position the leg from its centerpoint.

CENTER PIN. The whole key to this setup is to make sure you center the pin (a cutoff screw) on the end of the leg. If the pin is centered, the leg will automatically come out with identical tapers on all four sides. This must be done before you set up anything else on the jig.

To center the pin, you need to find the center of the leg itself. Draw a pair of intersecting layout lines from corner to corner on the end of the leg (see photo above). The spot where these two lines meet is the center of the leg, so this is where you will drill the hole for the pin.

Drill the hole to match the size of the cutoff screw you are using for the pin.

LAY OUT TAPERS. The other thing you need to do before using the jig is to lay out lines on the bottom of the leg for the tapers.

This is simply a matter of deciding how much of a taper you want (how much difference in size you want between the top of the taper and the bottom of the leg). Then draw layout lines parallel to the outside edges that indicate the "cut lines" *(Step 1)*.

Note: If the layout lines do not intersect with each other at the center-finding lines you drew, the leg may not be square. Check this before continuing to set up the jig.

STEP-BY-STEP. To cut the tapers, follow the steps below. Once the jig is set up, every leg you cut on it should have consistent tapers.

1 After laying out the tapers on the end of the leg, drill a hole centered on the end of the leg to fit on the pin.

2 With the leg in place, adjust the hex nuts up or down so the leg sits flat on the platform.

3 Next, align the mark for the taper with the edge of the jig and tighten the adjustment nuts.

4 Now lay out the starting point of the taper and align the mark with the edge of the jig.

5 Slide the stop against the leg and lock it in place. Then tighten the hold-down on the leg.

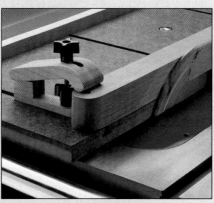

6 After cutting a taper on one side, rotate the leg and repeat the process for each side.

Tenoning Jig

Unlike some tenoning jigs, this version lets you cut both tenon cheeks without flipping the workpiece. It's easily adjustable, and a built-in spring-loaded clamp ensures accuracy pass after pass.

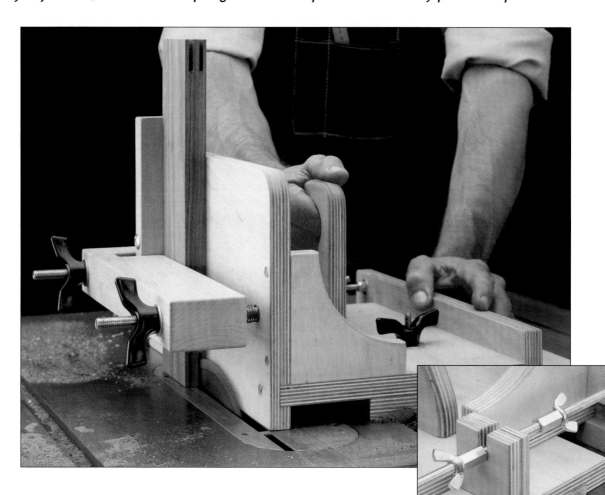

One of the fastest ways to cut tenons on the table saw is to use a tenoning jig. The typical versions of these jigs allow you to hold the workpiece *vertically* so you can cut one cheek of the tenon in a single pass over the saw blade.

But these jigs have a couple of drawbacks. First, to make the second cheek cut you need to unclamp the workpiece, flip it around, and clamp it in place again. Second, it's difficult to cut an accurate *offset* tenon (a tenon that's *not* centered on the thickness of the workpiece).

DOUBLE-STOP SYSTEM. So I built this tenoning jig with a double-stop system

that solves both problems. Once the stops are adjusted, you can make both cheek cuts without removing the workpiece (see inset photo).

In addition, this jig makes it easy to adjust the width and position of the tenon on the end of the workpiece.

BACK STOP. Another interesting feature of this tenoning jig is the back stop. The back stop supports the workpiece as it's pushed through the blade. It can be adjusted up and down so you won't cut through the stop when cutting tenons.

HOLD-DOWN BAR. To cut accurate tenons, the workpiece needs to be clamped securely to the tenoning jig. The

problem with most clamps is you need three hands to use them — two to hold the clamp, and one to position the workpiece. So instead, I added a spring-loaded hold-down bar to hold the workpiece.

MORTISES. Of course, a tenon is only half a joint. Before cutting tenons with this jig, I start by making the mortises. The drill press table and fence shown on page 82 is perfect for drilling out the majority of the waste of a mortise. Then it can be cleaned out with a chisel.

EXPLODED VIEW

OVERALL DIMENSIONS:
15W X 14L X 8½H

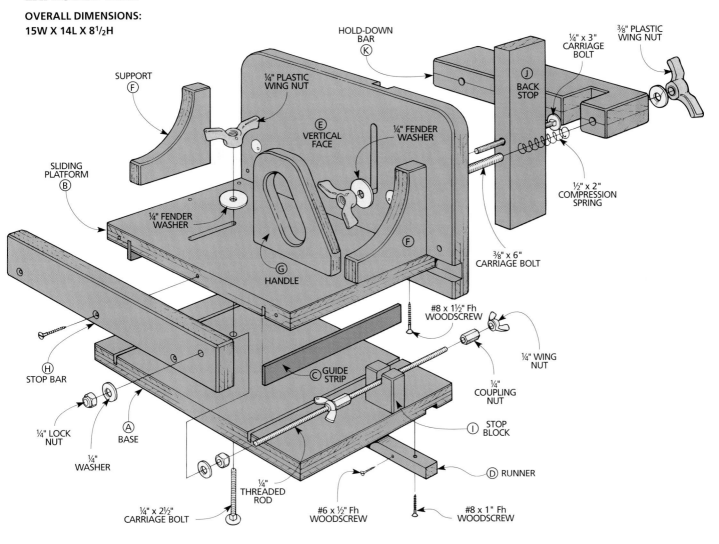

HOLD-DOWN BAR — K

SUPPORT — F

¼" PLASTIC WING NUT

E — VERTICAL FACE

¼" FENDER WASHER

SLIDING PLATFORM — B

¼" FENDER WASHER

G — HANDLE

BACK STOP — J

¼" x 3" CARRIAGE BOLT

⅜" PLASTIC WING NUT

½" x 2" COMPRESSION SPRING

⅜" x 6" CARRIAGE BOLT

F

#8 x 1½" Fh WOODSCREW

¼" WING NUT

¼" COUPLING NUT

C — GUIDE STRIP

STOP BLOCK — I

D — RUNNER

STOP BAR — H

¼" LOCK NUT

A — BASE

¼" WASHER

¼" x 2½" CARRIAGE BOLT

¼" THREADED ROD

#6 x ½" Fh WOODSCREW

#8 x 1" Fh WOODSCREW

MATERIALS LIST

WOOD

A	Base (1)	¾ ply - 9 x 14
B	Sliding Platform (1)	¾ ply - 8⅝ x 12¼
C	Guide Strips (2)	⅛ hdbd. - ¹¹⁄₁₆ x 8¼
D	Runner (1)*	⅝ x ¾ - 14
E	Vertical Face (1)	¾ ply - 8 x 14
F	Supports (2)	¾ ply - 4 x 4
G	Handle (1)	¾ ply - 5½ x 5½
H	Stop Bar (1)	¾ ply - 1¾ x 14
I	Stop Block (1)	¾ ply - 1¾ x 1¾
J	Back Stop (1)	¾ x 1¾ - 8
K	Hold-Down Bar (1)	1½ x 2½ - 11¾

* Size runner to fit your table saw.

HARDWARE SUPPLIES

(4) No. 6 x ½" Fh woodscrews
(3) No. 8 x 1" Fh woodscrews
(18) No. 8 x 1½" Fh woodscrews
(1) ¼" x 2½" carriage bolt w/fender washer
(1) ¼" x 3" carriage bolt w/fender washer
(2) ¼" plastic wing nuts
(2) ⅜" x 6" carriage bolts w/washers
(2) ⅜" plastic wing nuts
(2) ½" x 2" compression springs
(1) ¼" - 20 threaded rod, 10" long (rough)
(2) ¼" wing nuts
(2) ¼" coupling nuts
(2) ¼" lock nuts w/washers

BASE & SLIDING PLATFORM

A basic but important feature of this tenoning jig is the sliding platform. The platform slides back and forth on a fixed base (refer to *Fig. 2*). This sliding action allows you to adjust the jig to cut tenons of varying thickness.

GROOVES. To allow the platform to slide on the base without twisting or shifting, grooves are cut in both pieces for a pair of hardboard guide strips *(Figs. 1 and 2)*.

The tricky part is getting these grooves to align. To do this, start with an oversize blank and cut the grooves first. Then cut the base (A) and sliding platform (B) to size *(Fig. 1)*.

Note: The sliding platform is smaller than the base to allow room for a stop system that's added later.

SLOT. The sliding platform is held on the base with a bolt and a wing nut (refer to *Fig. 3*). To make the platform adjustable, a 3"-long slot is cut for the bolt to pass through *(Fig. 2)*. To cut this slot, simply drill a series of overlapping holes with a $1/4$" drill bit and clean up the slot with a file.

GUIDE STRIPS. The next step is to cut a pair of $1/8$"-thick hardboard guide strips (C) $8^1/4$" long. These will be glued into the grooves cut in the sliding platform *(Fig. 2)*.

Note: For clearance, the width of these guide strips ($^{11}/_{16}$") is $1/16$" less than the combined height of the two grooves (Side View in *Fig. 2*).

STOP BAR. Next, I added a stop bar (H) *(Fig. 3)*. (The stop bar is part of the double-stop system. Refer to page 113 for more on this.)

The stop bar is cut to match the length of the base (14") and to a width of $1^3/4$". It is then screwed to the edge of the sliding platform with three No. 8 x $1^1/2$" flathead woodscrews.

LOCATE HOLE. With the stop bar in place, the next step is to locate the bolt hole in the base.

The important thing here is to position the platform so there's a $3/8$" lip on the right side of the base *(Fig. 3)*.

Note: This lip will fit into a dado that's cut in the vertical face (E) later (refer to opposite page).

With the platform in position, drill a counterbored hole in the base for the $1/4$" x $2^1/2$" carriage bolt. Then slip in the bolt and washer, and thread on a wing nut.

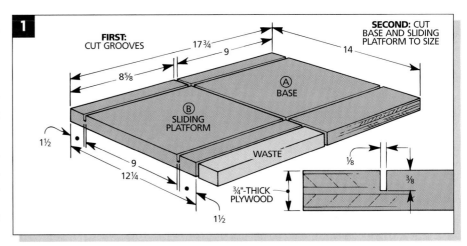

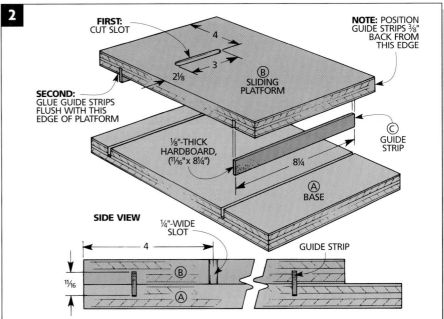

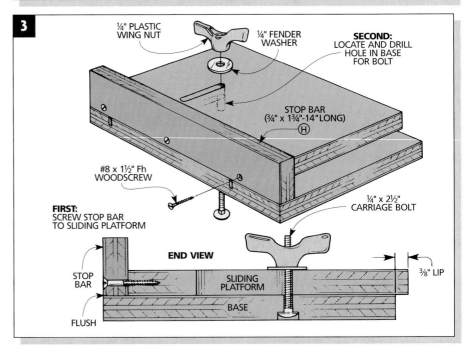

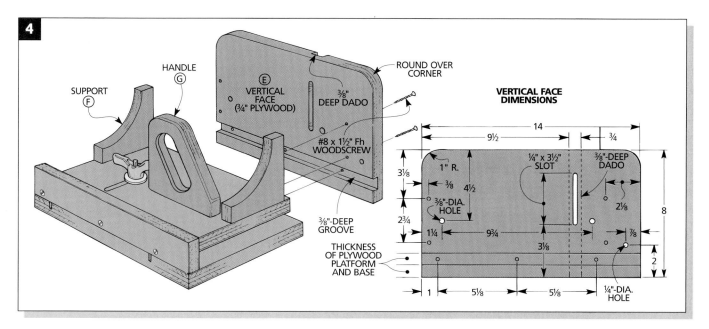

4

HANDLE (G)

SUPPORT (F)

(E) VERTICAL FACE (¾" PLYWOOD)

ROUND OVER CORNER

⅜" DEEP DADO

#8 x 1½" Fh WOODSCREW

⅜"-DEEP GROOVE

THICKNESS OF PLYWOOD PLATFORM AND BASE

VERTICAL FACE DIMENSIONS

14
9½
¾
3⅛
1" R.
⅜
4½
2¾
⅜"-DIA. HOLE
1¼
9¾
3⅛
1
5⅛
5⅛
¼" x 3½" SLOT
⅜"-DEEP DADO
2⅛
8
⅞
2
¼"-DIA. HOLE

VERTICAL FACE

With the base and sliding platform complete, the next step is to add the vertical face *(Fig. 4)*.

VERTICAL FACE. The vertical face (E) is screwed to the sliding platform and is designed to support the workpiece during a cut *(Fig. 4)*. It's nothing more than a piece of ³/₄"-thick plywood with the top corners rounded.

The only unusual thing about this vertical face is that you need to cut a groove, a dado, and drill screw and assembly holes before attaching it to the sliding platform.

GROOVE AND DADO. The groove is cut near the *inside* bottom edge, and sized to accept the ³/₄" plywood sliding platform *(Fig. 4)*.

The dado is cut vertically on the *outside* of the face. This dado forms a channel for a back stop that's added later (refer to page 114). A slot cut through the dado allows the stop to move up and down *(Fig. 4)*.

DRILL HOLES. Next, drill four countersunk shank holes for No. 8 x 1¹/₂" flathead woodscrews in the face (Vertical Face Dimensions in *Fig. 4*).

Note: There's also three holes (used later to assemble the jig) to drill: two ³/₈"-dia. holes and a ¹/₄"-dia. hole *(Fig. 4)*. Now you can screw the face (E) to the sliding platform (B).

SUPPORTS. To hold the vertical face in place, I added a pair of supports (F) *(Figs. 5 and 5a)*. Each support starts as a 4" square blank of ³/₄" plywood. Then a 3" radius is cut out of one corner.

When they're cut out, they can be screwed to the sliding platform and the vertical face *(Fig. 5)*.

To make sure the vertical face stays 90° to the saw table, clamp each support to the platform and vertical face *(Fig. 5)*. Then drill holes and screw them in place.

HANDLE. Finally, to make it safe and easy to push the tenoning jig, I added a slotted handle (G) cut from ³/₄" plywood *(Fig. 6)*.

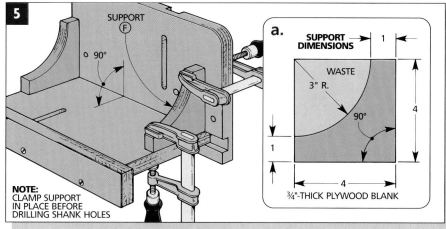

5

SUPPORT (F)

90°

NOTE: CLAMP SUPPORT IN PLACE BEFORE DRILLING SHANK HOLES

a. **SUPPORT DIMENSIONS**

1
WASTE
3" R.
90°
4
1
4
³/₄"-THICK PLYWOOD BLANK

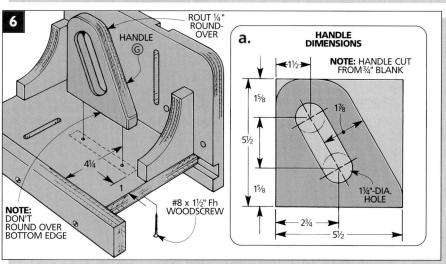

6

ROUT ¼" ROUND-OVER

HANDLE (G)

NOTE: DON'T ROUND OVER BOTTOM EDGE

4¼
1
#8 x 1½" Fh WOODSCREW

a. **HANDLE DIMENSIONS**

NOTE: HANDLE CUT FROM ¾" BLANK

1½
1⅝
5½
1⅝
1⅞
1¼"-DIA. HOLE
2¾
5½

Adjustable Runner. *The runner is cut to fit in the miter gauge slot of your table saw (with a little clearance). Screws in the side of the runner allow you to adjust the fit to compensate for seasonal changes in humidity.*

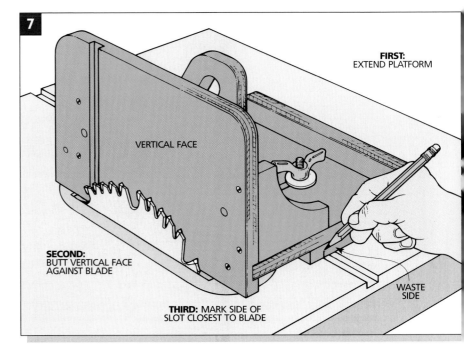

7

FIRST:
EXTEND PLATFORM

VERTICAL FACE

SECOND:
BUTT VERTICAL FACE
AGAINST BLADE

THIRD: MARK SIDE OF
SLOT CLOSEST TO BLADE

WASTE
SIDE

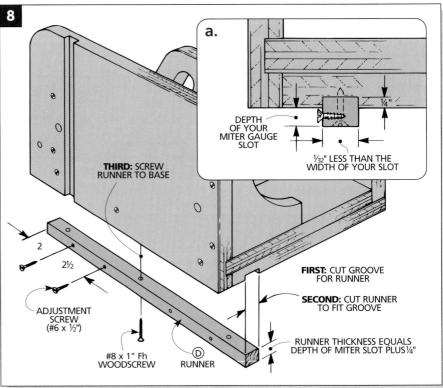

8

a.

THIRD: SCREW
RUNNER TO BASE

DEPTH
OF YOUR
MITER GAUGE
SLOT

$\frac{1}{4}$"

$\frac{1}{32}$" LESS THAN THE
WIDTH OF YOUR SLOT

2

2½

ADJUSTMENT
SCREW
(#6 x ½")

#8 x 1" Fh
WOODSCREW

D RUNNER

FIRST: CUT GROOVE
FOR RUNNER

SECOND: CUT RUNNER
TO FIT GROOVE

RUNNER THICKNESS EQUALS
DEPTH OF MITER SLOT PLUS ¼"

RUNNER

After the handle is attached, the next step is to add a hardwood runner. The runner fits in a groove cut in the bottom of the base and keeps the jig (and workpiece) parallel to the blade.

The only problem with using hardwood for the runner is that it can expand and contract with seasonal changes in humidity.

To solve this, I made the runner narrower (about $\frac{1}{32}$") than the miter gauge slot. Then I added adjustment screws (see photo above).

This way, the runner can be adjusted at any time for a fit that's snug, but still slides smoothly.

TWO STEPS. Installing the runner is a two-step process. First, you need to locate and cut a groove in the bottom of the base (A). Then cut the runner to fit the groove.

GROOVE. To locate the groove, start by extending the sliding platform (B) as far out as it will go *(Fig. 7)*. Then raise the saw blade and butt the vertical face against it.

Next, make a mark on the base where the side of the miter slot is closest to the blade *(Fig. 7)*. Now cut a $\frac{1}{4}$"-deep groove on the waste side of this mark, about $\frac{1}{32}$" less than the width of your miter gauge slot *(Fig. 8a)*.

RUNNER. After the groove is cut, the next step is to make the runner (D) *(Fig. 8)*. (I used maple, but most any hardwood will work fine.) The length

and width are easy. Cut the runner to match the length of the base (14") and to width to fit the groove you cut earlier in the base.

But the thickness may vary depending on the depth of your miter gauge slot. To determine the thickness of the runner, measure the depth of your slot, and then add $\frac{1}{4}$" for the groove in the base. Then cut the runner to this thickness.

Before attaching the runner to the base, drill countersunk holes in the side of the runner *(Fig. 8)*. Then add the adjustment screws (No. 6 x $\frac{1}{2}$" flathead woodscrews), and screw the runner to the base.

ADJUSTMENT. Finally, you can adjust the runner by backing out each adjustment screw the same amount until the runner slides smoothly in the miter gauge slot.

The double-stop system is an important feature of the tenoning jig. It's designed so you can accurately preset the movement of the vertical face.

This allows you to cut both cheeks of a tenon *without* flipping the workpiece. Then you can cut tenons more quickly and easily. (For more on this, refer to page 115.)

STOP BLOCK. I started work on the stop system by making the stop block (I) *(Fig. 9)*. This stop block is just a $1^3/_4$" square piece of plywood with a notch cut in it for a length of $^1/_4$" threaded rod.

NOTCH. The trick is to cut the notch so it aligns with the hole you drilled earlier in the vertical face (for the threaded rod) *(Fig. 9a)*. I made the notch by first drilling a $^1/_4$"-dia. hole using the vertical face as a template *(Fig. 10)*.

To do this, first clamp the stop block on the inside of the vertical face (E) *(Fig. 10)*. Then, use the $^1/_4$"-dia. hole in the vertical face (that you drilled for the threaded rod) to guide the drill bit through the block.

After the hole is drilled in the stop block, complete the notch with a jig saw or band saw. File or sand it smooth if necessary.

STOP BAR. The next part to cut is the stop bar (H). A hole drilled in the stop bar supports the other end of the threaded rod.

To drill this $^1/_4$"-dia. hole, I used the notch in the stop block as a guide. Simply clamp the stop block (I) to the stop bar (H), rest the drill bit in the

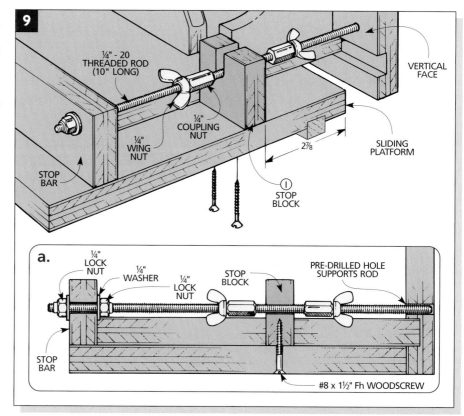

bottom of the notch in the stop block, and drill the hole *(Fig. 11)*.

Once this hole is drilled, screw the stop block to the sliding platform (refer to *Fig. 9*).

HARDWARE. With the stop block in place, the last step is to add the threaded rod and hardware.

A 10"-long piece of $^1/_4$" - 20 threaded rod runs through the stop bar, stop block, and into the vertical face (refer to *Figs. 9 and 9a*).

Threaded onto this rod (on each side

of the stop block) are a coupling nut and a wing nut.

The coupling nuts butt up against either side of the stop block and allow you to preset one of the cheek cuts. The wing nuts then serve to lock the coupling nuts in place after they've both been positioned.

To keep the threaded rod from spinning when the wing nuts are tightened down, I used two lock nuts and washers to secure the rod to the stop bar (refer to *Fig. 9a*).

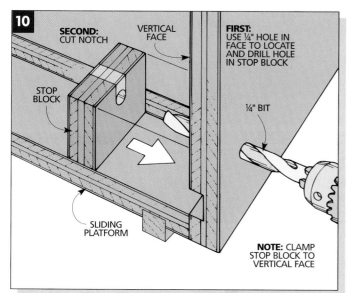

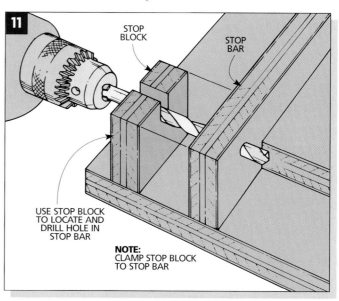

BACK STOP

The back stop (J) of the tenoning jig helps keep the workpiece vertical throughout a cut. And it acts like a push block to push the workpiece through the saw blade *(Fig. 12)*.

SLOTTED DADO. The back stop is just a $3/4$"-thick piece of hardwood. It is cut to a width of $1^3/4$", and to length to fit in the dado you cut earlier in the vertical face (E). The slot that was cut in the dado is what makes the back stop adjustable *(Fig. 12a)*.

The back stop is held in place with a $1/4$" x 3" carriage bolt and a wing nut. (I used a large plastic wing nut to make it easy to tighten.)

To locate the hole for the carriage bolt, first insert the back stop in the dado. Make sure it's flush with the bottom of the base (A).

Then make a mark near the bottom of the slot. Finally, drill the hole through the edge of the back stop and bolt it in place *(Fig. 12a)*.

HOLD-DOWN BAR

To keep the workpiece in place during a cut, I added a spring-loaded hold-down bar (K) *(Fig. 13)*. This bar is $1^1/2$" thick (I glued it up from two pieces of $3/4$"-thick stock). Cut it to a width of $2^1/2$" and a length of $11^3/4$".

NOTCH. The next step is to cut a 1"-wide, $1^3/4$"-long notch near the end of the hold-down bar to fit around the back stop (J) *(Fig. 13a)*.

CARRIAGE BOLTS. The clamping power comes from a pair of $3/8$" carriage bolts and wing nuts.

The bolts run through the hold-down bar and pass into the $3/8$"-dia. holes in the vertical face you drilled earlier *(Fig. 13)*.

To mark the holes in the hold-down bar, use the holes in the vertical face as a template. After the holes are drilled, install the carriage bolts.

SPRINGS. Next, I slipped a pair of $1/2$" compression springs over the carriage bolts to automatically push open the hold-down bar when the wing nuts are loosened.

FINISH. With the hold-down bar complete, there are only a couple things left to do. First, soften the sharp edges on all the parts of the jig to make it comfortable to handle. Then apply a finish. (I wiped on two coats of tung oil.) ■

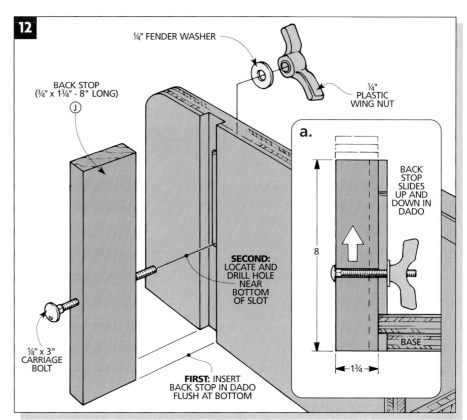

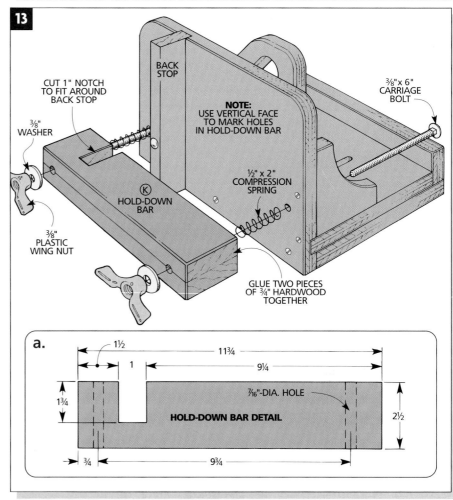

TECHNIQUE .... *Using the Tenoning Jig*

Using the tenoning jig is a fairly simple four-step process. But there are things to be aware of before you begin.

MORTISES. As was mentioned in the opening, a tenon is only half of a mortise and tenon joint. You can cut this joint in either order, but I always prefer to cut the mortise first, and then cut the tenon to fit. That's because I cut mortises on a drill press, and therefore am limited to the size of my drill bits. You have more flexibility when cutting a tenon.

SIZE. After you have drilled your mortise and cleaned out the waste, remember to cut the tenon a little *shorter* than your mortise (to allow room for clearance and glue).

1 First, lay out the tenon on the work-piece. Then butt the edge of the work-piece up against the back stop and clamp it in place with the hold-down bar. Next, adjust the height of the blade for the desired depth of cut (the length of the tenon).
Safety Note: *Remove the plug from the saw before setting up the jig.*

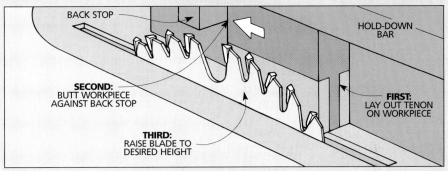

2 Once you have adjusted the height of the saw blade, you can adjust the back stop. To do this, slide the tenoning jig so the back stop is over the blade. Then lower the back stop until it just touches the saw blade at its highest point.

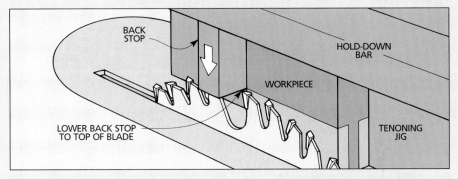

3 To set the cut for the inside cheek, slide the platform so the outside edge of the blade aligns with the inside layout line. Then thread the left coupling nut against the stop block and tighten the wing nut.

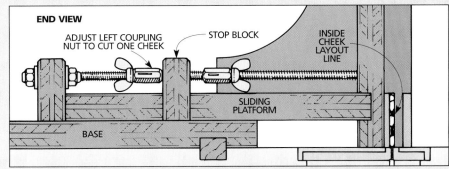

4 Now, move the platform so the inside edge of the blade aligns with the layout line for the other cheek. Then adjust the right coupling nut, tighten the wing nut, and make a test cut. To complete the tenon, remove the work-piece and make the shoulder cuts. (To do this, lay the piece flat on the saw table and use a miter gauge to cut the shoulders and waste.)

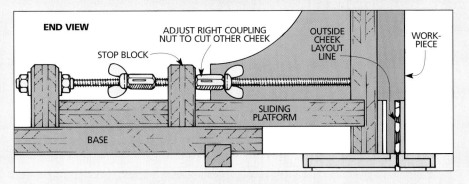

WOODWORKER'S NOTEBOOK

SHOP-MADE KNOBS

Make use of scrap pieces of wood that are headed for the trash to make customized knobs for a variety of applications.

MITER GAUGE HANDLE

This miter gauge handle is just a tall dowel that replaces the handle that came with the gauge. You'll want to try different sizes to find the most comfortable grip. (I used a 1¼"-dia. dowel.)

The dowel screws onto the threaded stud of the miter gauge. A nylon insert tapped to the same thread size as the stud is epoxied in the dowel *(Fig. 1)*.

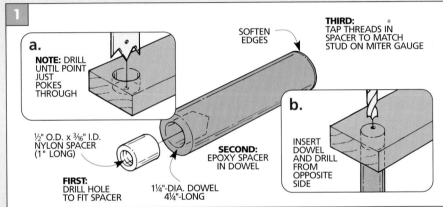

1

a.

NOTE: DRILL UNTIL POINT JUST POKES THROUGH

SOFTEN EDGES

THIRD: TAP THREADS IN SPACER TO MATCH STUD ON MITER GAUGE

½" O.D. x ³⁄₁₆" I.D. NYLON SPACER (1" LONG)

FIRST: DRILL HOLE TO FIT SPACER

SECOND: EPOXY SPACER IN DOWEL

1¼"-DIA. DOWEL 4¼"-LONG

b.

INSERT DOWEL AND DRILL FROM OPPOSITE SIDE

TWO-BIT TRICK. To center the hole for the insert on the end of the dowel, start with a spade bit that's the same size as the dowel and drill into a scrap until the point just pokes through *(Fig. 1a)*.

Insert the dowel in the hole and drill from the opposite side with a smaller bit to create a centerpoint *(Fig. 1b)*. Then drill a hole to fit the insert, epoxy it in the dowel, and tap the threads.

STAR KNOB

This knob is large enough to apply plenty of pressure for a jig (to lock down a fence for example). And the scalloped edges provide a sure, comfortable grip.

LAYOUT. To lay out a knob, start with a square blank of ³⁄₄"-thick hardwood *(Fig. 1)*. Then divide it into eight equal parts by drawing layout lines through the centerpoint. This same centerpoint is used to draw two circles. A small

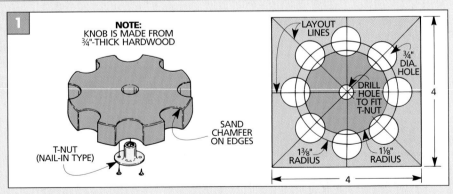

1

NOTE: KNOB IS MADE FROM ³⁄₄"-THICK HARDWOOD

SAND CHAMFER ON EDGES

T-NUT (NAIL-IN TYPE)

LAYOUT LINES

³⁄₄" DIA. HOLE

DRILL HOLE TO FIT T-NUT

4

1⅜" RADIUS

1⅛" RADIUS

4

diameter circle marks the outside edge of the knob. And the large one is used to lay out the finger recesses.

RECESSES. The scalloped recesses are formed by drilling holes where the large circle intersects the layout lines.

Cut to the small circle on a band saw or jig saw, and chamfer the edges.

T-NUT. To "thread" these knobs, use an ordinary T-nut. Epoxy and nail it in a hole that's drilled to fit the T-nut.

Protect the knob with paint or finish.

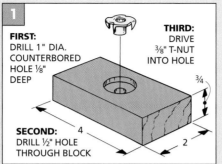

1

FIRST:
DRILL 1" DIA.
COUNTERBORED
HOLE 1/8"
DEEP

THIRD:
DRIVE
3/8" T-NUT
INTO HOLE

SECOND:
DRILL 1/2" HOLE
THROUGH BLOCK

4

2

3/4

2

WASTE

1/4

2

3/8

1

WASTE

■ Using a large wing nut makes it easier for me to get a good grip. This is especially important when I'm tightening down the fence on a jig. But instead of going out to buy a plastic version of this handy accessory, you can make your own using just a T-nut and a piece of scrap wood.

To make this shop-made wing nut, start with a 3/4"-thick block of wood *(Fig. 1)*. I'll generally use a piece about 4" long. But since you'll be making it to

fit your hand, pick whatever length you need for a comfortable grip. Take the time to experiment a little to find the proper size, and you'll be glad you did later on.

Note: Use a scrap piece with a tight wood grain (like maple or walnut) so the wing nut won't split when it's being tightened down.

The first step is to drill and counterbore the block to fit the size of the T-nut that you'll be using *(Fig. 1)*.

I'll install the T-nut in the block before cutting the knob to shape. That

way the block sits squarely on the workbench, which makes driving the T-nut in easier and more accurate.

Now mark the locations for the cuts on the sides of the block (top drawing in *Fig. 2*) and use a band saw to remove the waste.

Then mark the location for the bevels on the bottom (bottom drawing in *Fig. 2*). It's easy to sand the beveled angle with a disc or belt sander. Finally, round all the edges of the wing nut with sandpaper to get a comfortable grip and eliminate splinters.

■ Sometimes a simple knob just doesn't provide enough leverage. Your fingers simply don't have the strength you get from your wrists and arms. So to make things easier on my hands, I use a shop-made crank.

The crank shown here can be used as a replacement for a knob on a stationary tool. It would also be ideal for adjusting large shop machine accessories (raising and lowering an outfeed table, for example).

This crank has two parts: an arm that attaches to the shaft of an adjustment

mechanism, and a handle to turn the arm *(Fig. 1)*.

ARM. I wanted to make the arm strong (yet still easy to work). So instead of using wood or hardboard, I made it from a 1/2"-thick piece of phenolic (see page 126 for sources).

To make the arm, start with a piece of phenolic that is 4" long and 1" wide *(Fig. 1a)*. A large hole is drilled in one end of this piece to fit the shaft of the adjustment mechanism.

To secure the arm to the shaft, you'll also need to drill an intersecting hole through the edge that's tapped for an Allen screw *(Fig. 1a)*. And finally, there's a small hole that's drilled and tapped in the opposite end of the arm for the handle.

HANDLE. When the arm is completed, you can add the handle. It's just a short dowel that attaches to the arm with a carriage bolt.

The carriage bolt passes through a counterbored and slightly oversize shank hole in the dowel and threads into the arm. A nut "locks" the bolt in the threaded hole and allows the handle to spin freely.

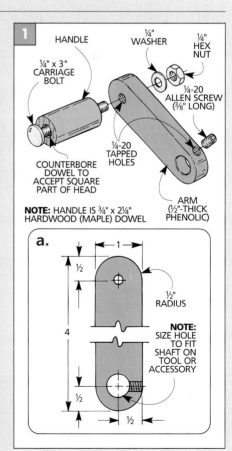

1

HANDLE

1/4"
WASHER

1/4"
HEX
NUT

1/4" x 3"
CARRIAGE
BOLT

1/4-20
ALLEN SCREW
(3/8" LONG)

1/4-20
TAPPED
HOLES

COUNTERBORE
DOWEL TO
ACCEPT SQUARE
PART OF HEAD

ARM
(1/2"-THICK
PHENOLIC)

NOTE: HANDLE IS 3/4" x 2¼"
HARDWOOD (MAPLE) DOWEL

a.

1

1/2

1/2"
RADIUS

4

NOTE:
SIZE HOLE
TO FIT
SHAFT ON
TOOL OR
ACCESSORY

1/2

1/2

Box Joint Jig

This shop-made jig lets you "dial in" perfect-fitting box joints on your table saw or router table. The unique micro-adjustment system and locking feature make it easy and accurate.

The thing that impresses me most about this box joint jig isn't the tight-fitting joints you can make with it. After all, that's what you expect from a precision-made jig. What's unique is how quickly and easily it can be adjusted.

Unlike most box joint jigs I've used that require an almost endless amount of "tweaking," this jig can be set up in a matter of minutes. The secret is a built-in system that lets you adjust the jig in extremely small increments.

MICRO-ADJUSTMENT SYSTEM. This system is designed to adjust both the *size* and *spacing* of the pins and slots that make up a box joint. By simply turning a knob, the jig can be set to cut

slots that range in size from a width of $1/4$" to $13/16$". A second knob changes the spacing of the pins and slots. This tightens (or loosens) the joint which allows you to sneak up on a perfect fit.

KEY. The adjustment system works by moving two metal brackets. The brackets form a "key" that automatically positions the workpiece so each slot is cut a uniform distance apart. This creates a series of pins and slots that fit together like fingers in a glove.

LOCKING FEATURE. To prevent the key from "creeping" once it's been adjusted, a pair of plastic knobs locks it

securely in place. The result is perfect fitting box joints.

TWO TOOLS. Another nice feature of this box joint jig is that it can be used not only on the table saw (see large photo above), but also on the router table (see inset photo).

MATERIALS. With the exception of a $1/4$" hardboard backing plate, all the main parts of the box joint jig are made from $1/4$" or $3/4$"-thick hardwood.

EXPLODED VIEW

OVERALL DIMENSIONS:
4W X 19¼L X 6¼H

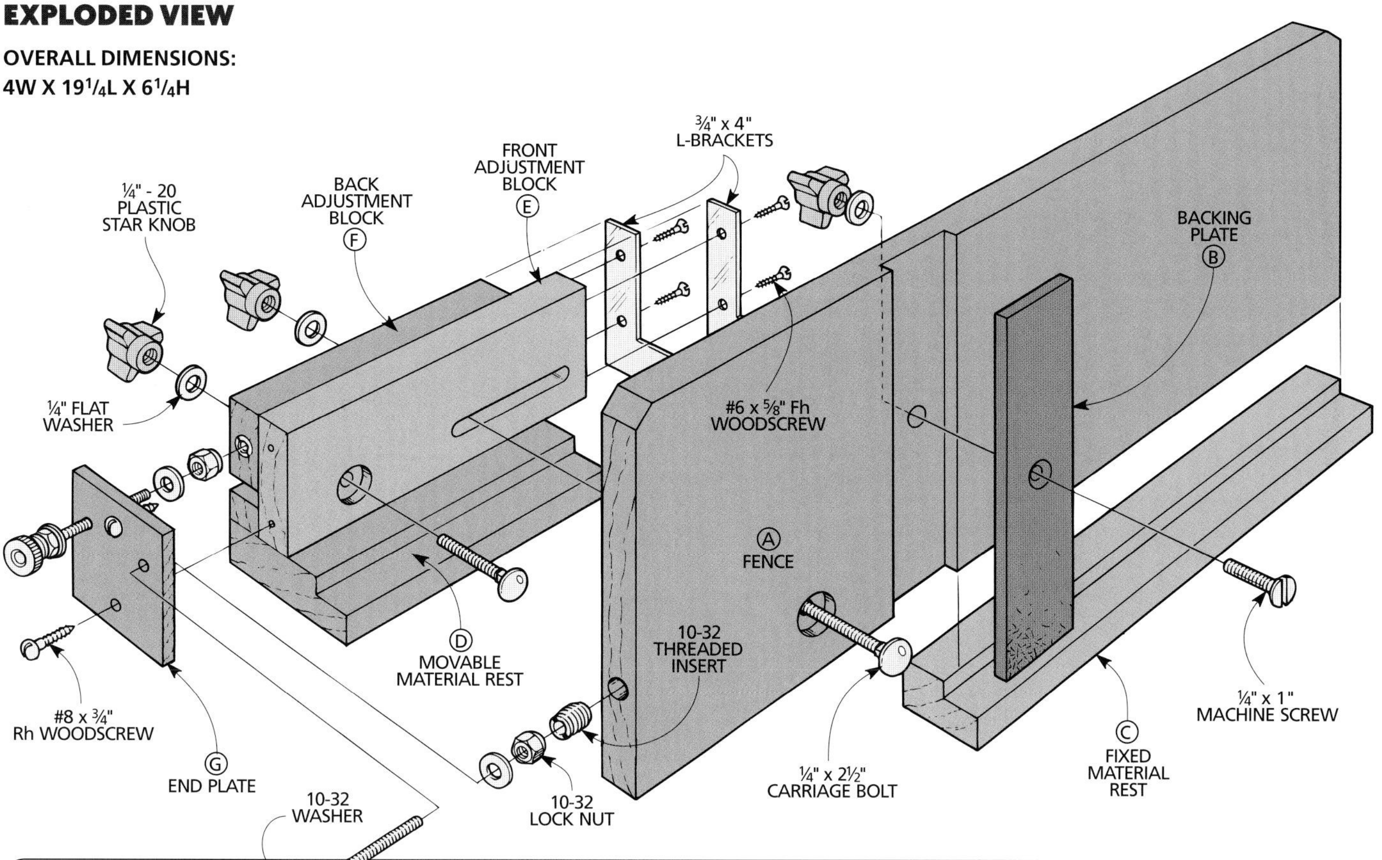

¼" - 20 PLASTIC STAR KNOB

BACK ADJUSTMENT BLOCK

FRONT ADJUSTMENT BLOCK (E)

¾" x 4" L-BRACKETS

BACKING PLATE (B)

¼" FLAT WASHER

#6 x ⅝" Fh WOODSCREW

(A) FENCE

(D) MOVABLE MATERIAL REST

10-32 THREADED INSERT

10-32 LOCK NUT

#8 x ¾" Rh WOODSCREW

(G) END PLATE

10-32 WASHER

¼" x 2½" CARRIAGE BOLT

(C) FIXED MATERIAL REST

¼" x 1" MACHINE SCREW

TOP VIEW

10-32 HEX NUT

10-32 THREADED ROD (2½"-LONG)

10-32 KNURLED KNOB

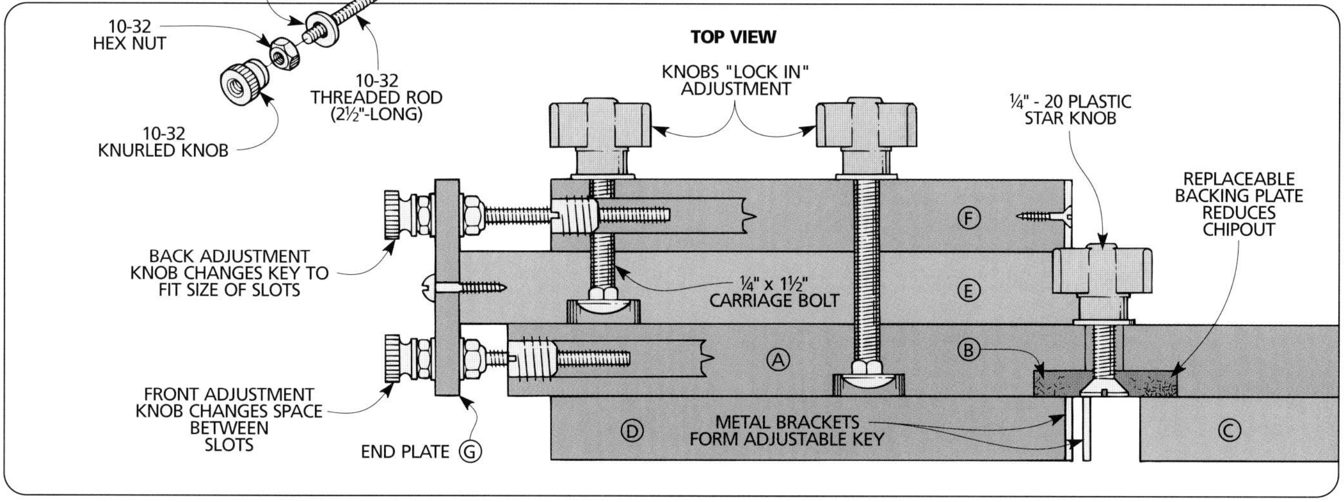

KNOBS "LOCK IN" ADJUSTMENT

¼" - 20 PLASTIC STAR KNOB

REPLACEABLE BACKING PLATE REDUCES CHIPOUT

BACK ADJUSTMENT KNOB CHANGES KEY TO FIT SIZE OF SLOTS

¼" x 1½" CARRIAGE BOLT

FRONT ADJUSTMENT KNOB CHANGES SPACE BETWEEN SLOTS

END PLATE (G)

METAL BRACKETS FORM ADJUSTABLE KEY

MATERIALS LIST

WOOD

A	Fence (1)	¾ x 5½ - 18
B	Backing Plate (1)	¼ hdbd. - 1½ x 5½
C	Fixed Mat. Rest (1)	¾ x 1½ - 11⅜
D	Movable Mat. Rest (1)	¾ x 3 - 5⅜
E	Front Adj. Block (1)	¾ x 2 - 6½
F	Back Adj. Block (1)	¾ x 2 - 5⅜
G	End Plate (1)	¼ x 2 - 2¼

HARDWARE SUPPLIES
(5) No. 6 x ⅝" Fh woodscrews
(2) No. 8 x ¾" Rh woodscrews
(1) ¼" x 1" machine screw

(3) ¼" - 20 plastic star knobs
(3) ¼" flat washers
(2) ¾" x 4" L-brackets*
(1) ¼" x 1½" carriage bolt
(1) ¼" x 2½" carriage bolt
(2) 10-32 threaded inserts
(4) 10-32 washers (brass)
(2) 10-32 lock nuts
(2) 10-32 hex nuts (brass)
(2) 10-32 knurled knobs (brass)
(2) 10-32 threaded rods - 2½" (brass)
* Also sold as mending plates

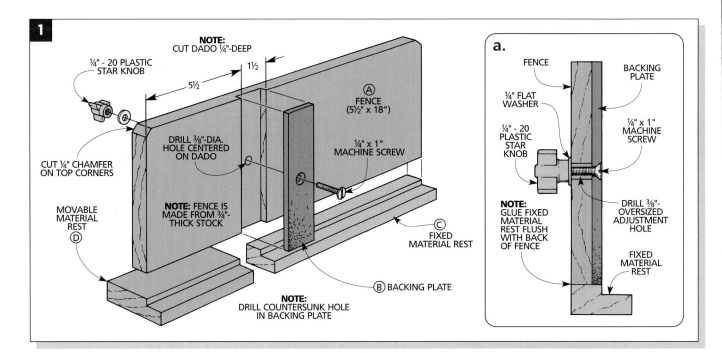

NOTE: CUT DADO ¼"-DEEP

¼" - 20 PLASTIC STAR KNOB

1½

5½

Ⓐ FENCE (5½" x 18")

DRILL ⅜"-DIA. HOLE CENTERED ON DADO

¼" x 1" MACHINE SCREW

CUT ¼" CHAMFER ON TOP CORNERS

NOTE: FENCE IS MADE FROM ¾"-THICK STOCK

MOVABLE MATERIAL REST Ⓓ

Ⓒ FIXED MATERIAL REST

Ⓑ BACKING PLATE

NOTE: DRILL COUNTERSUNK HOLE IN BACKING PLATE

a.

FENCE

¼" FLAT WASHER

¼" - 20 PLASTIC STAR KNOB

BACKING PLATE

¼" x 1" MACHINE SCREW

NOTE: GLUE FIXED MATERIAL REST FLUSH WITH BACK OF FENCE

DRILL ⅜"-OVERSIZED ADJUSTMENT HOLE

FIXED MATERIAL REST

FENCE

The box joint jig is designed with a tall fence that supports a workpiece when you stand it on end. This lets you cut slots on the end of the workpiece by pushing the jig through the table saw blade (or router bit).

FENCE. The fence (A) is just a piece of ³/₄"-thick hardwood (maple) with the top corners chamfered *(Fig. 1)*. To provide plenty of support, the fence is 5¹/₂" tall (wide) and 18" long.

BACKING PLATE. After you've cut the fence to size, the next step is to add a replaceable backing plate. This plate will help prevent the wood fibers around the back of the slot from chipping out as the blade passes through the workpiece.

So why doesn't the fence alone solve the problem of chipout? It will, but only the first time the jig is used. Because as the jig passes over the blade, a slot is cut in the fence itself as well as in the workpiece. Once that slot is cut, you've removed the support.

That's where the backing plate (B) comes in. It's just a piece of ¹/₄" hardboard that fits in a shallow dado in the fence *(Fig. 1)*.

To make it easy to replace when it gets chewed up, the plate is held in place with a machine screw and knob (or wing nut) *(Fig. la)*.

Note: If you cut a lot of box joints, you should cut a few extra backing plates now to have on hand later.

MATERIAL REST

With the fence complete, the next step is to add a material rest. The material rest serves as a "shelf" that raises the end of the workpiece above the saw or router table.

Because it's raised above the table, the workpiece spans any irregularities in the table insert that can cause the depth of the slots to vary.

TWO PARTS. The material rest consists of two separate parts. The first is a fixed rest (C) that's attached permanently to the jig. The second is a movable material rest (D) that slides from side to side *(Fig. 1)*.

This two-part rest creates an opening that provides clearance for an adjustable "key" that's added later (refer to opposite page).

The two-part design also lets you slide the jig through the blade without cutting into the material rest.

BLANK. Both parts of the material rest are cut from one ³/₄"-thick blank *(Fig. 2)*. After cutting a rabbet on one edge to form the shelf, the two parts are cut to final length.

Then the fixed rest is trimmed to width (1¹/₂") and glued to the bottom of the fence *(Fig. 1)*. The movable rest will be used later as a platform for the adjustment system.

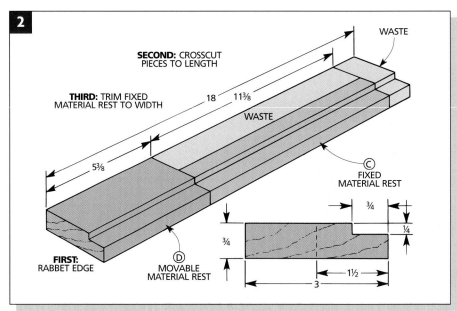

SECOND: CROSSCUT PIECES TO LENGTH

THIRD: TRIM FIXED MATERIAL REST TO WIDTH

18

11³/₈

WASTE

WASTE

Ⓒ FIXED MATERIAL REST

5³/₈

¾

¾

¼

1½

3

FIRST: RABBET EDGE

Ⓓ MOVABLE MATERIAL REST

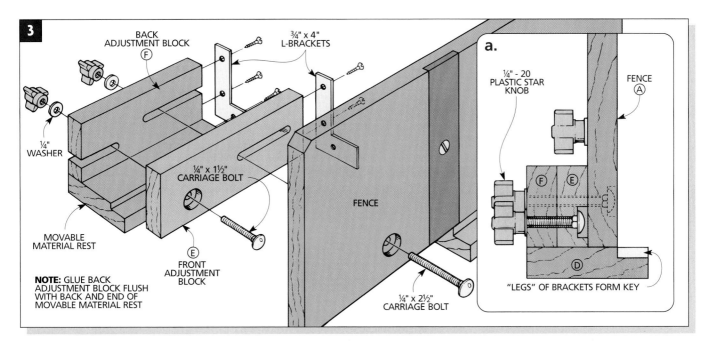

3

BACK ADJUSTMENT BLOCK (F)

¾" x 4" L-BRACKETS

¼" WASHER

¼" x 1½" CARRIAGE BOLT

MOVABLE MATERIAL REST

FRONT ADJUSTMENT BLOCK

NOTE: GLUE BACK ADJUSTMENT BLOCK FLUSH WITH BACK AND END OF MOVABLE MATERIAL REST

FENCE

E

¼" x 2½" CARRIAGE BOLT

a.

¼" - 20 PLASTIC STAR KNOB

FENCE (A)

F E

D

"LEGS" OF BRACKETS FORM KEY

ADJUSTMENT SYSTEM

After completing the material rest, work can begin on the adjustment system. This is the part of the jig that lets you make micro-adjustments to the size of the box joints you're cutting.

Basically, this system consists of the movable material rest you cut earlier, two adjustment blocks, and a pair of L-shaped metal brackets *(Fig. 3)*. The blocks and brackets work together to form a "key" that adjusts to the desired size and spacing of the slots that make up the box joint.

CUT BLOCKS. Start by cutting the front adjustment block (E) and the back adjustment block (F) to size from ³/₄"-thick stock *(Fig. 4)*.

Note: The back adjustment block is cut to match the length of the movable material rest (D), but the front adjustment block is longer (6¹/₂").

ADJUSTMENT SLOTS. To make the key adjustable, slots are cut in the front (E) and back adjustment blocks (F) *(Fig. 4)*. Then the back block is glued to the movable material rest (D) that was made earlier to create an L-shaped assembly *(Fig. 3)*.

KEY. When the glue dries, the next step is to add the adjustable key. To do this, the L-brackets are attached to the ends of the blocks. These brackets are just 4" mending plates that I picked up at the local hardware store. (See page 126 for other sources.)

The only unusual thing is the brackets need to be modified slightly to fit the adjustment blocks. This requires trimming the ends and drilling an additional mounting hole in each bracket *(Fig. 5)*. Note that the legs of the brackets are two different sizes.

ATTACH BRACKETS. Now the brackets can be screwed to the ends of the two

adjustment blocks so the bottom "legs" are flush with the front edge of the material rest (D). After the adjustment system is assembled, the legs will extend in front of the fence and form the key that's used to position the workpiece (refer to *Fig. 3a*).

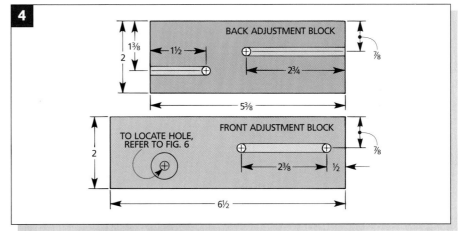

4

BACK ADJUSTMENT BLOCK

1³/₈

2

1½

2¾

⅞

5³/₈

FRONT ADJUSTMENT BLOCK

2

TO LOCATE HOLE, REFER TO FIG. 6

2³/₈

½

⅞

6½

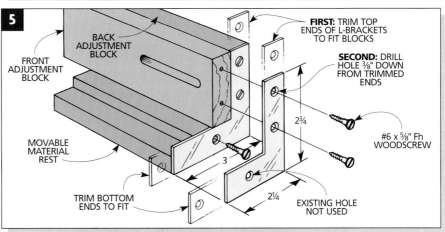

5

FRONT ADJUSTMENT BLOCK

BACK ADJUSTMENT BLOCK

MOVABLE MATERIAL REST

TRIM BOTTOM ENDS TO FIT

FIRST: TRIM TOP ENDS OF L-BRACKETS TO FIT BLOCKS

SECOND: DRILL HOLE ³/₈" DOWN FROM TRIMMED ENDS

2¾

3

2¼

#6 x ⁵/₈" Fh WOODSCREW

EXISTING HOLE NOT USED

The two adjustment blocks (E, F) allow you to set the size and spacing of the key. To prevent this key from moving once it's adjusted, I installed a special locking system.

This system consists of two separate "locks" — one for the size of the key, and one for the spacing between the key and the blade.

SIZE LOCK. To lock in the size of the key, the adjustment blocks are held together with a carriage bolt and knob (refer to *Fig. 3a*).

The bolt passes through a hole drilled in the front block (E) and through the short slot in the back block (F) *(Figs. 6 and 6a)*.

TEMPLATE. To ensure the hole in the front block aligns with the slot, I used the back block as a template *(Fig. 6)*. With the ends of the blocks flush, a $^1/_4$" brad point bit can be used to mark the center of the hole at the end of the slot *(Figs. 6 and 6a)*.

DRILL HOLE. After locating this centerpoint, drill a shank hole for the carriage bolt.

Then to recess the head of the bolt, I used a Forstner bit to drill a counterbore (I made this $^3/_4$"-dia. counterbore $^1/_4$" deep).

Now the two adjustment blocks can be fastened together with a carriage bolt, washer, and plastic knob (or wing nut) *(Fig. 7)*.

SPACING LOCK. The next step is to provide a way to lock in the spacing

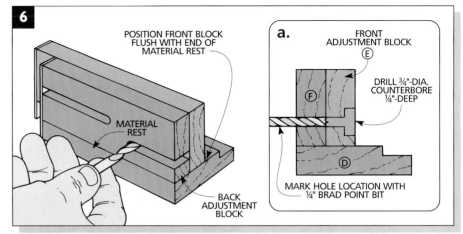

6
POSITION FRONT BLOCK FLUSH WITH END OF MATERIAL REST
MATERIAL REST
BACK ADJUSTMENT BLOCK

a.
FRONT ADJUSTMENT BLOCK
(E)
DRILL $^3/_4$"-DIA. COUNTERBORE $^1/_4$"-DEEP
(F)
(D)
MARK HOLE LOCATION WITH $^1/_4$" BRAD POINT BIT

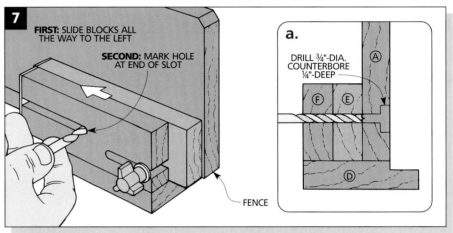

7
FIRST: SLIDE BLOCKS ALL THE WAY TO THE LEFT
SECOND: MARK HOLE AT END OF SLOT
FENCE

a.
DRILL $^3/_4$"-DIA. COUNTERBORE $^1/_4$"-DEEP
(A)
(F) (E)
(D)

between the key and the blade. Here again, a carriage bolt is used. But this time it passes through a hole in the *fence* and the long slots in *both* adjustment blocks.

To locate this hole, place the assembly under the fence. Then slide

the blocks to the left as far as possible, and make a mark for the hole at the end of the slot *(Fig. 7)*.

All that's left is to drill a counterbored shank hole in the fence *(Fig. 7a)*. Then install a carriage bolt, washer, and knob as before.

SHOP JIG . . . . *Vertical Drilling Guide*

Holding a long workpiece (like the box joint jig) steady when drilling holes in end grain can be a challenge. So when I drilled the holes for the adjusting rods, I decided to build a simple jig (see photo).

It's nothing more than a couple of pieces of wood, held together at a right angle, and a triangular support piece (see drawing).

To center the hole on the bit, the base is clamped to the drill press table so the upright extends over the edge. Then, with the work clamped to the upright, loosen the table and swing the workpiece under the bit.

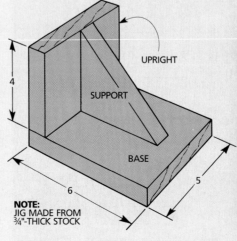

UPRIGHT
SUPPORT
BASE
4
6
5
NOTE: JIG MADE FROM $^3/_4$"-THICK STOCK

MICRO-ADJUSTMENT SYSTEM

The most innovative (and useful) feature of the box joint jig is the micro-adjustment system. This system lets you "fine tune" the key to the desired size and spacing of the slots.

ADJUSTING RODS. The secret to this system is a pair of adjusting rods. One rod threads into the end of the back adjustment block, and the other rod threads into the fence *(Fig. 8)*.

By turning these adjusting rods, you slide the adjustment blocks from side to side, which positions the key. (For more on using the micro-adjustment system, see page 124.)

ADJUSTMENT ASSEMBLY. To make this system work, an adjustment assembly is attached to the front adjustment block (E) *(Fig. 8)*. This assembly consists of a thin wooden end plate and several pieces of hardware.

END PLATE. Before installing the hardware, I cut an end plate (G) from a piece of 1/4"-thick hardwood *(Fig. 9a)* to dimensions of 2" x 2 1/4". Then, four 3/16"-dia. holes are drilled through the end plate.

After drilling these holes for the adjusting rods and two mounting screws, the plate can be used as a template to mark the corresponding holes in the end of the jig *(Fig. 9)*.

DRILLING JIG. Marking these holes in the end of the jig is the easy part. The trick is actually holding the jig steady to drill the holes. Since this part of the jig will be used to make micro-adjustments, you want to make sure the holes are drilled accurately.

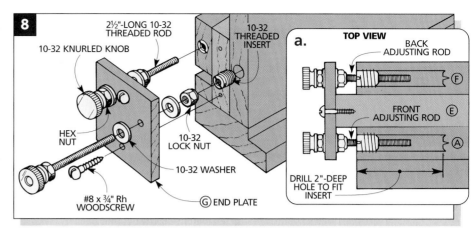

8
2 1/2"-LONG 10-32 THREADED ROD
10-32 KNURLED KNOB
10-32 THREADED INSERT
a. TOP VIEW
BACK ADJUSTING ROD
F
FRONT ADJUSTING ROD
E
A
HEX NUT
10-32 LOCK NUT
10-32 WASHER
DRILL 2"-DEEP HOLE TO FIT INSERT
#8 x 3/4" Rh WOODSCREW
G END PLATE

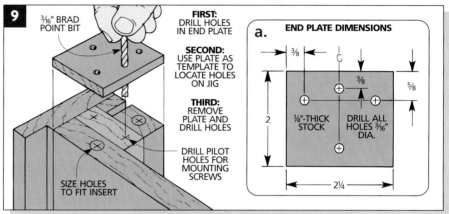

9
3/16" BRAD POINT BIT
FIRST: DRILL HOLES IN END PLATE
a. END PLATE DIMENSIONS
3/8
3/8
5/8
SECOND: USE PLATE AS TEMPLATE TO LOCATE HOLES ON JIG
THIRD: REMOVE PLATE AND DRILL HOLES
2
1/4"-THICK STOCK
DRILL ALL HOLES 3/16" DIA.
DRILL PILOT HOLES FOR MOUNTING SCREWS
SIZE HOLES TO FIT INSERT
2 1/4

To do this, I built a simple drilling jig (see the Shop Jig box on the opposite page). Once the holes are drilled, the micro-adjustment system can be assembled as shown in *Fig. 8*.

The 2 1/2"-long adjusting rods are cut from a piece of 10-32 threaded rod. To accept these adjusting rods, threaded inserts are installed in the fence (A) and back block (F). The actual adjusting pressure is created by a "stop" on each

side of the plate.

The stop on the inside of the plate is a washer and lock nut *(Figs. 8 and 8a)*. Another washer and a knurled knob that's tightened against a nut forms the outside stop.

MITER GAUGE

The last step is to attach the jig to the miter gauge. The idea here is to position the jig so you can cut the largest possible slot without cutting into the material rest.

This requires mounting your widest dado blade (or largest bit, if you plan on using the router table). In my case, this was a 13/16" dado blade *(Fig. 10)*.

Note: Since I don't like to remove that much material with a router (for safety reasons), the largest router bit I use is a 1/2" straight bit.

To complete the jig, check that the miter gauge is square to the blade. Then position the fixed rest against the saw blade, and screw the gauge to the fence *(Fig. 10a)*.

Note: If you prefer, you can use machine screws and threaded inserts to mount the jig (refer to the Miter Gauge Fence article on page 78). ■

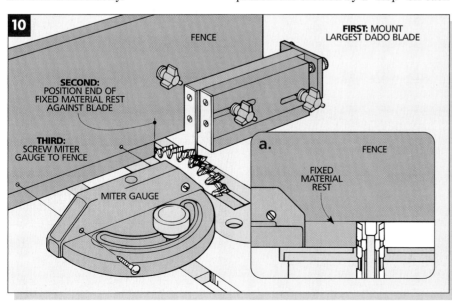

10
FENCE
FIRST: MOUNT LARGEST DADO BLADE
SECOND: POSITION END OF FIXED MATERIAL REST AGAINST BLADE
THIRD: SCREW MITER GAUGE TO FENCE
MITER GAUGE
a. FENCE
FIXED MATERIAL REST

TECHNIQUE .... Making Box Joints

Basically, there are only two requirements for making accurate fitting box joints. The first is perfect spacing between the pins and slots. The second is getting the ends of the pins flush with the side of the adjoining piece (see photo at right).

Using the micro-adjustable box joint jig solves the first problem — cutting identically spaced pins and slots.

FLUSH PINS. But the jig itself only helps so much. In order to solve the second part of the problem (getting the ends of the pins flush with the side of the adjoining piece), there are two other things you'll need to take into account: the *length* of the pins and the *thickness* of the workpieces.

In an ideal situation, the length of the pins would match the thickness of the workpieces exactly. So start out by checking that all the pieces are the same thickness.

Note: While you're at it, "thickness" a few test pieces to use when adjusting the jig.

1 *To produce a box joint with the ends of the pins flush with the side of the adjoining piece, raise the blade to match the thickness of the workpiece.*
Note: *This is the distance from the material rest to the top of the blade.*

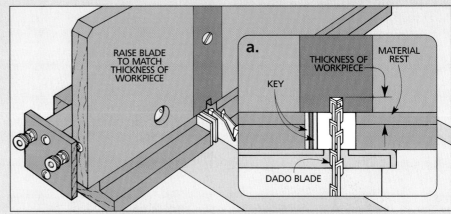

2 *Using a slot cut in a test piece, the key is adjusted to match the width of the slot. To do this, loosen the locking knobs and turn the back adjustment knob until the slot fits snugly over the key. Then tighten the outside locking knob.*

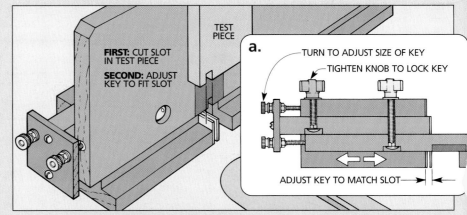

3 *Now turn the front adjustment knob to set the spacing between the slots. After positioning the key the width of one slot from the blade, tighten the inside knob. Then make a test joint and readjust if necessary. Moving the key closer to the blade loosens the joint. Moving it away tightens the fit.*

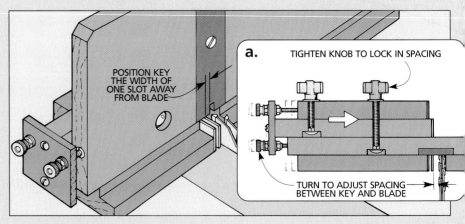

After checking the thickness of all the pieces, the next step is to determine the length of the pins (in other words, the depth of cut).

To do this, I use a test piece (the same thickness as the workpieces) as a set-up gauge. I then raise the blade to match the thickness of the piece (refer to *Step 1*). Then I use a slot cut in the test piece to set the width of the key. and adjust the spacing *(Steps 2 and 3)*.

APPEARANCE. While it doesn't "make or break" the box joint, I like the look of a full pin (or slot) on the end of each piece. So I cut each board to length, but decided to leave the boards actually *wider* than necessary for the project I'm working on. Then, after completing all the slots, the extra width can be trimmed to leave a full pin (or slot) at the end.

Note: Marking the extra width (as "waste") helps keep track of which edge to position against the key *(Steps 4 through 6)*.

TRIAL JOINTS. Once the pieces are cut to "working" size, it's a good idea to make a trial joint.

The goal is to slide the pins into the slots with a "friction" fit (they should require a few light taps to come together, but not be so tight that you need to force them). This may require some readjusting of the jig to get a perfect fit. But the end result will be worth the effort.

MAKE JOINTS. Now it's just a matter of cutting matching slots on each workpiece *(Steps 4 through 6)*.

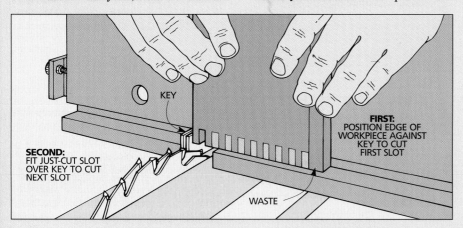

KEY

SECOND:
FIT JUST-CUT SLOT
OVER KEY TO CUT
NEXT SLOT

FIRST:
POSITION EDGE OF
WORKPIECE AGAINST
KEY TO CUT
FIRST SLOT

WASTE

4 With the edge of the workpiece against the key, cut the first slot. This creates a pin on the end of the piece. Then position the workpiece to cut each of the remaining slots by straddling the key with the slot that was cut last.

**FLIP WORKPIECE
TO CUT MATCHING
SLOTS ON OTHER END**

NOTE:
HOLD WORK TIGHT
AGAINST FENCE AND
MATERIAL REST

WASTE

5 To cut matching slots on the opposite end, flip the workpiece so the waste edge is oriented to the same side. Then, with the work held firmly against the fence and the material rest, cut slots on the opposite end of the workpiece, using the same procedure as before.

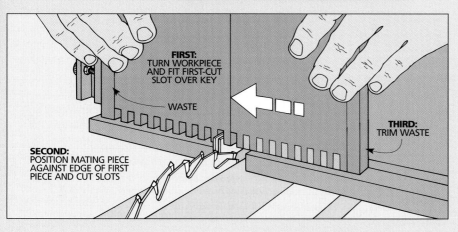

FIRST:
TURN WORKPIECE
AND FIT FIRST-CUT
SLOT OVER KEY

WASTE

SECOND:
POSITION MATING PIECE
AGAINST EDGE OF FIRST
PIECE AND CUT SLOTS

THIRD:
TRIM WASTE

6 To form pins that match the slots on the adjoining piece, use the first piece as a setup gauge. Just turn it around so the waste edge is on the opposite side and the slot that was cut first fits over the key. After cutting the first slot on the adjoining piece, set the first piece aside and complete the box joint.

Most of the supplies for the projects in this book can be found at hardware stores or home centers. But sometimes you may have to order through the mail. So we've tried to find reputable mail order sources with toll-free numbers (see box at right).

In addition, *Woodsmith Project Supplies* offers hardware for some of the projects in this book (see below).

WOODSMITH PROJECT SUPPLIES

At the time of printing, the following project supply kits and hardware were available from *Woodsmith Project Supplies*. Some of them can be seen at www.woodsmithstore.com. (The kits include hardware, but you must supply any lumber, plywood, or finish.) For current prices and availability, call toll free:

1-800-444-7527

Flush Trim Jig
(pages 32-37) ....No. 6834-100

Shelf Pin Drilling Guide
(pages 38-43) ....No. 6828-100

Dovetail Jig (1/2" template)
(pages 66-75)
Hardware Kit (includes all hardware, but no lumber) ..No. 758-310

Ready-to-Assemble Kit (everything needed to build the jig, including lumber) .....No. 5002-200

Miter Gauge Fence
(pages 78-81) ....No. 6814-100

Bevel Grinding Jig
(pages 86-89) ....No. 6803-100

Sliding Crosscut Box
(pages 90-95) ....No. 6827-200

Band Saw Circle Jig
(pages 96-101) ....No. 6815-100

Taper Jig
(pages 102-107) ....No. 6833-100

Tenoning Jig
(pages 108-117) ....No. 6806-500

Box Joint Jig
(pages 118-125) ....No. 6808-100

KEY: TL03

MAIL ORDER SOURCES

Some of the most important "tools" you can have in your shop are mail order catalogs. Those listed below are filled with special hardware, tools, finishes, lumber, and supplies that can't be found at a local hardware store or home center. Many of the supplies for the projects in this book can be found in one or more of these catalogs.

Note: The information below was current when this book was printed. Time-Life Books and August Home Publishing do not guarantee these products will be available nor endorse any specific mail order company, catalog, or product.

THE WOODSMITH STORE

2625 Beaver Avenue
Des Moines, IA 50310
800–835–5084
Our own retail store filled with tools, jigs, hardware, books, and finishing supplies. Though we don't have a catalog, we do send out items mail order. Call for information.

WOODCRAFT

560 Airport Industrial Park
P.O. Box 1686
Parkersburg, WV 26102-1686
800–225–1153
www.woodcraft.com
A must! Has all kinds of hardware for jigs including knobs, bolts, acrylic plastic, self-adhesive measuring tape, clamps, and safety accessories. Also hand and power tools.

WOODHAVEN

501 West 1st St.
Durant, IA 52747-9729
800–344–6657
www.woodhaven.com
A wide selection of auxiliary router bases, plus phenolic plastic and lots of ready-made jigs and accessories.

GRIZZLY INDUSTRIAL

P.O. Box 2069
Bellingham, WA 98227
800–523–4777
www.grizzlyindustrial.com
Another good source of power and hand tools and accessories. You'll find sanding drums, hold-down clamps, self-adhesive measuring tape, router bits and guide bushings.

TREND-LINES

135 American Legion Highway
Revere, MA 02151
800–767–9999
www.trend-lines.com
Another complete source for power tools and accessories. They also offer some of the hardware and supplies frequently used to build jigs, including self-adhesive measuring tape.

CONSTANTINE'S

2050 Eastchester Road
Bronx, NY 10461
800–223–8087
www.constantines.com
One of the original woodworking mail order catalogs. A good collection of hold-down clamps, other hardware, lumber, and finishing supplies.

WOODWORKER'S SUPPLY

1108 North Glenn Road
Casper, WY 82601
800–645–9292
An excellent source for power tools and accessories, hardware, self-adhesive measuring tape, and finishing supplies.

ROCKLER WOODWORKING & HARDWARE

4365 Willow Drive
Medina, MN 55340
800–279–4441
www.rockler.com
One of the best all-around catalogs for general hardware and specialty hardware for jigs. It's also a good "idea-starter" for projects with a variety of tools, accessories, and lumber.

President & Publisher: Donald B. Peschke
Executive Editor: Douglas L. Hicks
Art Director: Steve Lueder
Creative Director: Ted Kralicek
Senior Graphic Designers: Chris Glowacki, Cheryl Simpson
Assistant Editors: Joseph E. Irwin, Craig Ruegsegger
Graphic Designer: Vu Nguyen
Design Interns: Janet Graeve, Katie VanDalsem

Designer's Notebook Illustrator: Mike Mittermeier
Photographer: Crayola England
Electronic Production: Douglas M. Lidster
Production: Troy Clark, Minniette Johnson, Susan Rueve
Project Designers: Ken Munkel, Kent Welsh, Kevin Boyle
Project Builders: Steve Curtis, Steve Johnson
Magazine Editors: Terry Strohman, Tim Robertson
Contributing Editors: Vincent S. Ancona, Tom Begnal, Jon Garbison, Bryan Nelson
Magazine Art Directors: Todd Lambirth, Cary Christensen
Contributing Illustrators: Mark Higdon, David Kreyling, Erich Lage, Roger Reiland, Kurt Schultz, Cinda Shambaugh, Dirk Ver Steeg

Controller: Robin Hutchinson
Production Director: George Chmielarz
Project Supplies: Bob Baker
New Media Manager: Gordon Gaippe

For subscription information about
Woodsmith and *ShopNotes* magazines, please write:
August Home Publishing Co.
2200 Grand Ave.
Des Moines, IA 50312
800-333-5075
www.augusthome.com/customwoodworking

Woodsmith® and *ShopNotes*® are registered trademarks of August Home Publishing Co.

LIBRARY OF CONGRESS CATALOGING-IN-PUBLICATION DATA
Shop-built jigs & fixtures / by the editors of Time-Life Books and Woodsmith magazine.
  p. cm. – (Custom woodworking)
  ISBN 0-7835-5952-6
  1. Woodworking tools–Design and construction. 2. Woodwork–Equipment and supplies–Design and construction. 3. Jigs and fixtures–Design and construction. I. Title: Shop-built jigs and fixtures. II. Time-Life books. III. Series.

TT186 .S57 2000
684'.08–dc21
                                        99-057546

Time-Life Books is a division of Time Life Inc.

TIME LIFE INC.
President and CEO: Jim Nelson

TIME-LIFE BOOKS
Publisher/Managing Editor: Neil Kagan
Senior Vice President, Marketing: Joseph A. Kuna
Vice President, New Product Development: Amy Golden

CUSTOM WOODWORKING
Shop-Built Jigs & Fixtures
Editor: Glen B. Ruh
Design Director: Kate McConnell
Assistant Art Director: Patricia Bray
Cover Concept: Phil Unetic/3R1 Studios

Director of Marketing: Wells P. Spence
Marketing Manager: Jennifer C. Williams

Correspondents: Maria Vincenza Aloisi (Paris), Christine Hinze (London), Christina Lieberman (New York)

Executive Vice President, Operations: Ralph Cuomo
Senior Vice President and CFO: Claudia Goldberg
Senior Vice President, Law & Business Affairs: Randolph H. Elkins
Vice President, Financial Planning & Analysis: Christopher Hearing
Vice President, Book Production: Patricia Pascale
Vice President, Imaging: Marjann Caldwell
Director, Publishing Technology: Betsi McGrath
Director of Editorial Administration: Barbara Levitt
Director of Photography and Research: John Conrad Weiser
Director, Quality Assurance: James King
Manager, Technical Services: Anne Topp
Senior Production Manager: Ken Sabol
Manager, Copyedit/Page Makeup: Debby Tait
Chief Librarian: Louise D. Forstall

School and library distribution by Time-Life Education, P.O. Box 85026, Richmond, Virginia 23285-5026.

TIME-LIFE is a trademark of Time Warner Inc. and affiliated companies.

Printed in U.S.A   R 10 9 8 7 6 5 4 3 2 1